D0916773

The Making of the Eritrean Constitution:

The Dialectic of Process and Substance

BEREKET HABTE SELASSIE

The Red Sea Press, Inc.

Publishers & Distributors of Third World Books

P.O. Box 1892

P.O. Box 48

Trenton, NJ 08607

Asmara, ERITREA

The Red Sea Press, Inc.

Publishers & Distributors of Third World Books

P.O. Box 1892  P.O. Box 48

Trenton, NJ 08607   Asmara, ERITREA

Cover and book design: Roger Dormann

Library of Congress Cataloging-in-Publication Data

Bereket H. Selassie.
  The making of the Eritrean constitution : the dialectic of process and substance / Bereket Habte Selassie.
    p. cm.
Includes bibliographical references and index.
  ISBN 1-56902-160-0 (hardcover) -- ISBN 1-56902-161-9 (pbk.)
  1. Eritrea. Qewaam (1997) 2. Constitutional history -- Eritrea.
I. Title.
  KRN207.A311997 B47 2002
  342.635'029--dc21

                           2001008101

Contents

I dedicate this book to my parents of blessed memory:
—to my father, Qeshi Habte Selassie Gulwet,
revered community elder,
inspiring pastor and lawyer, and
—to my mother, Lete-Haimanot Negassi, the most
generous and gentlest of mothers.

Foreword

This book has been in the making for over four years. By May 1998, I had gathered and collated most of the necessary data and written three out of the twelve chapters. Then the war between Eritrea and Ethiopia changed everything; it was impossible to concentrate on one's work when war had become the dominant reality in the lives of a nation and its unfortunate people. A once promising region had suddenly become embroiled in a devastating war—waged by erstwhile allies. It was a tragedy that gives renewed meaning to the notion of hubris. Hubris was a contributory factor, if not the main cause of the war. Can we learn from it? Time will tell, but I, for one, am now inclined to believe the dictum attributed to Hegel: "Man learns from history that he cannot learn from history."

This book was designed not only as an academic exercise but (I had hoped) as a guide to practitioners as well. It was the result of a labor of love, and it is intended to celebrate our people's love of justice under law as well as to contribute to an understanding of the universal values underlying modern constitutional government. I am indebted to the countless Eritreans whose views expressed in many village and town meetings, during the three-year period of constitution making (1994-1997), enlightened us all and enriched the process. It has been a rare privilege and distinct honor for me to have helped design and manage the process that enabled people to air their views. It is hard to record faithfully and completely the views of so many compatriots from whose wisdom I learnt a great deal during the three-year period of constitution making, including particularly the members of the Constitutional Commission. My deepest thanks to all of them, and I hope that they can see in some of its parts a reflection of their contribution and the genius of our people's age-old traditions of respect for law and justice. To that end I hope that the book will be translated into Eritrean languages in order to reach the non-English speaking majority among them.

The first part of the book on the process of constitution making naturally makes mention of several aspects of the work of the Constitutional Commission of Eritrea, notably the Proposals and the specific tasks assigned by the Commission throughout the four phases of the process. The book discusses in some detail the origin and use of such method and its impact on the process as well as on the product, i.e. the text of the Constitution. Such reference constitutes a celebration of the work of the Commission, an homage to all its members who went about their duty and spent much time and expended a great deal of effort as a kind of labor of love, not just a matter of obligation. To all of them, I say, thank you, and may your labors be rewarded with the implementation of the Constitution that you worked so hard to help produce.

I also wish to thank friends and colleagues who kindly offered valuable comments and criticisms on different parts of the book. I am particularly indebted to Professors Owen Fiss of Yale Law School, Makau Mutua of SUNY Buffalo Law School, Rich Rosen of UNC Law School, Herman Schwartz of the AU Washington College of Law, Mark Tushnet of Georgetown University Law Center, and Isaac Unah of UNC Political Science Department. Their critical reviews and suggestions for improvement on parts of the draft have been valuable. I am most grateful to them but must, of course, issue the customary disclaimer that they do not bear any responsibility for any deficiencies in the book, which is solely mine.

I would also like to express my appreciation of the generous funding and logistical support given to me during parts of the research by Oxfam Canada, the Center for Democracy and Human Rights of Canada, The United States Agency for International Development, the United States Institute for Peace and the Fund for Peace. Above all, I wish to take this opportunity to express my heart-felt gratitude to my University, the University of North Carolina at Chapel Hill (UNC). What Howard, my previous employer of seventeen years, had failed to do, UNC did. UNC enthusiastically welcomed the idea of one of its faculty chairing a commission entrusted to draft the Constitution of a new country. The concerned leaders of UNC, not only welcomed me, with an endowed Chair to boot, but gave me ample leave of absence. To those who made this possible—to Craig Calhoun, Steve Birdsall, Julius Nyang'oro, Dick McCormick (Provost at the time) and Dick Richardson—I say: I hope this book justifies your belief in me and especially your trust in the promise that Eritrea held to all of us.

Last but not least, I express deep appreciation and thanks to my friend and publisher, Kassahun Checole, for his patience and understanding in the face of my failure to complete the book on time. And to the type-setter, Roger Dormann, go my thanks for his courtesy and consummate professionalism throughout our collaboration in in finalizing the publication of this book.

Bereket Habte Selassie
Chapel Hill, NC

Introduction

Eritrea's constitution was ratified on 23 May, 1997, on the eve of the sixth anniversary of the country's independence from Ethiopian rule. It is the first constitution created by the Eritrean people themselves, as a free and sovereign nation and, as such, carries enormous symbolic significance. In contrast, the 1952 constitution was imposed on the Eritrean people under a UN-arranged federation, brokered by the United States, in which they had no say and under which they had no sovereignty.[1]

The aim of this book is twofold. The first is to offer students of constitutional law and government, both Eritreans and interested foreigners, a text book, providing a backdrop to the Eritrean constitution making process with a concise discussion of the product of that process, i.e., the constitution. To that end, Part One of the book attempts to acquaint the reader with the highlights of the three-year process of constitution making, while Part Two engages the constitution itself, in a chapter-by-chapter analysis and commentary. In much of the book, reference is made, in comparative perspective, to literatures pertaining to other jurisdictions in the hope of encouraging the interested readers—and especially Eritrean young professionals—to enrich their knowledge further. To the same end, I have made an attempt to provide as much theoretical grounding as possible in discussing the provisions of the Eritrean Constitution.

The second aim of the book is to provide members of the legal profession (judges, prosecutors and practicing attorneys), legislators and other policy makers with reference material which might help them in their respective works, at least as a point of departure for further inquiry and debate on constitutional issues.[2]

In this Introduction, I try to pull together and comment on certain recurring themes of African history, society and politics, including those of Eritrea and other countries of the Horn of Africa. In doing so, I hope to put the subject matter of the book in a larger, historical and global perspective.

Regional History and Geopolitics

Eritrea is part of the Horn of Africa, a strategically located and potentially rich region which has been associated with war and famine in recent years. Lying astride the northwest Indian Ocean and the Red Sea, across from the Arabian Peninsula and the Gulf region, the Horn of Africa has been a crossroads of history between Africa and Asia. The combined effect of history and geography is reflected in the region's demographic makeup, culture, national identities, and religion. Its close proximity to the cradles of Christianity and Islam facilitated the early spread of these two great religions which acted as centralizing and harmonizing factors, and occasionally as causes of conflict. They have both left an indelible mark on the life and peoples of the region.[3]

More recently, European colonial rule has left its mark on the region as in much of Africa, notably in the realm of governance, political economy and in the colonially fixed boundaries, cutting across ethnic lines and defining the nation/state identity of the five countries—Sudan, Eritrea, Ethiopia, Djibouti, and Somalia.[4] The political economy of the region, as of much of Africa, is a study in squandered resources and missed opportunities caused by disastrous policies and politics. Failed development models, mostly inspired by external sources of finance, have left the populations burdened with huge debts. That in turn has conditioned the policies and behaviors of the governments, leaving the people worse off, for the most part. The region's economic potential—both human and material—thus remains virtually unrealized.

Conflicts provoked by the ambitions of individual politicians and built-in tensions created by artificial boundaries form a backdrop of political crises that have plagued the region as a whole and the Horn of Africa in particular. This situation is complicated by the politics of exclusion and domination in most States and exacerbated by flawed development policies. External forces have inevitably intervened to complicate and prolong local conflicts with tragic consequences in death and devastation. Foreign intervention typically has involved the infusion of massive quantities of arms that have been costly and destructive. This has resulted in the militarization of society in the whole region and the brutalization of its peoples. Thus, on the whole, political instability has characterized the region against a grim background of economic stagnation, social unrest, and ethnic cleavage. Even Djibouti, which enjoyed relative calm and stability for over a decade, has begun to experience conflicts based on competition between its two ethnic groups, the Issa and the Afar.

In Sudan, a civilian parliamentary government, to which the departing British transferred power in 1956, was overthrown two years later by a military takeover. Since then civilian and military governments have exchanged power four times. The civilian side of the equation has been dominated by the Umma, a sectarian party, continually challenged by another sectarian party, a condition that facilitated military intervention. The reigning military regime has been backed by a new religious party, the National Islamic Front, with its policy of Islamization of all Sudan. Hence rebellion in the south of the country has continued.

In Ethiopia, Emperor Haile Selassie's "modernizing" monarchy was overthrown by a radical military group which, led by colonel Mengistu Haile Mariam, imposed a Soviet-style one-party rule on the country. Marxism-Leninism was written into the 1984 Constitution as a guide and arbiter of politics and society, with suffocating effect.

Somalia began with a Westminister-type parliamentary government in 1960. However, Somali politics proved to be clannish and fractious, precipitating a military coup in 1969, led by General Mohamed Syiad Barre. The military regime established one-party rule with "scientific socialism" as its guiding ideology. The promised healing and unifying quality of this ideology was short-lived, overwhelmed as it was by clan politics.

The overthrow of the Syiad regime in early 1990, and of the Mengistu regime in May 1991, raised hopes of democracy, equal rights, and self-determination in the region. In Somalia, fractious clan competition stood in the way of a pan-Somali nationalist reconstruction of the State.[5] The Somali are still a nation in search of a State. Ethiopia began with a transitional government led by the Ethiopian Peoples Revolutionary Democratic Front (EPRDF) and proposed to restructure the empire state through an ethnic-based federal system. Empire die-hards denounced the scheme as a prescription for disintegration to which the EPRDF responded by saying that an ethnic-based federal system was the only way of maintaining the unity of the Ethiopian state. The EPRDF proceeded to create a Constitution to underpin the restructuring agenda.[6]

Eritrea, Africa and the Colonial Legacy

Like most African countries, Eritrea was a creation of European colonial history and, as elsewhere in Africa, the boundaries that define it as a nation state, were fixed during the colonial period. Presently numbering some three million and half, comprising nine ethnic groups and more or less evenly divided between Christians and Muslims, Eritreans were brought together as a nation under the white heat of alien rule. It was aided and abetted by a powerful, tradition-shattering monetary economy with a colonial administrative and security apparatus serving as handmaiden. In addition to the defining borders, therefore, Eritrea's colonial legacy included a market economy and the colonial laws and institutions imposed upon an already established, indigenous system.

Eritrea shares these colonial legacies, together with the problems incidental to them, with much of the rest of Africa. The current problems of Africa—problems of development, of stability, of democratic transition and transformation, etc.—are Eritrea's problems as well. The majority of African statesmen of the first years of decolonization, when confronted with the question of how to deal with the colonial legacy, particularly as regards the colonially fixed boundaries, decided to accept them as irreversible. These leaders chose to find post-colonial solutions to all problems arising from these legacies, having been convinced that it was neither possible nor desirable to go back to the pre-colonial status quo. President Kwame Nkrumah of Ghana preached pan-Africanism and waged a valiant, but losing battle to establish a United States of Africa. Nonetheless, on the occasion of the creation of the Organization of African Unity (OAU) in 1963, he was persuaded to suspend his insistence on the creation of a United States of Africa, in the interest of a united front. He thus became a reluctant signatory of the founding Charter in Addis Ababa and, a year later, in Cairo, witnessed, in disbelief, the passage of the Resolution recognizing the colonial boundaries by which the post-colonial African state system was to be defined.

Africa reaffirmed colonial history by deciding to live with the colonial boundaries. Living as citizens of nations defined by these boundaries, Africans accepted their new identities in terms of these nations.[7] Indeed, ethnic-based reclamation of old identities was virtually unknown. The Somali example of irredentism was an exception that proved the rule, and even in that case, the Ogaden Somali seem to have accepted their Ethiopian identity under the new, post-imperial, dispensation.

The origins of Africa's colonial boundaries can be traced to the late 1880's and 1890's when several European powers carved up Africa in what became known in historiography as the scramble for Africa. They divided the continent, first into "spheres of influence," then into colonial territories, drawing artificial boundaries regardless of ethnic composition or indigenous political systems. These artificially constructed territories were the colonial antecedents of the present state system.

A late comer in the European scramble for Africa, Italy first acquired a maritime foothold at Asab in the southern end of the Red Sea and gradually expanded from the Red Sea coast upwards, into the highlands of present day Eritrea.[8] This process culminated in the creation of a full-fledged colonial state that the Italians baptized as Eritrea in January 1890. Italy's first colony, Eritrea shared the fate of Italian colonial rule with Somalia and Libya but unlike the two Eritrea's decolonization was to be more tortuous, as will be discussed later in more detail. Italian rule in Eritrea came to an end in 1941, replaced by a British "caretaker" administration (1941-1952).

The history of Eritrea's quest for self-determination and independence, pitted against Emperor Haile Selassie's acquisitive claims and the marriage of those claims with US strategic interests is a story of the triumph of Cold War politics over the principles of freedom and democracy. The reaction of the Eritrean people to these developments, which culminated in the victory of the protracted armed struggle, may be characterized, to paraphrase Samuel Johnson, as a story of the "triumph of hope over experience."

Eritreans live spread out on two different geographical divides: the mountainous landmass in the highlands of the central and northern areas, inhabited by settled farming communities; and the hot lowland areas along the Red Sea coast and in the western areas inhabited, for the most part, by nomadic herdsmen. The people living in the highlands are mostly Christian, while the lowlanders are predominantly Muslim.

Problems of Nation and State

If there was a common problem facing all African countries, it is nation building. Enclosed within the walls of artificially created boundaries, Africans of different ethnic groups were left to fend for themselves as best they could in all matters, including the matter of forging a nation out of diverse groups. Nation building became the primary task, and the most frequently voiced slogan of the new governments. But what did it mean?[9]

In ideological terms, nation building flowed from the nationalist sentiment that animated the first generation of African leaders. The experience of common oppression and the need to fight that oppression was a mobilizing weapon to organize the mass of African peoples. The primordial sentiment of outraged dignity suffered by Africans and their thirst for freedom acted as a matrix for the birth of African nationalism, the ideology that the leaders used to forge an idea of common destiny, a sense of nationhood. Articulated in these terms, it emboldened ordinary Africans, enabling them to see things with different eyes. In their daily encounters with agents or symbols of colonial rule—the police, the judge, the tax man, and even the missionary and his benevolent attitudes and useful services—Africans began to apprehend things in light of their own needs and wants. Eventually, these scattered sentiments were joined, mobilized and given organized expression by the emerging African independence parties or movements. Thus, in the heady days of the early independence era, nationalism's seductive appeal was compelling and all-embracing. It acted at once as a mobilizing and unifying force. "Tribal" division was rare and, where it occurred, short-lived. The millennium seemed at hand. The leaders appeared to be invincible with their messianic aura, and the jubilant masses cheered and spurred them on. And this, eventually, became part of the problem. Then everything changed.

Differences began to emerge, manifested along different axes of division—personal rivalry, ethnic hostility, factional feuds and ideological rifts. In several cases, internal (intra-state) strife was followed or accompanied by inter-state conflicts. Before long, people began to see the distinction between state and nation in the post-colonial situation –a continuation and confirmation of the colonial experience with the difference that Africans now occupied the seats of power. The classical, European, conception of the state, as distinct from the nation, became part of the African experience. The divorce of the nation from the state was a rare phenomenon in the African traditional context. In the post-colonial situation, the state and its most visible manifestations (the police, the judge, the tax collector and the bureaucrat) and their increasing alienation from the rest of society soon created the notion of "Them" and "Us."

Meanwhile, a middle class of merchants and traders emerged alongside state apparatuses. Money talked louder than the most eloquent pleas of the ordinary person. The public at large soon perceived the bureaucracy, by and large, as serving the interest of the urban middle class. The gap between promise and performance in government affairs was reflected in a widening gap between rich and poor. "Class consciousness" and "class struggle" suddenly became part of the lexicon of African political discourse and as international connections reinforced the post-colonial reality of an emerging business class and its bureaucratic ally, public alienation from the state deepened. Discontent began to flare up in complaints and open protests. Clearly, African leaders needed a binding ideology to hold their nations together, an ideology transcending ethnic and class divisions. They looked north for inspiration.

Enter Socialism.

Socialists of different stripes, from Soviet-style Marxists and their Chinese counterparts to democratic socialists (and a few propagating "African socialism") preached the gospel of national unity under the banner of socialism. Some used it sincerely, if not effectively, others used it as a fig leaf for naked power. Despite a rhetorical commitment to democracy, many used national unity as an overriding reason or pretext for repressing public protests that were made on different occasions for differing reasons.

Nation building as a clarion call was compelling in the early days and served a unifying purpose in the face of a common enemy. Absent that enemy, and in view of the divisions noted above, nation building, though commonly invoked as a universal ideal, begged many questions. Eventually, its invocation by corrupt and irresponsible leaders who relied on brute force to maintain "national unity" raised questions about the very idea of national unity. Questions multiplied and the young educated posed them boldly and unequivocally. Unity for what, and for whose benefit? What had independence brought the ordinary African? What about democracy and human rights? In raising these and related questions, even non-Marxists quoted Marx about the necessity of class struggle!

Governments and party bureaucrats became targets of ridicule and scathing criticism. In reaction, preventive detention, banishment and other forms of punishment for the "trouble makers" followed. An irony of African history and politics is that the new African leaders resorted to the same tactics as their European predecessors in the characterization and treatment of their critics or opponents. No less nationalistic, they invoked the inspirational ideas of nationalism and socialism as weapons on behalf of what they considered to be the disenfranchised and dispossessed members of society. The struggle continues in different forms. Nation building cannot be achieved by heavy-handed tactics in the absence of a clear vision of what it means and how it can be achieved, that is through the creation of a political framework and social environment that ensures the participation of all members of the nation. Political inclusion and equitable distribution of resources should be the key ingredients of national policy. Yet the problem of nation building is critically linked with the problem of democracy and development.

Problems of Democracy and Development

The problem of democratic politics is part of the development problematic. The subject has been debated among scholars and practitioners for some time. My approach is to think of democratic politics and development in dynamic terms, as a sort of work in progress, rather than as settled matters fixed in a time warp. This is not to say that there are no fundamental principles governing the subject. In chapter nine, I provide a historical survey of the concept of democracy, of its evolution and some of the mechanisms of its application. Here, I shall address, in outline, the question of democratic transition and development in the African context.

Democratic transition represents a worldwide phenomenon and even die-hard dictators pay lip service to its principles. What is often missing, and what people committed to the democratic ideal have been insisting on, is that in addition to commitment to principles, mechanisms of control should be put in place and their operation watched with vigilance in order to hold governments accountable. Accountability, as I will show in later chapters, is the key principle in this matter. Being part of the development problematic, democratic transition involves a complex process depending on a number of related factors. By way of generalization, I submit the following three primary factors which I think are controlling: 1) government commitment, 2) public support, and 3) vigorous institutions.

1. Government commitment
Generally, the function of government is to maintain the status quo. But government is also—perhaps even essentially—about change. And governments possess the means to carry out changes. Thus, without government providing leadership and resources, not much progress can be expected.

2. Public support
Government needs public support for its programs of change. The public must be actively involved in the process of translating principles into practice. To that end, a successful government with competent and wise leadership needs to persuade and organize the public for the realization of the democratic ideal and development. This is the main reason why dictators pay lip service to democracy.

3. Vigorous Institutions
There must be institutions with constitutionally guaranteed powers to ensure integrity in the process of building, uphold-

ing and defending democratic principles. This may sound redundant in that government necessarily implies institutions. However, even when the immediate interests of governments –and of those in power at any given moment—are affected, institutions that uphold and defend democracy must be in place and assiduously cultivated. Hence the need of constitutional guarantees.

The combined effect of these factors put a nation on the path of sustainable democratic development. Their absence constitute the principal problem of democratic transition. Yet the following can also constrain an African government's democratic transition.

a. Traditional Values and Attitudes.
A yet unanswered question is whether there are elements in traditional African institutions and values that can be used as building blocks for democracy. The failure of the ideology of modernization as a goal of development in the 1960's and 1970's has caused eminent African scholars to wonder about the relevance of tradition for development.[10]

Mazrui argues, for instance that, regarding simplistic opposition of the modern and the traditional, "traditional wisdom is beginning to regain respectability," and ethnicity as the "fountain of tradition must also have its credentials reassessed."[11] It is worth noting, in this connection, that the ethnic politics as the foundation of the federal structure in Ethiopia was not based on such reassessment but rather, as a matter of necessity.[12]

b. Autocratic, Colonial Legacy and State Alienation from the Public.
Basil Davidson asserts that the crisis of the African state is "the crisis of institutions" which were imposed by colonial rule.[13] If true, the current democratic agenda is doomed to

failure because it is premised on the necessity of state institutions which are modeled on European institutions of governance—Parliaments, Executive and Courts together with the administrative and security bureaucracies.

Some dismiss Davidson's thesis as unrealistic. Nonetheless, it needs serious consideration because, to the extent that it goes to the root of the democratic agenda, it entails a review of the fundamental assumptions about such an agenda and its applicability to Africa.

c. Underdevelopment of Democratic Institutions.

The dichotomy of representative versus direct democracy notwithstanding, direct (Athenian-style) village democracy has long existed in much of Africa. How can such direct democracy be organized in ways that local governments can enable citizens to be involved in their own affairs and, thereby, help redress the balance vis-a-vis central government power? Direct democracy, cannot, of course, replace representative government which seems to have come to stay. The problems of adequate and proper representation of all citizens and the methods of ensuring such representation, including electoral laws, will be discussed in detail in chapter nine.

d. Underdevelopment of Judicial Institutions.

Assuming that institutions of European provenance, including an independent judiciary, are not only unavoidable but necessary, a strong judiciary is an essential element of democratic governance. The constitutions of all African governments subscribe to the principle of judicial independence. The question is what has been the role of the judiciary and what has been done, or should be done, to strengthen the institution? Can it be realistically expected that a strong Executive will permit the emergence of a vigorous judiciary?

e. The Professional Class.

This category includes lawyers, journalists and other members of the professions. At issue are education and the overall development of human resources. That trained human power is critical to a country's development, including political and economic development, is beyond dispute. Equally important is civic education to raise citizens' awareness of their rights and duties. Maximum possible commitment of resources towards professional development is an imperative.

f. Democracy and the Public at Large.

In recent years, expanding public education on democracy and human rights has become a popular theme of seminars and conferences of private voluntary groups throughout the world. They demonstrate a need for balance between nation building and state construction and between state and civil society. Ideally, the two should go hand in hand, with neither being allowed to wax great while the other wanes. But, as already seen, the state has its own laws of growth and behavior, so that a vigorous and vigilant civil society is needed to redress the balance. The issue of ethnicity and how ethnic groups can be allowed optimum space within a framework of national unity is a recurring theme. In this respect, Ethiopia's experiment should be watched with great interest. A caveat must be issued nonetheless, that in this age of triumphalist capitalism, when the dominant public discourse insists on privatization, the public domain should not be abolished or even narrowed down. The challenge is to work out the right balance between the public and private space. A Constitution should provide the framework and principles for such a balance.

g. Democracy and Economic Growth.

A distinction must be drawn between development and economic growth. Economic growth is measurable in terms of the quantities of goods produced and services provided over a given time frame, usually a year, tons of steel, bushels of wheat, kilowatts of electricity, etc. Thus the gross national product of a country (GNP) is the amount of goods and services produced in a year. On the other hand, the definition of development includes something qualitative in addition to growth. The nature of that "something qualitative" may vary from case to case, depending on differences in culture, philosophy and policy, among countries. A simple definition of development should include: 1. Having more, 2. Doing more, 3. Knowing more, and 4. Being more. Having, doing and knowing more represent, respectively, more goods and services, more activity, and more knowledge and, as such, are necessary ingredients for economic growth. The use of the word more implies addition to existing goods and services and of knowledge.

Being more (being) transcends quantity and implies existential questions involving aspirations, attitudes, sentiments, and philosophies of life embedded in a country's culture, as by-products of its history. A country's leaders should ask about the impact economic growth can have on such qualitative considerations. Furthermore, economic planners and project designers should also grapple with them, even though hard-boiled economists may contend that such existential questions, however acceptable in theory, may slow down or even impede economic growth. In this respect, India and Japan provide different approaches to this problem which may be instructive for Africa.

Is economic growth a precondition for democratic transition, or vice versa? Is there a golden rule of a right balance that must be struck between optimal economic growth and sustainable democratic transition? Are "bread and liberty" irreconcilable opposites or two sides of the same coin? Such dichotomy is false. Democracy and development are dialectically connected concepts, not irreconcilable opposites, though there is nothing new or revolutionary about this view. Locke's conception of liberty,[14] for instance, subsumes property as a necessary condition for the enjoyment of liberty. What was revolutionary in Locke's time was the notion that those who invest their efforts (labor and talent) in creating things should be rewarded with having title on the products of their efforts. Even though this right was limited to a minority segment of society at the time, that is, the then ascendant middle class, Locke's idea had revolutionary implications, as later generations would discover. As a guiding ideology in the hands of the American revolutionaries, it cleared the way for a future dynamic polity and society. In their hands, the marriage of liberty and property was consummated. Democracy and development must go together. One cannot do without the other. While there are universal principles of democracy to which almost all nations subscribe as we shall see below, each nation can also find its own solutions to problems of democratic transition and development according to specific national needs and aspirations, and in consonance with overall cultural heritage.

Notes

1. See Bereket Habte Selassie, Eritrea and the United Nations, 1989. On the brief constitutional experience of Eritrea under the UN-arranged federation, see Tekie Fessehatzion, A Brief Encounter with Democracy: From Acquiescence to Resistance During Eritrea's Early Federation Years, in Eritrean Studies Review, Volume 2, Number 2, 1998, pages 19-64. Tekie argues in this work that Eritrean nationalism and constitutional consciousness was raised in the early period of the Federation, as the flegeling Eritrean government fought off Emperor Haile Selassie's

encroachment on internal Eritrean affairs, in violation of the UN Resolution.

2. A translation of the book into some Eritrean languages is being negotiated with a funding agency.

3. Much of the content of this section is based on my entry in the Oxford Companion to Politics of the World, OUP, 2001 edition.

4. In recent years, Kenya has been added to the Horn of Africa sub-region, which is also at times referred to as North-Eastern Africa. The US strategic policy under the Clinton Administration even included Uganda and other states in the Great lakes under the rubric Greater Horn of Africa Strategic Initiative, primarily designed to fight Islamicist governments.

5. See Said Samatar et al Somalia: A Nation in Search of a State. Boulder: Westview Press, 1987.

6. See Bereket Habte Selassie, Self Determination in Principle and Practice: The Ethiopian-Eritrean Experience, Columbia Human Rights Law Review, Volume 29, Number 1, Fall 1997.

7. See, generally, Robert July, A History of African People 4th edition 2001.

8. See below for reference to the treaty of Wuchale. On Menelik's dealings with Italy, see generally Carlo Rossetti, Storia Diplomatica dell'Etiopia, 1910.

9. As Thomas Hodgkin has written, in Nationalism in Colonial Africa (1956), the rise of African nationalism has been analyzed as "the final stage in a chain reaction, deriving its operative ideas originally from the French revolution—the doctrine of the 'Rights of Man' interpreted as the rights of nations." (page 17).

10. See, for example, Ali Mazrui, The Bondage of Boundaries, The Economist, September 11, 1993.

11. Ibid.

12. See Bereket Habte Selassie, op cit.
13. See Basil Davidson, Black Man's Burden. New York: Times Books, before 1992.
14. John Locke, Second Treatise on Civil Government. New York: Times Books, 1992.

PART ONE:
The Making of the Constitution

ONE
Historical Context

"And when what had been done in the heart of darkness was repeated in Europe, no one recognized it. No one wished to admit what everyone knew...You already know that. So do I. It is not knowledge we lack. What is missing is the courage to understand what we know and draw conclusions." (SVEN LINDQVIST, EXTERMINATE ALL THE BRUTES.)

History is everything. Without understanding the history of a country, it is impossible to understand fully its current reality. And a precondition of understanding is knowledge—knowledge of the essential facts of the history of a country. Much of Eritrea's problem during the liberation struggle had to do with lack of knowledge of its history, or rather a consumption of a distorted version spun by the scribes of succeeding Ethiopian regimes. In the struggle for the hearts and minds of policy makers, therefore—in the arduous work of diplomacy, the propagation of the correct version of Eritrean history played a major part.

In this chapter, a summary account of the history of Eritrea will be given, starting with pre-colonial times and ending with the Referendum of 1993. This will be followed by a brief account of the transitional period from the Referendum to the establishment of the Constitutional Commission.

A. PRE-COLONIAL AND COLONIAL HISTORY.

Pre-colonial History

The country now known as Eritrea was a creation of Italian colonial adventure of the late 19th century. In pre-colonial times, Eritrea, known by various names, experienced different systems of government and was an arena of population migration, intermingling and cultural evolution. Historians record that as early as the third century BC, the port of Adulis (near today's Massawa) was frequented by ships coming from Greece and Egypt.

It is a matter of controversy—albeit academic—whether Adulis was founded and developed before the rise of Axum, Ethiopia's ancient city, where Christianity was first introduced in the fourth century AD. At any rate, the rise and expansion of the Axumite empire included much of present day Eritrea as a core part of its central territory. In short, Ethiopia's ancient city is also Eritrea's, a point which succeeding Ethiopian regimes used in support of their claim over Eritrea, especially during the time of the independence struggle.

Before the rise of Axum, in times when the coastal regions, in and around Adulis, were frequented by Greeks, Egyptians, Romans and other sea-faring peoples, the highlands were inhabited by Nilotic peoples, later mixed with Kushitic tribes coming from the North and West, i.e., from

4

present day Sudan. These populations were later invaded by waves of immigrants from the Arabian peninsula, mostly present Yemen, during the five centuries before the Christian era. Historians refer to these generically as Sabeans and cite numerous inscriptions on stelae and other items such as incense-burners which are comparable to those found in Arabia. The development of the Geez language and culture is undoubtedly the most convincing evidence of the Trans-Red Sea crossings and the advent of the Sabeans.[1] Following the advent of Christianity which eventually dominated the outlook of the governing elite of the Axumite state and defined its culture, the rise of Islam gradually laid the foundation for a competing faith and corresponding culture and way of life. The two religions lived side by side, at times giving rise to strife and religiously-inspired wars, but by and large, co-existing in harmony. The periodic strife was driven by external powers such as the Ottoman Turkish empire and its 19th century Egyptian successors under Khedive Ismail.

Italian Colonial Rule

Italian colonization of Eritrea began with the purchase of Asab in November 1869, by an Italian monk, Giuseppe Sapeto, from three local chiefs.[2] The purchase was made on behalf of an Italian private enterprise, the Rubattino Shipping Company, but with the blessing of Italian king Vittorio Emanuele II.[3] Following two years of problems, Italy established Asab as a beachhead for future colonization of the hinterland. With British encouragement, aimed at frustrating French colonial designs in the area, the Italians were able in consolidating their beachhead and gradually expanding further into the interior.

The Italians landed in Masawa in 1885 and occupied

Keren in 1888. Ethiopian Emperor Yohannes was killed fighting the Sudanese Mahdists in March 1889, and a couple of months later the succeeding Ethiopian Emperor, Menelik, signed the treaty of Wuchale (March 2, 1889) recognizing the border between Ethiopia and Eritrea. Eritrea was officially proclaimed as a colony of Italy on January 1, 1890.

In fifty one years of colonial rule the Italians built railway lines and roads connecting major urban centers, and agricultural and mineral enterprises.[4] By the beginning of the Second World War, Asmara had a population of more than one hundred thousand. Italy under Mussolini (1922-1943), embarked upon a revanchist scheme to avenge the shame Italy suffered in its defeat at Adua in March 1896 at the hand of the Ethiopian army. Mussolini invaded Ethiopia in 1935. Within a few months of their victory, the Italians issued a decree on June 1, 1936, redrawing the map of the Horn of Africa region and calling it *Africa Orientale Italiana*, regrouping Ethiopia, Eritrea and Italian Somalia. Eritrea and Somalia had been used as launching pads for the invasion of Ethiopia which was Italy's historic objective from the time of the acquisition of Asab, and later Masawa.

Eritrea went through a boom as a result of the invasion of Ethiopia. The roads were enlarged and improved and industry expanded to include some two thousand factories and workshops. Masawa's port was enlarged and improved, and urbanization accelerated changing the social landscape, with shanty towns housing an increasing urban population to which rural people streamed. The conscription of young men to the Italian armed forces who were trained and armed to fight, earlier in Libya , later in Ethiopia, added a critical catalytic factor to the rural-urban influx, thus affecting the socio-economic life of the country side.

Then Mussolini entered the Second World War on Hitler's side in June 1940, with dramatic consequences. The defeat of Italy in the African theater of war early during the war brought Italy's African colonial adventure to an abrupt end. Italy lost her colonies and a new chapter was opened in the history of African peoples, including the Eritrean people who in fact became among the first in the demand and struggle for independence from colonial rule. Unfortunately for Eritreans, a defeated former colonial master was replaced by another colonial master, under a different guise, entailing post-war political and strategic complications that would haunt them for forty years.

British Occupation.

Italy signed a peace treaty in 1947 renouncing her claims on her former colonies, including Eritrea.[5] Meanwhile, Britain replaced Italy as the Administering Authority (1941-1952). During the ten-year British care-taker administration, Eritrea's fate was the subject of two main opposed claimants: Eritrean nationalist forces demanding independence, and Ethiopian acquisitive claims.[6] The contending sides organized and agitated for public following and international support.

During the first phase of the British occupation (1941-1946), Eritrea was administered by the military under the British Middle East Command. Then it was placed under a civilian control while the major allied powers of the Second World War (the Big Four: The US, UK, France and the USSR) and later the UN debated its future. Two Commissions were appointed to investigate the situation, focussing on the wishes of the Eritrean people: The first was the Four-Power Commission appointed in October 1947 which submitted its report in August 1948. The Report reflected a divided opinion and, in any case, none of the opinions supported the case for self-determination of the Eritrean people.

7

Ethiopia's demand was viewed favorably by the United States. The British also expressed partial support as borne out by the Bevin-Sforza scheme designed to partition Eritrea under which the Western (Muslim) lowlands would be joined with Sudan, then under British rule, and the central (Christian) highlands would go to Ethiopia. The Bevin-Sforza plan was scuttled principally due to a united Eritrean opposition.

A Commission of Enquiry was then set up in September 1949 by the General Assembly of the United Nations, comprising five members, Burma, Guatemala, Norway, Pakistan and South Africa. With a clear mandate to ascertain the wishes of the inhabitants of Eritrea, to examine the future fate of the country and consider proposals which would be acceptable to all concerned, and report to the UN General Assembly. The Commission submitted a divided report, with Norway proposing union with Ethiopia, while South Africa and Burma proposed federation with Ethiopia, and Guatemala and Pakistan advocating independence for Eritrea. The United Nations voted for a federal union between Ethiopia and Eritrea "under the sovereignty of the Imperial Crown", which gave Eritrea a modicum of autonomy.[7]

The UN General Assembly Resolution became the basis for the "Federal Act," the legal instrument that put the Resolution into effect. A UN Commissioner was appointed to prepare a Constitution for Eritrea, which he did within a year of his appointment.[8] The British Administering Authorities organized the election of an Eritrean Assembly to approve the Federal Act and the Constitution. The election took place in March 1952. The majority of the 68 members of the Assembly were elected by an indirect suffrage: by representatives of the regional families or *Enda*'s—save for Asmara and Massawa where direct elections were held.

The federation came into force on Sept. 15, 1952.[9]

8

Federation and Annexation

The federation between Ethiopia and Eritrea lasted ten years (1952-1962). The Federal arrangement provided for an autonomous Eritrean government with legislative, executive, and judicial powers over internal (Eritrean) affairs, with matters of defense, foreign affairs, currency and finance as well as foreign and "inter-state" commerce and communication reserved for federal (i.e. Ethiopian) jurisdiction.

It was a lopsided arrangement and made for an uneasy relationship from the start. Sir Ivor Jennings, one of the panel of experts appointed to assist the UN Commissioner in drafting the Eritrean constitution, wondered how one could write a constitution " for a democratic state federally united with Ethiopia", which was a feudal state?[10] To begin with, the anomaly alluded to by professor Jennings was further complicated by the absence of an essential federal principle that there must be equality among the component parts of the federation with a "neutral" arbiter to settle any conflicts arising between them. Not only was Eritrea an unequal partner but no provision was made to settle such conflicts. Indeed, Ethiopia had made sustained efforts to interpret the UN Resolution in ways that would give the Emperor power to reduce to naught the autonomy of Eritrea stipulated under the resolution.

The Ethiopian government of Emperor Haile Selassie systematically subverted the working of the Eritrean government and drove the first Chief Executive of Eritrea out of office. This provoked mass protests which led to the suppression of the civil and human rights of Eritreans guaranteed under the constitution. In September 1961, the underground resistance exploded into an armed rebellion led by the Eritrean Liberation Front (ELF). On November 14, 1962 Emperor Haile Selassie dissolved the federation, declaring

Eritrea his 14th province. The city of Asmara was the scene of a highly visible Ethiopian military, including a police contingent that stood guard around the Eritrean Parliament, when the Emperor's proclamation was read to a hostage Parliament by the hand picked Chief Executive. The dissolution of the UN-arranged federation was announced as the decision of the Eritrean Parliament.[11]

The dissolution of the federation was followed by the introduction of Ethiopian laws and institutions into Eritrea, including feudal institutions. Thus, a more backward social formation was forced on a relatively more advanced one, inconsiderate of local interests and insensitive to local laws and customs, a condition that reinforced Eritrean resistance and drove out more Eritreans to join the armed rebellion that was to last thirty years.

In the views of Eritreans, Emperor Haile Selassie's annexation of their country violated international law which gave added legitimacy to the armed rebellion. UN Commissioner Anze Matienzo had approvingly quoted the opinion of a panel of legal experts in his final report to the UN General Assembly that the UN Resolution on which Eritrean autonomy was based would remain an international instrument and that, if violated, the General Assembly "could be seized of the matter."[12] But the UN did not choose to be "seized of the matter". On the contrary, the UN lent a deaf ear to all pleas and peaceful protests of the Eritrean people.[13] Cold War diplomacy and Ethiopia's growing alliance with the United States foreclosed Eritrean rights, thus leading to armed struggle, as the only option.[14]

Emperor Haile Selassie's prominent position in African international relations, backed by US diplomacy, reduced any discussion on Eritrea to a simplistic and distorted equation of the legitimate claims of an African state versus an illegitimate secessionist rebellion. Following the creation of the

Organization of African Unity (OAU) in 1963, Ethiopian leaders successfully invoked "OAU principles" of non-intervention in the internal affairs of a state. The sensitivity of African states to the question of "secession" was highlighted by the Katanga rebellion in the early 1960's and Biafra in the late 1960's.

The "Pandora's box" argument (if Eritrea secedes it will inspire other secessions) carried favor in African political circles. Thus, to people unfamiliar with the historical and legal bases of the Eritrean case, the implications of the Pandora's box argument reduced the issue to such an emotional level that Eritreans faced extreme difficulty in making any headway in African diplomacy with a few notable exceptions.[15] This began to change gradually with the progress of the liberation war when the balance of forces tipped in favor of Eritrean freedom fighters, particularly after the victory at Afabet in May 1988.[16] War had indeed become the final arbiter.

From Military Victory to National Referendum.

As already noted, May 1988 marks a turning point in the Eritrean-Ethiopian war. The capture by the forces of the Eritrean Peoples Liberation Front (EPLF) of the garrison town of Afabet, where the best and largest Ethiopian regiment—the Nadow Front—was concentrated, tipped the scale in the war decisively in favor of eventual Eritrean victory. Basil Davidson, the British writer, who happened to be there at the time, compared the Eritrean victory at Afabet with Dien Bien Phu.[17] Analysts and politicians alike who had predicted Eritrean defeat changed their views and began to pay due attention and respect to the Eritrean side.[18]

Meanwhile, the Soviet Union which had become Ethiopia's ally since 1977, stepping into US shoes, warned

11

the Dergue government to go for a negotiated settlement. Soviet President, Mikhail Gorbachev, warned Ethiopian leader, Mengistu, that there would be no more unlimited arms assistance.[19] Everyone called for negotiation. Former US president Jimmy Carter even tried his hand at it, but events had produced their own momentum and the victory of the EPLF forces became a foregone conclusion. The capture of the port of Masawa on February 10, 1990 sealed the fate of the occupying Ethiopian forces.

On May 24, 1991 the EPLF forces entered the capital, Asmara, and four days later the allied forces of the Ethiopian Peoples Revolutionary Democratic Front (EPRDF), an ally of the EPLF, entered Addis Ababa. Mengistu had fled to Zimbabwe a few days earlier. The 30-year war in Eritrea was over.

Two years later, on April 23-25, 1993, an internationally-observed referendum was held in Eritrea. The Eritrean people voted in favor of independence by 99.8%. At the close of the referendum process, Mr. Samir Samba, a UN official, solemnly declared the referendum to have been fairly conducted. The Provisional Government of Eritrea had postponed declaration of independence by two years and insisted on a referendum, as it had done earlier before victory.[20] The referendum, to which the government submitted the fate of the country, consummated the military victory and laid to rest any question as to the historic wishes of the Eritrean people. Eritreans had won their rightful place among the family of nations after a long and tragic war, unlike most other African people who had been granted independence peacefully.

Eritrea's case, the world now knows, was not one of secession of an ethnic minority from a constituted state, but was one of *denied decolonization*. Eritrea's rightful claim to self-determination and independence, a right accorded to Libyans and Somalis had been sacrificed on the altar of Cold

12

War power politics. What was denied by diplomacy was claimed by force of arms at great cost.

B. TRANSITION TO CONSTITUTIONAL GOVERNMENT

After the formal independence of the country, following the April 1993 Referendum, a transitional government was established designated as the Government of the State of Eritrea.[21] The government was charged with the responsibility, inter alia, of preparing the ground and laying the foundation for a democratic system of government. The Constitutional Commission of Eritrea was established in fulfillment of this responsibility.[22]

During the two years between military victory on May 24, 1991 and the establishment of the transitional government in 1993, the government which was established under Proclamation No. 1/91 was called Provisional Government. That law provided for the legislative, executive and judicial organs of government which was formed by the transformation of the principal organs of the EPLF into a proper government organ. The chief executive was titled Secretary-General of the government (later president) and the heads of the departments (later ministries) were designated as Secretaries.[23]

The provisional government enacted several transitional laws, including transitional codes.[24]

The EPLF-based government also passed other laws, one of the most important being Proclamation No 26 of 1992 providing for the establishment of regional government. The law dealt with the territorial division of the country (numbering ten at the time), the composition and function of the regional authorities, their relationship with the central (national) government, and the nature and extent of power sharing. It is noteworthy that, under that law, the judiciary is declared to be independent from the executive and legislative powers at all levels of the administration.[25] This law has been replaced by Proc. No. 86/1996 reorganizing the territorial division and reducing the number of region from ten to six.

The post-liberation period was a time of transition, transition from a devastating war and its consequences to peaceful reconstruction and rehabilitation. Transition also from a government of military provenance to one of democratic constitutionalism. It is worth reiterating that the EPLF was an armed political organization whose principal aim was liberation of the country from alien occupation. That task having been accomplished, the foundation was laid under Proclamation No. 1 to organize a society that would be ruled by a democratically elected government.

To that end the Eritrean government established the Constitutional Commission with the following mission:

(1) to draft a constitution on the basis of which a democratic order would be established, and which, as the basic law, would be the ultimate point of reference of all the laws of the country, and the final arbiter of all basic issues in dispute,

(2) in pursuit of the objective set forth above, to organize and manage a wide-ranging and all-embracing national debate and education through public seminars and lecture series on constitutional principles and practices."[26]

The Commission began its work in late April, 1994. The law establishing the Commission provided for a body with a membership of 50 people representing a cross-section of Eritrean society. The structure and function of the Commission and the strategy and methodology it adopted will be discussed in detail in the next chapter, together with its challenges and achievements. At this point reference will be made, by way of introduction, to two sets of questions that must be asked by those engaged in the task of constitution-making.

First, what are the values and goals that constitution-makers need most emphatically to promote, nurture and protect? The constitution must be both an embodiment and a consequence of a proper attachment to such values and goals.

Second, what are the main constitutional issues that a Constitutional Commission and the public must select for debate and eventual inclusion in the constitution?

Concerning the first question, the Charter of the Front for Democracy and Justice of Eritrea (PFDJ), the governing political organization (EPLF's successor body), set forth five major national strategic goals which the Constitutional Commission of Eritrea took as a significant source of national consensus and a point of departure for the public debate in which Eritreans were engaged since the beginning of the process. These goals and values are:-

1. Stability and National Unity;
2. Democracy;
3. Economic Development;
4. Social Justice;and
5. Human Rights.

The validity of these goals and values is not at issue. A civil order cannot be viable without such central goals and values, and the Constitution is the primary instrument of expressing them. There can be no civil order where there is no stability and national unity, as the experiences of Somalia, Liberia, Sierra Leone and Rwanda demonstrate. Nor is there any serious dispute as to the critical link between democracy, economic development, human rights and social justice. It has been aptly said, in this respect, that "...the pursuit of political virtue in the form of a vibrant democracy need not come at the expense of the drive for economic development."[27]

The public debate on the constitution confirmed the Commission's initial assumption of a national consensus on the goals and values: the public was asked on a number of occasions whether there were any alternative, or opposed visions, and none were forthcoming that questioned or challenged the vision of a future Eritrean society based on the five fundamental goals or values listed above.

With regard to the second question, namely, the constitutional issues that must be debated, this was confronted by the Commission at its first meeting. The Commission began its work by drawing up a list of 23 constitutional questions to guide its work of research and study and eventual drafting of the future constitution. The Commission selected 12 key issues for special attention and prepared papers on them, eventually turning these papers into concrete proposals for public debate. This will be discussed in detail together with the strategy and modalities adopted by the Commission to fulfill its mission.

Notes

1. See Jean Doresse, *Ethiopia, Ancient Cities and Temples*, London Elek Books 1959.
2. An Italian monk, Giuseppe Sapeto, arranged the sale of a strip of land around the port of Asab from some local chiefs. Giuseppe Sapeto who was knowledgeable of Ethiopian languages and culture, acted as agent of the Rubattino company.
3. Note that the purchase of Asab took place some ten

months before Italy's unification. Also, the Suez Canal construction was nearing completion, and the good monk's aim was to enable Italian ships to use Asab as a coaling station after the opening of the Suez Canal.

4. The Italians built roads, railways, and telecommunication facilities and expanded the port of Masawa.

5. See Bereket Habte Selassie, *Eritrea and the United Nations*, Trenton: Red Sea Press, 1989.

6. Ibid.

7. UN General Assembly Resolution No. 390 (V) Dec 2, 1950.

8. The commissioner was assisted by a panel of experts who agonized over Eritrea'a democratic future under a union with Ethiopia. See Ivor Jennings, *Approach to Self-government*, Cambridge University Press, 1956.

9. The constitution was approved on July 10, 1952. The Federation came into effect on Sept 15, 1952.

10. See note 8 supra.

11. The Emperor had prepared a Proclamation dissolving the federation several months before the Eritrean Parliament was presented with the fait accompli and asked to dissolve itself. The author had conversations with the then legal advisor at the Prime Minister's office, to the effect that the said Proclamation was being drafted for approval by the Emperor.

12. See the Report of the Panel of Legal experts whom Matienzo cites that the UN General Assembly had jurisdiction over the matter and that it could be seized of it. Final Report to the United Nations of the UN Commissioner to Eritrea, Chapter II, paragraph 201.

13. See Bereket Habte Selassie, op cit.

14. Ibid

15. The notable exceptions were Somalia and Guinea under Sekou Toure. The Somali government provided assistance

to the Eritrean struggle from the beginning to the end, except for a brief period when Siad Barre and Mengistu had agreed to suspend assistance to their respective opposition movements.

16. The government representatives at the Unite Nations, where I acted as representative of the Eritrean Peoples Liberation Front, began to be more receptive and helpful.
17. Mr. Davidson spoke to the BBC from the war front and thus helped broadcast the Eritrean victory to the world.
18. The case of Mr. Paul Henze who was an opponent is a good example.
19. As told to the author by persons close to the Soviet Mission at the United Nations.
20. The EPLF offer of a referendum in the mid 1980's was rejected by the Mengistu regime.
21. See Procl. No 37/93
22. Procl. No. 55/94
23. This was the title under the 1952 Const.
24. Civil Code, the Transitional Civil Procedure Code, the Transitional Penal Code, the Transitional Commercial Code, the Transitional Maritime Code and the Transitional Labour Law Code.
25. See chapter 11 for discussion on the judiciary.
26. Procl. No. 55/1994, article 4(2)
27. See J. Bhagawati, "The New Thinking on Development," Journal of Democracy Vol. 6. No. 4 Oct. 1995. PP. 51-64

Two

The Politics of Constitution Making

The question of our age...is whether a constitution can give recognition to the legitimate demands of the members of diverse cultures in a manner that renders everyone their due, so that all would freely consent to this form of constitutional association. Let us call this first step towards a solution 'mutual recognition' and ask what it entails (JAMES TULLY)[1]

Popular Participation, The Litmus Test.

When the Constitutional Commission of Eritrea embarked on its constitution-making mission in April 1994, none of its members had heard of the author of the above-quoted epigraph. Nor did, or could, any one of its fourteen-person panel of foreign advisors make any reference to his book which was published a year later, the book from which the quote was taken, although the question of popular participation in constitution-making was regarded by the Commission as a strategic point of reference and no one disputed the validity of this point.

Eritrea's constitution represents in fact a new approach in African constitution-making not dissimilar to the one advocated by Tully, with certain unique features of its own. This new approach marks a break with the past when constitutions used to be drafted by experts to the virtual exclusion of the public. I have called the old approach the Lancaster House model.[2]

The point of the epigraph quoted above is that there should be a radical paradigm shift in the matter of constitutionalism. This approach poses a serious challenge to the prevailing school of modern Western constitutionalism, a challenge backed by a historical and critical survey of over three hundred years of European and non-European constitutionalism. It has been called a post imperial approach to the organization of political community.[3] The approach calls for the conciliation of different claims for recognition over time through constitutional dialogue, in which citizens reach agreement on appropriate forms of accommodation of their cultural differences, guided by constitutional rules.

Despite the difference in the language, the approach followed in Eritrea's constitution-making approximates to this radical, "post-imperial," prescription. A "post-imperial" consciousness thus seems to be emerging, challenging the dominant paradigm in which a popularly grounded basis of consent which accommodates all the component elements of a society is the critical requirement for creating a country's constitutional system. In the spirit of such consciousness, the present book is an attempt to examine the Eritrean experience of constitution making by explaining the process that produced the constitution and commenting on the articles of the constitution itself—the product of the process.

The Constitutional Commission of Eritrea worked out a

strategy and organized research and public consultation efforts on the conviction that the process is as important as the product. Process and product are dialectically linked: the end prescribes the means, and the means impinges on the end. Process involving the public constitutes empowerment, giving the members of the public a sense of ownership of the constitution and providing them with an opportunity to air their views on a range of critical issues concerning their lives. There are several ways of writing a constitution, reflecting the history and politics of a given country. But there are certain key elements that are common to all democratic constitutions and the process of making them. The overriding consideration is that the people must play an active role in one form or another in the making of their constitution. This, as already noted, is an essential requirement of creating a constitutional system in a "post-imperial" condition.

Historically, we can discern three main methods of constitution making. The first, classical, example of constitution-making may be called the Philadelphia model. The Philadelphia constitutional Convention of 1787 comprised representatives of the then 13 states and combined the function of a drafting Commission as well as (partially) of a Constituent Assembly. The constituent character of the Convention was partial in that the Draft coming out of the Philadelphia convention had to be ratified by the legislature of each one of the several states.

The second example is a model followed by countries with established democratic systems. Under this model the drafting is left to the Parliament, or a committee of Parliament, and the ratification of the Draft is done by a larger majority (e.g. two-thirds) of the next Parliament or by popular referendum. The assumption on which this model proceeds is that Parliament represents all the constituent members of the political community in the country con-

21

cerned, which may not be necessarily the case. In fact, there may be instances in which Parliament is simply "an imperial center" in Tully's sense. A recent example of this is the attempt by the Scottish nationalists to obtain sovereignty for Scotland through the Scottish Parliament which was defeated by the Parliament in Westminister(the imperial Parliament), a defeat which the nationalists hope to reverse with the support of a labor government.

The third example is typified by the use of constitutional commissions. In recent years the use of a specially mandated drafting Commission and an elected Constituent Assembly to ratify the draft has gained currency. This has been the case with the recently promulgated constitutions of Ethiopia and Uganda, while in Namibia the elected Parliament turned itself into a Constituent Assembly. The time frame used for drafting the constitution, including public debate, varies from place to place: one year in Ethiopia and over five years in Uganda. In Eritrea the time frame originally proposed by the Commission was two years, but it turned out that an additional year was needed.

The common feature of this new politics of constitution-making in Africa is that it marks a break with the past when constitutions used to be drafted by experts in the capitals of the Metropolis (London, Paris or Brussels) or even in the African capitals, and in which debate was limited to a select few among the ruling elites. This is what I have called the Lancaster House Model.

The Significance of the Eritrean Experience.

The transitional government of Eritrea[4] and the Constitutional Commission which it established[5] were committed to the principle that the constitution must be written with the active participation of the people. There are two reasons for such commitment, historical and theoretical.

Historically, Eritreans owe their success in their lonely struggle against overwhelming odds, to the active participation of the people. Their adversaries, both under Emperor Haile Selassie until 1974, and under the military government of Mengistu Haile Mariam until 1991, were economically, diplomatically and militarily superior, and were alternately supported by the United States and the Soviet Union. Moreover, in the referendum of April 1993 to which the government submitted the fate of Eritrea, popular participation consummated the military victory and enhanced the role of the public in determining their fate. This historic event proved to the international community that Eritrea was able to win the war not only by military prowess, i.e. by the skill, tenacity and resilience of its fighters, but above all through reliance on the democratic process and on the support of its people.[6]

The popular participation of Eritreans in such historical processes relied on the inherent wisdom of encouraging and organising the people to be involved in decisions affecting their lives in all instances. This makes sense theoretically, and conforms to universal principles of democracy. It also accords with the historically evolved system of village democracy in which village communities governed themselves democratically through periodically elected assemblies. This village democracy forms a central part of Eritrean customary laws[7] and was preserved and utilized during the period of armed struggle.

The Role of the Constitutional Commission.

The law establishing the Constitutional Commission charged the Commission, as already noted, with the duty of organizing and managing "a wide-ranging and all-embracing national debate and education through public seminars and lecture series on constitutional principles and practices."[8] The law also provides that, following public debate on a constitutional Draft, the Commission must submit the Draft to the National Assembly, having taken the views of the public into account. The approved Draft must then be submitted to a Constituent Assembly for ratification.[9]

The establishment of the Commission was envisaged in the law which reorganized the government of Eritrea in the post-referendum period.[10] That law charged the government, inter alia, with maintaining the unity and territorial integrity of the country; guaranteeing the fundamental rights and liberties of its citizens; planning, organizing and directing the reconstruction and rehabilitation of the war-ravaged national economy; and, "above all, *preparing the ground and laying the foundations for a democratic system of government.*" (Emphasis added).[11]

The National Assembly established the Constitutional Commission in fulfillment of the last of the above-mentioned goal.[12] Proclamation No. 55/1994 which established the Commission provides that the members of the Commission shall comprise "experts and other citizens with proven ability to make a contribution to the process of constitution-making, and charged with the responsibility of drafting a constitution and organizing popular participation in such a process of constitution-making..."[13]

The Commission, which was accountable to the National Assembly, was composed of a Council of fifty members and an Executive Committee of ten people drawn from the Council. As noted before, the mission of the Commission was defined under Article 4(1) of the law which established it, as follows:

"To draft a constitution on the basis of which a democratic order would be established, and which, as the basic law, shall be the ultimate point of reference of all the laws of the country, and the final arbiter of all basic issues in dispute."

In pursuit of the objective set forth above, the Commission was authorized to organize and manage public debate and education. It was also authorized "to seek and receive assistance in funds, written materials and additional expert opinion on different constitutional practices" for the proper carrying out of its mission.[14]

The Commission was headed by a Chairman who presided over both the Council and the Executive Committee, assisted by a Vice-Chairman and a Secretary. All three officers were named and appointed by the National Assembly.[15] The Chairman was authorized, on behalf of the Commission, to direct and coordinate the activities of its various organs and to supervise the activities of the Secretary and of the various committees. Additionally, the Chairman was enjoined to encourage the participation and contributions of Eritreans and foreign experts and to organize *ad hoc* advisory boards of experts "to help expedite the process of preparing the Draft Constitution."[16] The Secretary's duties were to direct the secretariat of the Commission which handled all administrative and logistical matters.[17]

In order to carry out its tasks properly, the Commission established four research-oriented committees and one committee charged with organizing and managing civic education and public debate. The four research-oriented committees were:

Committee on Governmental Institutions and
   Human Rights;
Committee on Economic Issues;
Committee on Social and Cultural Issues; and
Committee on Governance and Related Issues.

The Commission also formed two Advisory Boards pursuant to Article 16(4) of the law: one to render advice on the experience of other countries, and another on Eritrean customary law. The Chairman of the Commission chose professor Owen Fiss of Yale University School of Law to chair the foreign Advisory Board.[18]

The Commission began its work by asking itself the following questions, in its first meeting:

- How do constitutionmakers go about the business of drafting a constitution of a country?
- What lessons, if any, do historical experiences offer in this respect?
- Do such experiences yield helpful models or guidelines?
- Is it desirable, or practicable, to use models: are they transferable like some technology?
- What, after all, are the values and goals that a nation needs, most emphatically, to promote, nurture and protect, and how should these be incorporated in a constitution?
- Should such values and goals be so incorporated, or should they be left to be determined and developed extra-constitutionally, i.e., in the crucibles of political action and social interaction—in the daily discourse of culture?
- What form of government would be best suited for Eritrea?
- What degree of decentralization should there be?
- Should there be an official language, or languages: if so, which ones do we select and why?

It was quite clear from the outset that some things could be appropriately left out of the constitution while others could not, which made the question susceptible to debate. There were other questions of detail, including some pertaining to technicalities such as the size of the constitution: should it be long or short? All in all, the Commission listed 23 questions with which it launched its historic mission.

The Commission organized its work methodically, dividing its two-year mandate into four phases. Phase One, beginning on Inauguration Day (April 16, 1994) and lasting until December 1994, involved the establishment of a headquarter; setting up and assignment of tasks of the five committees; conducting preliminary public meetings to introduce the work of the Commission on the subject of constitutional government; and fund raising and related logistical matters. The preliminary meetings were held inside Eritrea as well as abroad wherever Eritreans are found in large numbers.

During the same phase, the Commission translated into Tigrigna and Arabic and published several booklets including international legal instruments such as the Universal Declaration of Human Rights and all four of the 1966 UN covenants on political, social, economic and cultural rights. The Commission also published a handbook explaining, in simple language, constitutional principles and political ideas such as democracy , the rule of law, separation of powers and electoral systems. It organized a conference in mid-July designed to test its adopted method of constitution-making and to solicit the views of some experts, both Eritrean and foreign, including Ethiopian, Namibian, Egyptian and Swiss experts. Perhaps more important, it held a four day training seminar given to some 400 selected Eritreans who would play crucial roles in the civic education and public debates that followed in the second and third phases.

Phase two (January—May 1995) was principally concerned with civic education seminars explaining constitutional principles in more detail and reaching over half a million

Eritreans in village and town meetings throughout the country and abroad. On January 7-12, 1995, an international symposium was held in Asmara in which some 30 internationally known scholars and some 60 Eritreans participated and at which papers were presented on a number of constitutional and political issues.[19]

The Commission had prepared several Issue Papers on selected topics and sent them to the members of the Foreign Board of advisors for their comments which were voiced during the Symposium. Following the Symposium and before the large-scale civic education campaign was launched, the Commission reviewed its past activities and decided to consolidate the four research oriented committees into one Research Committee. The Civic Education Committee was strengthened and re-organized to carry out its function more efficiently. A Media Committee was added to organize and manage an intense publicity campaign using all available Media resources with the help of the Ministry of Information. Also during the latter part of Phase two the Commission transformed the Issue Papers into Proposals, which embraced the most critical of 23 issue which had been identified earlier.

In August 1995, in between Phases two and three, the Proposals were discussed and adopted by the Council of the Commission, published and distributed widely. The Proposals are a reflection and an outcome of research, public debates and expert views. The main objective of the Proposals was to raise more public awareness and to promote more focused debate on the most important constitutional issues before the first draft was written by the Commission.

In phase three (October—December 1995) the Commission organized wide-ranging public debates based on the concrete Proposals. The opinions of the people (both inside Eritrea and abroad) was meticulously recorded and collected. A summary of the questions raised and opinions given by the public was made and a draft constitution prepared for presentation to the Council of the Commission. The Council approved the draft on June 26, 1996. The approved draft was then presented to the National Assembly. The National Assembly approved the draft on July 3, 1996.

Thus began the final phase (phase four) of the process and continued with the publication and distribution of the approved draft. The public then held debates on the draft, between August 8 and November 1996. The Council reviewed the outcome of the final public debate and submitted the final draft to the National Assembly which approved it in December 1996. (See chapter 4 for details)

Challenges and Response: A Summing-up

The challenges facing the Constitution Commission from the start may be summarized under three main categories:

1. Ensuring maximum public participation;
2. Obtaining all the necessary personnel, equipment and facilities to accomplish its tasks; and
3. collecting and analysing opinions—both popular and expert—and selecting from them all the relevant points to be used in drafting the future constitution.

Public Participation

The most heartening feature of the Eritrean experience in constitution-making is the extent and quality of the public's involvement. The diffidence observed during the introductory phase was replaced by bolder and more candid participation in later meetings. During the second (civic education) phase the interest of the public—their eagerness to know—was pronounced. During the third phase, the distribution of concrete Proposals enabled the public to be more focused, to raise questions, air their views and express their concerns on a number of issues. It was clear that the people did indeed feel empowered, they became more keenly aware that they were determining their future system of government, thus amply justifying the Commission's approach.

Personnel Equipment and Facilities

With regard to the trained manpower needed for a satisfactory discharge of the Commission's duties, it should be borne in mind that Eritrea had suffered enormous loss as a result of the war-death and mass exodus to foreign countries. The impact of this loss is still being felt in all branches of government and in the society at large. The Commission made an effort to augment the work of the trained and experienced personnel found among its 50 members by tapping into all available national human resources throughout the first two phases of its life.

This was done by establishing several *ad hoc* sub committees for all the four committees. The Board of Foreign Advisors helped in this respect, as did individual scholars with whom some members of the Commission had previous professional contacts. The Law Schools of The University of North Carolina at Chapel Hill, Yale University and New York University provided invaluable help by supplying materials and making comments on a range of constitutional issues. The Board of Advisors on Customary Law made similar useful contribution in helping the Commission assess Eritrean native genius.

30

A number of Eritreans sent written comments and even detailed ideas on what should be included in the constitution. Needless to say, the final responsibility of what to include in the draft rested with the Commission.

In terms of equipment and facilities, the Commission's fund-raising efforts were crowned with success. The last batch of vehicles, audio-visual equipment parts and accessories arrived by the end of December 1995. The government of Eritrea made all necessary resources available to the Commission, starting with the provision of a handsome building for the Commission's headquarters and all media facilities as well as administrative and logistical support in the Commission's work in the rural areas. All of this government help was given with the utmost respect for the internal autonomy of the Commission and the integrity of the process.

Collection and Analysis of Views

This is an area where the Commission faced considerable challenge. The main concern was to make full and accurate record of the questions raised and views expressed by the public. It was important to ensure completeness and accuracy and also to make statistical analysis of the origin of the questions—region, age, gender, etc.., in order to be able to gauge public opinion in all its varied forms for drafting purposes and for future reference.

The main "tool" to achieve these ends was obviously an able personnel that took notes in every public meeting and dispatched them to the Commission headquarters. These manual methods of recording were supplemented by recording equipment—tapes, videos. The data was then collected and analyzed.

The bulk of the collected and analyzed data will be of

great historical interest. But the Commission's duty was to produce a draft that reflects public opinion as much as it was humanly possible.

Summing-up

It is one thing to write a good constitution. It is quite another to ensure constitutional rule. Looking beyond the time following the promulgation of the constitution of Eritrea what are the prospects for its successful application?

In the considered opinion of the Constitutional Commission, although having a constitution is important, an equally important—perhaps a more important—question is: building a vigorous political system. A constitution has to provide, among other things, the basic framework for building a viable government and political system.

The Commission worked in the belief that in order to be effective and enforceable a constitution has to fulfill the following basic conditions.

1. Its content must reflect present realities as well as be mindful of future developments in the society;
2. It must provide for the existence of government and social institutions that give it life and force and political and social forces that can enforce and defend it, forces with the necessary interest and capacities. [20]

In short, to be enforceable, a constitution needs institutions that put it into practice and political forces that build and develop these institutions. A constitution can only have force and effect where there is a political system that breathes life into it. There is no dispute on this point.

However, the history of other African countries teaches us that there has to be a balance between state construction and nation building, between state and civil society. The two go hand in hand; one should not grow at the expense of the other. Constitution makers have to be aware of this requirement and constitutionalize it as much as possible.

In the language of political science, one alternative is the Weberian ideal of a minimal state which has certain appeals as a useful tool, particularly under conditions where the state shows tendencies of overpowering and stifling civil society. In the ideal minimal state, government is conceived as a necessary evil; the best government is one that governs least, as Thomas Jefferson put it. Yet, in the African context, the case for a strong government is compelling, provided that certain conditions are satisfied. These conditions may be summed up in the doctrine of the rule of law and its related concept of human rights as well as separation of powers and government accountability.

Rule of law values must be embedded not only in the text of the constitution, but in the political system. There must be a bill of rights written in the constitution. There must be a judiciary with constitutionally guaranteed independence, acting as guardian of the rule of law, insulated from political pressures from both the executive and legislative branches.

A strong government must also be accountable primarily to an elected legislature. A legislature should not be just a deliberating body on bills proposed by the executive. It must have real power to legislate, and to challenge, and exercise oversight on, the activities of the executive. This function is best performed through a system of legislative committees with the authority to summon and question members of the executive. Hence the legislature must attract the best and brightest of the nation.

One critical function of legislative oversight, among others, concerns the military and security forces. A vigilant legislature must maintain a close scrutiny over these forces both to enable them to perform their duties properly and to exercise legitimate control. The military's intervention in politics has been a curse in African political development. In Eritrea, the military have a homegrown professional self-image as a result of their close link with the rest of the population during the protracted armed struggle. This is an invaluable asset which is absent in most of other African states. (For details on the Legislature see Chapter 9 below)

Notes

1. James Tuly, *Strange Multiplicity: Constitutionalims in an Age of Diversity*, Cambridge University Press, 1995. P.7.
2. In a paper titled "In Lieu of Lancaster House" delivered at Chatham House, January 10, 1996.
3. This characterization is made in the jacket of the book.
4. Established under Proclamation No. 37/1003.
5. Established under Proclamation No. 55/1994.
6. See Dan Connell, *Against All Odds*, Red Sea Press, 1993. The betrayal of of this democratic process has been the cause of crisis as explained in the Epilogue at the end of this book.
7. On Eritrean Customary Law. See Carlo Conti Rossini, *Diritto Consuetudinario del'eritrea*. Firenze 1938.
8. See Article 4(2) Proclamation No 55/1994.
9. Article 4(4)
10. Proclamation No 37/1993
11. Preamble to Proclamation No 37/1993, also reproduced in the Preamble of Proclamation. No. 55/1994.
12. Under the authority of Article 4(6) (a) and (b) of Procla-

mation No. 37/1993.

13. Preamble, paragraph 4.
14. Article 4(3).
15. Article 6(3).
16. Article 12.
17. Articles No. 3 and 4.
18. The Chairman had written a letter to Professor Fiss outlining the proposed role of the Board. Then both the Chairman and Professor Fiss consulted in choosing the other members. The members of the Board of Eritrean customary law experts were chosen in consultation with the appropriate local elders and the Ministry of Regional Government. Both Boards held two formal meetings, but informal consultations took place at various levels and times.
19. The proceedings of the Symposium are available in a bound volume at the Research and Documentation Center, Asmara and copies were distributed to government departments and interested persons.
20. Proposals.

Three
The Commission's Proposals

Our point of departure is the reality of our country, and the history, culture and political experience of our society, not any foreign model. The primary consideration would be to draft a constitution that could pass analytical and critical tests in terms of its suitability to our historical circumstances, its relevance to the overall aims and aspirations of our people, and its reflection of the principles of justice, human dignity, equality and democracy." (The Constitutional Commission of Eritrea)

> *Too many axes deforest the land*
> *Too many rules tie up the hand"*
> (A TIGRIGNA SAYING)

1. Background to the Genesis of the Proposals

The Proposals which the Commission prepared and published in August 1995 served the purpose of focusing the public mind on the most important issues that a constitutional debate must resolve before writing the draft for final debate. The Proposals themselves were the outcome of

37

meticulous research and vigorous discussion among the members of the Commission reinforced by expert consultations, both Eritrean and foreign. In tracing the origin of the Proposals, and the manner in which their final form was shaped, therefore, we need to outline the strategy of the Commission and the development of the ideas and issues which defined the public discourse from the inauguration meeting in April 1994 to August 1995.

As outlined in the last chapter, the Commission divided its mandate term into four phases. There were two intertwined golden threads running through four phases: public debate and expert consultation. Furthermore, the four phases were linked by what may be called conceptual continuum, in that, from the very beginning, the minds of the members of the Commission were continually engaged with the various issues as expressed in different ways, be it in civic education, seminars—both local and international—and the meetings of the Executive Committee and ad hoc committees. All these inter-connected activities aimed at producing an acceptable and workable constitution.

As already pointed out, the Commission started the process of constitution-making by drawing up a list of 23 basic questions and planning a strategy of expressing these questions in simple language that would be easily understood by the public. This was in keeping with the principal objective which placed the active participation of the people at the center of the process, eschewing the top-down approach adopted by other countries in previous constitution-making experience. Eritrea's preferred method may be likened to a gigsaw-puzzle, the different pieces coming from historical analysis and a careful reading of many constitutions. It involved a study of several constitutions, extracting from them all the important issues and deciding how the future Eritrean constitution should tackle them: To what extent and in what way they should be incorporated in the constitution.

The Chairman designate of the Commission had conducted a preliminary study of several constitutions, notably African, and prepared the list of questions, a few weeks before the inauguration of the Commission's work. The questions were presented to preliminary meetings of the Executive Committee along with other matters of administrative and logistical nature, including the budget of the Commission. Following discussion and concurrence of the Executive Committee, the list of questions was presented to, and exhaustively discussed by, the Council of the Commission at its first meeting, on April 17, 1994. This meeting took place a day after the inaugural meeting which combined a festive mood with a serious address by the President of the State of Eritrea.

The President's speech was concise and pithy, outlining his view on the purpose and function of a constitution, reminding the members of the Commission of their historic responsibility and wishing them success.[1]

The Commission embarked upon introductory public seminars in village and town meetings in late spring 1994. These seminars were designed to introduce the subject of constitution-making and constitutionalism, in broad outline, and to solicit views thereon. In this introductory exercise a pattern was established that would be followed, *mutatis mutandis*, right up to the end of the process. Meetings were held under the stewardship of members of the Executive Committee in the towns of the several regions, staring with Asmara, and abroad, among Eritreans in the Diaspora.[2] This was then followed by more meetings in other towns and villages in the course of the Summer and early Autumn of 1994 with the participation of the other members of the commission. In every meeting, a recording officer was assigned who dispatched to the headquarters the outcome of the meeting, noting all questions and answers and commenting on logistical and related problems, for future reference.

To these introductory public meetings was added what the Commission termed "a mini international conference" held in July 1994, designed as a testing ground for the approach followed by the Commission, as noted earlier. This particular conference which lasted four days aroused a great deal of curiosity among Eritrean intellectuals and was well attended. Important issues were discussed on the basis of a conference agenda related to the constitutional issues on which the four afore-mentioned research committees had conducted preliminary studies such as (1) government institutions, (2) human rights and the rule of law, (3) social and cultural issues and the constitution, (4) governance and the constitution, and (5) economic issues and the constitution. Eritrean intellectuals were identified and called upon to present papers addressing these issues. Additionally, four foreign experts were invited to submit papers highlighting the experience of their respective countries. These were: the former Chairman of the Constitutional Commission of Ethiopia, Mr. Kifle Wodajo, the Swiss Ambassador to Ethiopia and Eritrea, Dr. Peter A. Schweizer, the Namibian Ambassador to Ethiopia and Eritrea, Mr. Hinyangerwa P. Asheeke and an Egyptian constitutional Scholar, Professor Bedawi.[3]

These introductory seminars constituted the major portion of Phase One, which also saw the translation into Tigrigna and Arabic, and wide distribution, of several documents, notably international legal instruments including the following:

- The Universal Declaration of Human Rights.
- International Covenants on Economic, Social and Cultural Rights.
- International Covenant on Civil and Political Rights.
- Declaration on the elimination of discrimination

against women.
- Convention on the elimination of all forms of discrimination against women.
- Declaration on the principles and rights to development.
- Declaration on the principles of international cultural cooperation.
- Convention on the rights of the child.
- African Charter on Human and Peoples Rights.

Between the end of Phase One and the start of Phase Two, the Commission produced a handbook titled An Introduction to the Idea of a Constitution, in Tigrigna and Arabic, with a companion small volume in cartoons, illustrating basic constitutional concepts. In December 1994, the Commission organized a four day training seminar and workshops involving four hundred participants carefully selected to help the future civic education and public debate programs. To that end, a network of centers was established in each of the country's ten administrative regions. The centers were established to facilitate the transmission of information to, and receipt from, the public and to inform the Commission on local opinion concerning its work. Heading these centers were Seven provincial head offices and seventy-three local committees were formed to oversee and help organize the work.

Before the start of Phase Two (Jan-May 1995) which featured civic education, the on-going public consultation was climaxed in an international symposium, held in January 7-12, 1995. Before the symposium, the Commission's Executive Committee and its research committees held meetings specifically designed to extract from the initial list of questions the most basic set of issues in order to prepare what were termed Issue Papers. In other words, the initial issue-by-issue discussion strategy was replaced by aggregating the issues into major questions covering various topics such as legislative power, the structure of the judiciary, electoral systems, decentralization, fundamental rights and freedoms, social, economic and cultural rights, equality guarantees, and the structure of the executive.

The Issue papers prepared by members of the Commission with expertise on the respective topics were distributed among prominent Eritreans and the departments of the government. They were also sent to the Chairman of the Foreign Board of Advisors, Professor Owen Fiss, for distribution to the other members of the Board. Since the International symposium was designed, among other things, to examine these Issue Papers and offer comments, the members of the Board were requested to critique these papers.[4]

Following the conclusion of the Symposium, the Commission concentrated on civic education. To that end, it assigned the four hundred trained people civic education tasks, joining their efforts, when necessary, with those of members of the Commission assigned the same task. The committees established in foreign countries in which a large numbers of Eritreans lived, were also assigned similar tasks. Over half a million Eritreans participated in civic education seminars. Among the participants 40% were women. A break down of the number of participants inside Eritrea by province is shown in the following figures:[5]

Number of civilian Participants by Province.

Provinces	Number of Participants
Gash-Setiti	26,947
Asmara	52,169
Seraie	101,145
Akele-Guzay	83,713
Barka	17,129
Hamasien	51,939
Semhar	14,235
Denkel	11,997
Senhit	48,779
Sahil	12,030
Total	**420,092** [6]

During the latter part of Phase Two, the Executive Committee met to review its work and decide, among other things, to restructure the work of its *ad hoc* committees. Accordingly, as already noted, the four research-oriented committees were consolidated into one Research Committee. The Civic Education and Public Debate Committee was mandated to continue as before with a sharper focus on public debate. A Media Committee was established to help coordinate the Commission's public campaign activities with relevant government departments, notably the Ministry of Information.

The Executive Committee then discussed the Issue Papers in light of the outcome of the public seminars and expert opinion, particularly those provided at the International symposium. The Issue Papers, thus enriched, were transformed into Proposals comprising eight papers:

- Electoral System
- The Legislative Branch
- Women and the Constitution

43

- Decentralization
- Fundamental Rights and Freedoms
- The Executive Branch and the Structure of the Government (which system is appropriate for Eritrea?)
- The Judiciary
- Defense and Security Institutions
- Language Policy.

The Proposals were submitted to the Fourth Regular Session of the Council of the Commission on August 9, 1995, for debate and approval. After approval, the Proposals were printed in booklet form and widely distributed inside Eritrea and abroad. It bears repeating that these Proposals were the outcome of research, of wide-ranging public debate and expert comments and that their main objective was to focus public attention on the most important constitutional questions and thus raise public awareness and make the ensuing debate meaningful.

It is worth noting that the use of theater and musical groups in several languages proved extremely helpful in imparting knowledge and raising public awareness on constitutional issues and imbuing citizens with a sense of their own importance in making the basic law by which they would be governed. The use of theatrical and musical groups was started during Phase Two and continued through phase three. Radio drama and student contest on information about the constitution was also utilized. The Civic Education committee organized many student contests and mobile theaters. Elementary and Secondary school students were challenged to write poetry or essays touching on constitutional issues. Such student activities further enhanced parental interests in, and engagement with, the process. University students conducted panel discussions which were broadcast over the radio.[7]

2. The Content of the Proposals.

In offering the Proposals for public debate, the Commission explained in the Introduction to the Proposals that its contents reflected some of the principal issues determining the future constitution. Accordingly, the views that will be expressed and the position taken on the issues would shape the kind of constitution that the country will have. "The principal aim of these proposals", the Commission stated," is to generate views and encourage debates. We have great expectations that all citizens will participate in the coming debates"[8]

The Proposals were divided into two parts, Part One dealt with Constitution and Constitutional system and what type of Constitution Eritrea should have. Part two dealt with the following six major topics involving constitutional issues:

a) Type of Government—Legislative, Executive and Judicial Powers.
b) Fundamental Human Rights and Duties.
   Civil and Political Rights and Duties
   Social, Economic and Cultural Rights.
c) Administrative Arrangements
d) Electoral System
e) The Issue of Language(s)
f) Armed and Security Forces

Part One: Constitution and Constitutionalism

This section of the Proposals gives a succinct description of the main functions and objectives of a constitution. It explains the difference between, on the one hand, a constitution which contains the basic principles pertaining to the powers and responsibilities of government, and the rights and

45

duties of citizens and laws and regulations issued under the constitution, on the other. It also explains the difference between constitution and constitutionalsim. "A constitution without constitutionalsim is a lifeless document", it asserts, "In order for a constitution to be meaningful, therefore, it is necessary to have appropriate institutions and procedures that ensure popular support and participation."[9]

Constitutionalsim is linked with democracy and the rule of law. Indeed, democracy and the rule of law are posited in the Proposals as the foundation of a constitutional system. Institution building is thus emphasized in tandem with the sustained development of popular consciousness. This section of Part One of the Proposals sums up the Commission's view as follows:

> "....a constitution is the source of the basic rights and duties and the principal instrument of the objectives of a nation and the government. Therefore, the constitution that we draft must serve the following two aims:
> (1) to build an appropriate/vigorous political system:
> (2) to develop a democracy in tune with our national conditions".[10]

Part one of the Proposals also deals with the question of what type of constitution would be suitable for the country. The Commission is at pains to caution against copying foreign models. It recognizes the usefulness of learning from the experience of other countries but insists on maintaining "ideological and political independence". In addition to the two basic conditions stated above, the Commission argued that in order to be practical and enforceable a constitution must reflect the present realities of a country while being mindful of future developments of the society. It reiterated the need to secure the existence of governments and social institutions, "that give life and force" to the constitution and political and social forces that can enforce and defend it, forces with the necessary stakes and capacities.[11]

Part one ends with a summary discussion of the subject of building an appropriate/vigorous political system on which the fortune of a workable constitutional system is fastened. In the Eritrean condition, as perhaps in most modern governments, emphasis is laid on the issue of national unity or sense of nationhood transcending parochial interests, together with the building of a secular democratic ethos. Related to this is the need to ensure equal participation of all citizens in the life of the nation.

The Commission also stressed the imperative of building a system which is inclusive and which serves to strengthen "unity-in-diversity," citing the experience of the Eritrean revolution as proof that diversity can be a source of strength rather than of weakness.[12] Such diversity must respect the rights of everyone, maintaining a balance between the rights and duties of citizens and the powers and responsibilities of the government.

Modern versus Traditional Democracy

The subject of democracy will be discussed in greater detail in chapter 9 below. At this point, it suffices to explain briefly the distinction between substantive and procedural democracy. "Transition to Democracy" has become, these days, a rallying cry for people involved in the struggle to change oppressive, autocratic regimes, as well as for international "donors", both bilateral and multi-lateral like the World Bank as conditions for loans or assistance. This phenomenon presents an extraordinary challenge, intellectually as well as in practical terms.

This challenge is part of the dialectic of State-society relations and their relative strengths and weaknesses: of creating and maintaining a modern democratic, constitutional system. It is a challenge which is bound to test the quality of the leaders and citizens of a country alike. Leaders in emerging modern democracies are faced with cruel dilemmas, harnessed as they are to weak state institutions against a background of tradition-bound societies in most of which there are strong social forces opposed to progress. The challenge is further complicated by the fact that there are democratic traditions in much of traditional societies which must be identified reinforced and preserved.

The Proposals try to sharpen the debate by dividing the subject into substantive and procedural democracy. Both aspects of democracy are essential and should be properly understood and given a place in the scheme of things. One cannot do without the other. Thus, electoral law and politics represents the procedural aspect of democracy. It is vital in modern representative democracy as will be explained in more detail below. At the same time, the "bread and butter" aspect of political life—who gets what, when and how—is the central aspect of democracy which the procedural aspect must serve.

This subject has been a central part of political discourse for a long time. More recently, the debate has centered on whether democracy can, or should, be jettisoned, or make way for, national development. Some have argued that this is a risky venture that can be fatal to democracy. Others have contended that democracy dies hard. As Richard Sklar has put it "Democracy stirs and wakens from the deepest slumber whenever the principle of accountability is asserted by members of a community or conceded by those who rule.[13] Most leaders claim to respect democracy and the accountability principle on which it rests. But many leaders also contend, armed with a developmental ideology, that the imperatives of development are more compelling than the claims of democracy. The debate continues without resolution; it will be a foolish scholar, indeed, who asserts without allowing room for flexibility that there is one form of democracy applicable to all African countries. As Sklar pointedly contends democracy in Africa is as varied as "the ever-changing forms of government in more than fifty sovereign states. In his view, because democracy in Africa is an experimental process in a new generation of countries, we should study this process not only to learn about Africa, but also "to refresh our knowledge about the meaning of democracy itself."[14]

What the intellectual discourse cannot, and should not, ignore is the history of abuse and misuse of power in Africa and elsewhere, and that the principal source of this abuse and misuse is the absence of sufficient means of accountability. Thus, the first part of Sklar's statement, quoted above is of the essence, and its implied emphasis on the need to strengthen the "community" (i.e., civil society) cannot be overstressed.

Part-Two: Constitutional Issues

Using the discussion of Part-One as a point of departure, the Commission's Proposals then delve into the six principal issues listed above. The commission cautioned that the views expressed were preliminary in nature, to be modified through debate and further research, which would be the bases for further elaboration and expansion. With these cautionary remarks the Commission then discussed the issues one by one as summarized below.

a) Type of Government
The type of government that a constitution establishes is an

important constitutional question which determines the nature and quality of the political system. There are two related questions in this respect: the separation of power on the one hand, and the form of government (i.e. presidential or parliamentary), on the other.

The classical and near-universal division of government into the legislative, executive and judiciary is a model that one cannot avoid in this day and age. But in the Commission's view, a nation is not condemned to choose between the models of presidential or parliamentary system.

Separation of power, together with the related system of checks and balance, the Commission admitted, is an important historically developed principle viewed in conjunction with the expansion and strengthening of government power. "Regardless of the type of government we choose, this (basic) principle is fundamental. Regardless of the type of government we choose, if appropriate executive, legislative and judicial bodies are not established, the government becomes merely a skeleton."[15]

The Proposals then explain the nature and function of the three branches of government. The Legislature, the Commission holds, must have the ability to collect essential information on the country and its surrounding areas in order to make appropriate decisions or to pass legislation. It should be able to utilize research and studies and show willingness to accept expert advice, be open to people's views, and above all, "be an effective body that actually participates in leading the country and make the executive body accountable."[16]

The Commission observes that one of the most controversial issues in constitutional debates is the question: How can an executive body effectively carry out its responsibilities while obeying the rule of law and respecting the bounds of its power. "This question arises", the Commission states, "because historically, executive bodies have shown a persistent tendency to accumulate power in their own hands."[17] This raises the question of how we can develop an effective body, with delineated powers, which is accountable and functions openly. What is the appropriate and workable balance between effectiveness and power limitation"? The Commission sums up this particular discussion by pointing out that in Eritrea's current stage of nation building a strong leadership with clear vision is essential for the fulfillment of the major objectives and values of government and society.[18]

With regard to the judicial branch, the Commission asserts the principle of an independent judiciary as one of the pillars of constitutional government. The judiciary must be free from the interference of the other branches. At the same time the judges themselves must also be competent and free from corruption. A point of great interest which arose throughout the debates that followed concerned the question of what principle and institutional mechanisms should be adopted in order to secure judicial independence and ensure that there are competent and incorruptible judges.[19]

This section of the discussion concludes by stating that "the three government bodies are interrelated and must work together, checking each other while maintaining a proper balance. It is important to keep in mind that the health of each component of the system determines the overall health of the system, and vice versa."[20]

Next, concrete proposals are made on each of the branches. The Commission proposed that, based on the country's history and needs, a one-chamber legislature is the most suitable, and that the members should be elected for five years. The legislative body should elect a president from among its members to serve for five years with a two-thirds majority.[21]

The legislative body (Parliament) should also establish different standing committees to deal with areas such as economic, foreign relations, legal etc. It was proposed that there should be a standing body of the legislature composed of the chair (Speaker) of the Parliament and the chairs and members of the various standing committees. Parliament should have the power to impeach the president, with the support of three-fourths of votes, in the event that the president violates the constitution and commits an offense "harmful to national interest."[22]

The Proposals recommend that the executive power of the government should be vested in a president who should be elected for two terms of five years. The president can form a cabinet and appoint ministers, judges and other high-ranking officials of the government with the approval of Parliament. The details would be written in the draft constitution.

The Judiciary should be constituted by a Supreme Court and other courts functioning under it. The judiciary interprets laws and adjudicates cases presented to it. The power to interpret the constitutionality of laws and actions should be under the sole jurisdiction of the Supreme Court.

b) Fundamental Human Rights and Duties

The Commission's Proposals link human right with social justice as a prerequisite for the enjoyment of human rights. In the Commission's view, human rights remain abstract notions, for the majority of peoples, in the absence of the economic and social conditions that guarantee a certain degree of security. Human rights and social justice are thus inseparable objectives, and the Commission expressed the link by observing: "when we say social justice in Eritrea, we mean a system based on upholding human rights, ensuring balanced development and providing equal opportunities to all citizens."[23]

The Proposals then proceed to note two categories, the so called "generations", of human rights: civil and political rights, on the one hand, and social, economic and cultural rights, on the other. Such a distinction is useful not only for analytical or expository reasons, but because it obviates the task of careful drafting of the constitution, at the end of the process. Whereas the classical concept of rights—civil and political—is entrenched in constitutions virtually without exception, the inclusion of the "second generation" rights in the constitution is a matter of exception, and to the extent that they are included, it is not without qualification.

The Proposals declare that fundamental human rights of the classical variety—right to life, humane treatment of prisoners, right to belief, freedom of expression and the right to form association, etc.—should be enshrined in the constitution. The Proposals also insert a reminder that there must be corresponding duties which are assumed but often neglected in public discourse on the subject. Another pertinent issue, of relevance to the discussion, is the equality of citizens in the application of rights and duties, including gender equality. "On the basis of this equality", the Proposals assert, "the government and society have the responsibility to take the necessary steps to enable women to achieve equality in all areas."[24]

The Proposals also insert another reminder, namely that in the context of a given society the appropriate balance between individual rights and community rights requires special attention. "In theory, rights can be abridged for national security, health reasons, and during national emergency situations, (but) there are certain rights which cannot be violated even during a national emergency situation, and that the declaration of emergency should be lifted as soon as the conditions causing the emergency are non existent".[25]

The Proposals end this section of rights by recommending that rights should be written in simple and general terms which can be interpreted and expanded through application over time.

As regards social, economic and cultural rights the proposals reiterate that human rights cannot be complete without these rights. These rights include rights to education, health, balanced development, development of culture, languages, etc. A cautionary note is voiced by the Commission in its Proposals, namely that rights which cannot be implemented for lack of resources should not be listed as categorical imperatives. However, this does not mean that such rights should not be mentioned as goals to be achieved in time, as and when the nation acquires the necessary resources. Again, it is recommended that social, economic and cultural rights should be presented in general terms which can be expanded through parliamentary legislation and judicial interpretation as needs arise and resources permit.

c) Administrative Structure

A unitary (as against federal) government is the preferred option as being consistent with Eritrea's goal of building a unified and strong nation. At the same time a degree of decentralization is recognized as essential for peoples' participation and initiative at the regional or local level. It is the considered opinion of the Commission that the details on the degree of decentralization should be determined by legislation issued under the constitution rather than specified in the constitution. More power can be devolved to regional or local institutions with the economic and social development of the regions; it should not be forced through policy decision at the center alone.[26]

The regional administrative arrangement has been changed since the publication of the Proposals. The law now reduces the regions from ten to six, and there has been a redrawing of the maps. The major consideration in this new map of regions has been a developmental rationale which joins areas with geographic proximity, having a unified economic and social life. It also fulfills the primary goal of national unity.[27]

d) Electoral system

An electoral system involves a process that enables peoples' participation and representation in government. As such, it is a determining factor in the optimal performance of the political system. The Commission studied carefully a number of electoral systems, adopted by several countries including relative majority, and proportional representation. From this study, it became clear that the systems can change with changing political and demographic conditions. Accordingly, The Commission decided that it is not necessary to prescribe any particular system in the constitution. Rather, what needs to be stated in the constitution is the principle of fair representation and equal opportunity for all citizens to participate in the electoral process.[28] A Parliamentary Act can then prescribe the details.

e) Issue of Languages

Is language policy a constitutional issue? If so, what should that policy be? Should the constitution provide for an official language(s)? If so, which language or languages? These are questions which engaged the minds not only of the members of the Commission and government officials but the public at large. Depending on the history, ethnic composition and related political issues, the language question can be, and has been in several instances elsewhere in Africa, a sensitive matter.

The Commission's Proposals in this regard begin with a bold assertion: "Objectively speaking, there is no compelling reasons why the issue of languages should be a political issue. The people of Eritrea speak different languages...All people communicate in the language that is easy for them, and citizens learn more than one language."[29]

The Commission considered carefully the question of whether or not to include the question of language in the constitution and decided that, although it is not necessarily a constitutional issue, in Eritrea's case, it should be raised in the constitution. And it must be raised as a principle providing for the equality of all Eritrean languages. This principle of equality being the controlling factor, it meant that instead of providing for an official language(s), what should be given constitutional backing is what had already been a policy of the government—the policy of developing all languages.

The Proposals expressed this commitment in the strongest possible way:

"We must handle the issue of language in a way that serves and strengthens our basic goal of building a unified and strong nation. The equality of all Eritrean languages, the cultural and psychological importance of starting education with the mother tongue, the need for a common medium of instruction from the middle to higher levels of education, the right of every citizen to use in government activities any language he/she chooses, are important considerations."[30]

At the present time, Tigrigna, Arabic and English are the working languages in terms of the issuance of the country's laws and regulations. All three are taught in schools and English is the language of instruction at upper secondary school level and in the university. This being the case, parents who think of their children's future are expected to guide their children towards learning these languages as early as possible. But what cannot be overstressed is that all language groups have the right to develop their languages and the government is committed to the provision of the requisite resources and facilities in the realization of that objective.

f) Armed Forces and Security Institutions.
Of all the institutions of the modern African State none had drawn more curiosity—often morbid curiosity—of outside observers, than the armed forces. And none has been more critical in the life and fortune of the states. Indeed, the intervention of the military in politics and the consequent distortion of the democratic process is a natural subject for attention of scholars and policy-makers, be they domestic or foreign, and many volumes have been published on the subject. The topic of military coups d'etat is one that dominated newspaper pages and salon conversations, and the experience of Nigeria, among others, in recent years demonstrates that the subject will not go away.

The Commission starts the subject of military by stating that due to "the negative experience of many Third World countries, a question that generates the constitutional debates is: what guarantee is there that military coups will not occur?"[31] In answering this question, the Commission observes that the question is not susceptible to easy answers, that it cannot be answered out of the context of a country's general conditions and in particular without regard to the type of training and quality of the armed forces and security institutions. This is so, the Commission contends, because a coup is a symptom rather than the root cause of a country's problems. When the system lacks the capacity to resolve its political economic and social problems in a democratic manner, then a military coup or the recent phenomenon of state collapse ensues. The basic guarantee against the occurrence of coups is thus the establishment of an appropriate political system and effective institutions including the armed and security forces.

In Eritrea, these forces were built not as a separate caste, isolated from the rest of the society, but were an integral part of the society. This is one of the salutary legacies of the armed struggle. The core of the present armed and security forces is the former EPLF guerrilla army. "From the very beginning, its (the EPLF's) small band of guerrilla, while bearing arms, planted in people's minds the doctrine that politics command guns, articulating policies on the expression of popular will, of popular interests, needs and aspirations."[32]

The Commission's proposals take the experience of the armed struggle as basic condition for the development not only of the *esprit de corps* of the Eritrean armed forces but as the determining condition for their future behaviors and attitude *vis-a-vis* the constitution and the law. Their culture is popular and democratic, a factor which has been reinforced and maintained in the post-liberation situation. The armed forces and security institutions have been, and continue to be, national in composition and basic outlook, representing all segments of the nation and dedicated to uphold and defend the national interest. This is the first guarantee, the first line of defense of institutional rule.

The commission ends the discussion of this subject by stating that in order for the armed forces to be effective servants of the country, the President should be their commander-in-chief and the armed forces should be free from affiliations with any political party.[33]

3. The Public Debate on the Proposals.

The public debate on the Proposals was launched in mid-September 1995. Proposals had been distributed to the public and broadcast over the national radio beginning from the last week of August. As on previous occasions, the introductory meetings were launched by members of the Executive Committee of the Commission in all the main city centers and widely reported in the nation's Mass Media.

Before the start of the public debates, the Commission reorganized the implementation machinery dividing the country into four regions and counting the countries abroad in which Eritreans resided as a fifth region. One member of the Commission was put in charge of each region and the rest of the members of the Commission were assigned to manage the discussions or debates. At the highest level of the administrative region (*Zoba*) members of the Commission's Executive Committee started the debates, as noted above, by making introductory remarks, explaining the salient points of the Proposals. These meetings were attended by the leaders of the *Zoba*, including the Administrators, and their colleagues.

The meetings were then extended more widely encompassing the lower levels of the administrative structure, going down to the villages. When compared with Phase Two (Civic Education), this phase was less inclusive of the population. Phase Two was designed to spread knowledge about constitutional issues whereas the debate on the Proposals was principally meant to enable members of the community to review the Proposals and offer their views on them. Accordingly, quality of participation, rather than the sheer number of participants was the principal consideration. The nature of the questions raised and opinions given were thus of high quality, invariably accompanied by a lively spirit. On an average, meetings lasted not less than four hours. The reports coming from the majority of the various regions indicate that participants had carefully read the Proposals, judged by the number and quality of questions raised and points registered.[34]

The similarity of the opinions expressed and points raised between the debates taking place inside Eritrea and those abroad was striking. In some parts, such as major cities in the United States and Europe, educated Eritreans raised questions with considerable degrees of sophistication. But, by and large, there were very few questions arising outside the ambit

59

of the Proposals and the vast majority of views agreed with those expressed in the Proposals. However, many people offered alternative suggestions on a number of points raised in the Proposals. For example, the manner of the election of the President gave rise to different suggestions depending on the operating system in the host country. Eritreans living in the United States of America wondered why the Proposals did not adopt direct election of the President as in the United States. Those living in countries with Parliamentary systems in Europe tended to agree with the Commission's proposal for an indirect election by Parliament.

Other examples which provoked heated debate are language and the source from which people would be drawn for ministerial appointment by the President. Concerning the issue of language, those who strongly suggested that there should be an official language, or two, tended to be worried about the cost implication, both political and financial, of the principle of equality of languages, as mentioned already. With regard to the Proposals' suggestion that ministers can be appointed from among the members of Parliament as well as others outside it, concerns were voiced about the possible diluting effect this might have on the principle of separation of powers.

The Commission's Committee on Civic Education and Public Debate registered all questions and points raised and submitted a summary report for the consideration of the Commission in drafting the constitution. Most of what may be called new points—points not covered in the Proposals— were in the nature of details which would be covered in the draft constitution and answers were given to that effect at the meetings and noted in the reports accordingly. These points of detail demonstrate the seriousness with which Eritreans viewed the Constitution-making process and the time and other resources they were willing to spend on it, including travel and other expenses out of their own pockets.

All in all, public meetings were held, during this phase, in 157 different places inside Eritrea, involving over 110,000 Eritreans. These meetings started on September 17, 1995 and ended on December 27, 1995, covering over three months of public debate. It is the opinion of all the members of the Commission and other Eritreans who were actively engaged in the conduct of these meetings that they had great impact on Eritreans, imparting new knowledge or awareness or, in some cases, enhancing existing knowledge on constituionalism. Every one of those involved in the conduct of the debates came away impressed with the empowering quality of such debates as expressed by participants of the meetings. Earlier uncertainties and puzzlement were replaced by enthusiasm and, in several instances, appreciation for the degree of care and concern with which the Commission prepared the Proposals and the background research and other preparations that went into the making of the Proposals. The entire process thus contributed in instilling in the participants a sense of ownership of the future constitution.

The role of the Media in this respect was outstanding. There were reporters in most meetings held inside Eritrea reporting the event instantly and the national radio broadcast their reports. The reports were often accompanied or followed by commentaries on the event which added to the momentum, inducing more and better participation in meetings that followed. Some 35 Newspaper articles covering different constitutional issues were published by several commentators. There was also a TV broadcast of panel discussions in which some select experts participated.[35]

The views expressed and points raised throughout the debates were collected and analyzed by the Executive Committee of the Commission. A summary of points raised during the debates that would cause the Commission to adjust its previously held views was made for eventual inclusion in the draft. These will be mentioned in later chapters when the relevant provisions are discussed.

Notes

1. A copy of the President's speech delivered at the inauguration of the Commission's work in April 1994, is found in the archives of the Center for Research and Documentation, Asmara. It is fair to question the sincerity of the President in view of subsequent events, including his suppression of the ratified Constitution.
2. These included: Ethiopia, Saudi Arabia, Italy, Germany, UK, U.S.A, and Canada. In all of them committees were formed to organize public debate.
3. Professor Bedawi was sent courtesy of the Egyptian Embassy to Eritrea at the suggestion of their Ministry of Foreign Affairs.
4. Comments by members of the Board of Advisors on the Issue papers as well as on the constitutional draft are on file.
5. The Provincial system was changed in 1996.
6. In this table the number of members of the national service who participated in the seminars is not included.
7. The Radio broadcast news report and commentaries on the constitutional process, twice a week.
8. Proposals Introduction.
9. Proposals p.3.
10. Ibid. p.9.
11. Ibid. p.5.
12. Ibid. p.7.
13. See Richard Sklar, *African Studies Review*, Vols. 26, nos. nos. 3/4, September/December 1983. p. 11
14. Ibid.
15. Proposals

16. Ibid. p.16 and 17
17. Ibid.
18. Ibid.
19. See Chapter 11 below.
20. Ibid p.18.
21. This was later changed to a majority
22. Proposals, p.19.
23. Ibid. p.20
24. Ibid. p. 21
25. Ibid p. 22
26. Ibid. p. 23.
27 See Proclamation No. 86/1996
28. Ibid. p.24.
29. Ibid. P. 24
30. Ibid.
31. Ibid P. 25
32. Bereket Habte Selassie, "Reflections on the Future Political System of Eritrea." ERD Working Paper No. 3, Washington DC, June 1990. However, as this book goes to press, stories coming out of Eritrea indicate that the President of Eritrea, as the commander-in- chief of the armed forces, is decimating the rank of the former guerrilla army and replacing them with new recruits that have been baptized as "Warsai." This does not augur well for the country and has become a bone of contention and a serious issue discussed by Eritreans of all walks of life.
33. Proposals p. 25.
34. Concluding Report of Civic Education and Public Debate Feb 16, 1996.
35. Ibid.

Four

The Draft Constitution and its Ratification

(While) the will of the majority is in all cases to prevail, that will, to be rightful, must be reasonable. The minority possess their equal rights, which equal laws must protect, and to violate would be oppression.. If there be any among us who wish to destroy this union, or to change its republican form, let them stand undisturbed, as monuments of the safety with which error of opinion may be tolerated where reason is left free to combat it.
(THOMAS JEFFERSON, INAUGURAL ADDRESS, 1801)

Writing the First Draft

There are two principal and related questions which constitution makers must first address: what should be included in a constitution and how long should it be? These questions logically raise another one: how does one determine what should, or should not, be included in a constitution? Are there a set of universally applicable criteria, or is each country's choice determined by specific historical conditions in writing a constitution?

The detailed answer to the first two questions in the case of Eritrea will be provided in the discussion of the chapters of the Constitution (chapters 5-12). The answer to the last question must obviously be: both. From the writing of the American constitution in 1787, the first complete (and enduring) constitution of the modern epoch, constitutions have been modeled on preceding models or experiences. This is so not only in terms of form but content as well, because there are certain universally accepted principles of government. At the same time, the historical conditions of a given nation—its culture, social structure and governmental policies—inevitably play a modifying role. How much such modifying role affects some of the universal principles differs from case to case.

The Abbe Sieyes, the constitutional genius of the French revolution, provided some generalizations on writing a constitution, based on his own direct, first hand experience and from his reading of history and philosophy. His reading notably included French philosophers such as Montesquieu, Rousseau and Voltaire, as well as constitutional documents such as that of the United states of America, which was two years old at the time of the explosion of the French revolution.[1]

Writing a century after Sieyes, the British scholar, Lord Bryce, affirmed the rule of brevity, adding simplicity and precision of language as essential requirements for writing a good constitution. In his admirable summary of the essential elements that make the American constitution excel, he ranked it above every other written constitution "for the intrinsic excellence of its scheme, its adaptation to the circumstances of the people, the simplicity, brevity, and precision of its language, *its judicious mixture of definiteness in principle with elasticity in details.*"[2] [Italics supplied.]

Above all else Bryce's last phrase provides the key to writing a good constitution. Drafting a constitution may be likened to both a work of art and an engineering exercise because it can test the writing skill of the best draftsman in terms of the choice of language, its precision and clarity while, at the same time, requiring craftsmanship in building the edifice of state institutions. An edifice is built to last and in the case of a constitutional edifice, it has to be built so as to weather the storm, as it were, of changing political fortune. Having lived through the tumultuous times of the revolutionary period until Napoleon's coup d'etat, Sieyes' keen intellect and sensitive soul understood and articulated this point. Keep the constitution "neutral," he counseled, or at least open-ended in political-ideological terms (particularly in the Bill of Rights provisions). Otherwise, it may be too closely identified with "the transient fortunes of a particular political party or pressure group, and rise and fall with them".[3]

This counsel, among other reasons, justifies and explains the need for a professional, legal panel to lead the drafting of a constitution. "Neutrality" may be disputed as a controlling concept in this respect, but not objectivity. Even a partisan of a ruling party or group can objectively see the rationale behind Sieyes' counsel if he or she is forward-looking and can see the perils of being wrapped in present, parochial, or existential concerns only.

In the constitution-making experience of Eritrea, the Commission met this question head-on. The Commission's Proposals addressed this issue, as noted already, by insisting that the contents of the constitution "must reflect present realities as well as be mindful of future developments of the society." The concluding paragraphs of the first part of the Proposals state:

> our constitution has to be concise, clear and forward-looking, it has to be written in a general way rather than in detail, such that it will be amenable for

future developments through a process of interpretation in response to future events. Its detailed implementation should be left to ordinary legislation.[4]

With these general considerations in mind, the Executive Committee of the Commission sat down to review the mass of documents which were the product of two years of research, seminars, conferences and public debate, before writing a Working Draft Constitution for discussion. On that basis the Chairman of the Commission prepared the Working Draft, which was then distributed first to the members of the Executive Committee, and studied and debated by them for over two weeks. This debate was one of the most stimulating, free-flowing discussions this writer ever had the pleasure of leading or experiencing. The person assigned to act as secretary of the Committee to record the main points of the discussion, herself a member of the Council of the Commission and responsible for the logistics of the public debates, recorded that the meetings "were characterized by openness and candor."[5]

On the basis of the Executive Committee's debate, several amendments were made on the Working Draft. Members of the Committee were reminded and/or kept reminding each other of the guiding principles summarized above, of the Commission's Proposals as a basic point of departure, as well as of what came from the public debates during Phase Three. The final draft constitution, coming out of the discussions of the Executive Committee and submitted for the approval of the Council of the Commission, reflected the outcome of the discussions containing the proposed changes. Simply noted at this point, they will be discussed in detail in later chapters. Noted here, they will be in the order of their appearance in the Draft.

First, there is the question of a secular state. Section 2(3)(6) of the Proposals had posited secularism as one of the elements that must be incorporated in the constitution. While there was a commitment to the idea, the Draft did not specifically mention secularism for reasons which will be noted in the discussion on the General Provisions of the constitution.

Second is the question of affirmative action on behalf of women. The Draft omitted this but reinstated it following debate at the Council meeting.[6]

Third, the Proposal's statement made on the armed forces contained a categorical injunction prohibiting the armed forces from any affiliation with any political party. The text of the Draft was silent on this point.[7]

Perhaps the most controversial issue concerned the election of the President. The original proposal for a parliamentary election of the president was retained, but the percentage required was reduced from two-thirds to an absolute majority of all the members of the National Assembly. Retained as originally proposed was also the three-fourths majority required for impeachment of the President. The minimum and maximum age of the President was a question that occasioned some discussion during the public debates. The original Draft provided for a maximum age, leaving the minimum age to be determined by Act of Parliament. This was changed, leaving the maximum age open-ended.

The presidential term limit (two terms of five years each) was also the subject of much controversy. Many people tended to focus on the present President. Why, they wondered, should the country be deprived of such leadership? But a simple answer prevailed. The constitution had to be forward-looking, providing for posterity and not bound by present conditions. Term limit was a sure guarantee against the abuse or corruption of power to which limitless occupancy of position would make the occupant susceptible. Term limit also helped to institutionalize orderly succession to high office and thus avoid invidious and deadly struggle between competing individuals or forces. The latter point was stressed by

President Isaias in the National Assembly at the session to which the chairman of the Constitutional Commission and two other members were invited to attend in order to explain certain aspects of the Draft.[8]

Matters which had not been specifically mentioned in the Proposals but which came up repeatedly in public debates included: principles and mechanisms for ensuring the independence of the judiciary, whether there should be a Constitutional Court and the place of customary law in the Constitution.

The answer to the first point was related to the establishment of a Judicial Service Commission to oversee the entry into, progress within and exit from the judicial service, as well as conditions of service, including matters of discipline of judges. Judicial independence as a basic principle was guaranteed in the Draft and no one raised any question on it. As for the question on whether it was better to have a Constitutional Court, the answer was given earlier in the public debate: that in Eritrea's present condition it was better to leave the jurisdiction interpreting the constitution to the Supreme Court.[9]

The question of customary law was problematic. The issue had to be treated in relation to the supremacy principle. The Draft disposed of this issue by asserting that the constitution was the supreme law of the country and "...all laws, orders and acts contrary to its letter and spirit shall be null and void." The implication of this provision to the future of customary law will be discussed in greater detail in the appropriate section of the chapter on law and justice.[10]

Approval Process

There were three separate steps in the matter of the approval of the Draft Constitution. The first concerned the approval by the Council of the Commission of the Draft prepared by the Executive Committee. The latter was designated as a drafting committee at the fifth regular meeting of the Commission in August 1995. The second step was the approval by the National Assembly of the text approved by the Council. The third step, the ratification by a Constituent Assembly, was the culminating point of the whole process.[11]

The law establishing the Commission provided that among the functions of the Commission was the duty to prepare a Draft Constitution and submit it to the National Assembly and to distribute the Draft and to receive the comments (to be) made on it by regional assemblies, localities, and members of professional, business and civic organizations as well as by individual citizens.[12]

The first Draft prepared by the Executive Committee was distributed to the members of the Council of the Commission, some two weeks before the meeting scheduled to be held June 14-16, 1996. The Council of the Commission spent three days of intense debate during which the draft was read article by article with introductory remarks given by the chairman on each article, as appropriate. After each reading the floor was open for questions or comments and debate.

In opening the meeting, the chairman gave an introductory speech summing up the experience of the previous two years and laying emphasis on some of the main topics which may be subject to controversy.

The topics were grouped under three headings:

(a) The meaning and implication of strong government and how it is related to the rule of law;
(b) Democracy and its challenges, and
(c) Development, Social Justice and Human Rights.

Except for national unity and stability, which were too obvious to need further discussion, the topics covered under these headings were connected with the five basic objectives and values to which reference was made above on which national consensus was a pre-condition for the public discourse on the constitution. The chairman's aim in reviewing those topics at the start of the most important meeting of the Council was to help focus the attention of the members to the central principles underlying the articles of the Draft and thus provide a framework for the debate that was to follow.

After three days of intense debate, the Council approved the Draft with some amendments and a couple of additional sections. There were attempts made by a few members of the Council, some of them prominent members to revive debate on some of the issues that were controversial during the debate on the Proposals. But the majority did not support their point of view. It was clear that the public debate during Phase Three had proved to be a chastening experience in terms of the support of the Proposal by the overwhelming majority of the members of the population who participated in the meetings. Yet the initial expression of dissent by a few individuals on some issues at the Council's meeting, was given ample time for debate; indeed, a disproportionate amount of time was spent on debating such issues. In the end, however, the members who supported the minority position volunteered to go along with the majority with the result that the entire Draft was approved by unanimity.

The approved Draft was transmitted by the chairman to the President, in his capacity as chairman of the National Assembly. A cover letter briefly outlined the issues that occasioned controversy with an understanding that the minutes of the meeting would be submitted on time.

The President convened a meeting of the National

Assembly on July 2, 1996. After a two day meeting, the National Assembly approved the Draft with a few amendments. In the morning of the second day, July 3, the Chairman of the Commission and two other members of the Executive Committee, were summoned to appear before the National Assembly to explain a few articles of the Draft. The first topic on which the National Assembly sought further clarification concerned the provision for the establishment of a Judicial Service Commission. Members of the National Assembly wanted to know the reason for this in light of its historical origin, its adoption in others constitutions and its policy implication in terms of judicial independence and accountability. To whom, they wanted to know, would the Judicial Service Commission be accountable? What would be its relation with the Ministry of Justice?

Another question related to the Inspectorate Commission, a sort of Ombudsman. Some members also wanted to know the historical origin and use of commissions in general and why the Constitutional Commission singled out some for inclusion in the Constitution, and not others. All were legitimate questions. The Chairman of the Commission and his colleagues answered all questions at length, to the satisfaction of the National Assembly.

Public Debate on the Draft and Changes Introduced by the Council

Public debate on the draft was launched in mid-August 1996, a few weeks later than originally planned, for logistical reasons. The Draft was published in Tigrigna, Arabic and English and widely distributed throughout Eritrea and shipped abroad for distribution among Eritreans in the Diaspora in advance of the start of the debates. The Draft was also published in the weekly newspapers in the same three languages and broadcast on the radio. As in the previous phases of the constitution making process, the introductory meetings were launched by members of the Executive Committee of the Commission in the main urban centers.

The organization and management of the task was basically the same as in the debates on the Proposals and, as on previous occasions, the introductory meetings were attended by leaders of the respective regions, including administrators and their senior colleagues. Several members of the Executive Committee were also charged with conducting meetings in foreign countries where there was a large concentration of Eritreans, as was done for the debate on the Proposals. For the first time, a member was sent to Australia and another member went to Syria and Lebanon which also had not been covered before. In North America, the coincidence of the annual Festival of Eritreans held in the Washington DC area with the start of the debates was taken into account in planning the launching of the debates in that part of the world. The Chairman of the Commission undertook the task of introducing the debate on the Draft on September 1, 1996 to an audience of Eritreans, living in the United States and Canada, who came to attend the Festival. Two weeks later, four members of the Commission, including the Chairman, began to address meetings in several cities throughout the United States and Canada, explaining the articles of the Draft and answering questions.

Inside the country, meetings were organized throughout Eritrea, extending to the village level, starting in late September.

As the reports of those in charge of organizing the meetings at all levels indicate, the meetings were well attended and involved vigorous debates and probing questions, illustrating the interest of the Eritrean people in the constitution making process and in the content of the constitution.

The Committee in charge of Civic Education and Public Debates compiled lengthy reports of all the debates on the Draft as it did on the Proposals. These reports included the discussions of the Draft by members of the public, throughout the debates, from the Preamble right up to the last article. With respect to the Preamble, the discussions were mainly concerned more with style and language than with substance. With regard to the main text of the Draft, there were more questions on substance than on style and language. Questions were asked and opinions offered on all the articles of the Draft. All in all, over seventy different questions or opinions were recorded.

A comparison of the Draft and the final text reveals what questions or opinions were taken into account and accepted by the Commission. While later chapters will offer further detail three examples will suffice for now. The first concerns the duties of citizens stipulated under article 25 of the Draft, in which seven duties are listed. Sub-article 4 changes with the elimination of the requirement, in the original version, of the duty to advance "the well-being of the people." Similarly, in sub-article 5, the requirement of the citizens' duty to know the constitution is deleted. Also, the requirement to "respect the rule of law" is omitted in sub-article 7.

All three changes were debated at length by the Council of the Commission, as were others that had been proposed during the debate.

A second example of change was the addition of a new article, requiring the establishment, by the National Assembly, of a standing committee to deal with citizens' petitions. This provision was the outcome of an extensive debate regarding the need of an entity that could perform the function of what was called "Ombudsman" function in other countries. Some constitutions preferred to call it a "Human

Rights Commission". The need for such an entity as a safety-valve for the governmental machine was not disputed; the variety of its form and name was in accord with the peculiarities of the histories of individual countries. In Eritrea for example, there had been a committee answerable to the highest leadership of the liberation front (the EPLF) that fulfilled the function of Ombudsman. The decision to assign this task to a special committee of the National Assembly was in accordance of this specific history.[13]

A third example concerned the oath of office, both for the President and the members of the National Assembly. Under the original Draft, these office holders were required to swear an oath in the name of the Eritrean martyrs. In a very religious country, it was expected that this would raise objections. But the extent of the objection and the vehemence with which it was expressed gave the Commission food for thought. An oath, it was said repeatedly, should be sworn in the name of the Creator, by whatever name He is known (God, Allah...etc). Some articulate members of the debating audiences even held the Commission to the logic of its own strong commitment to religious freedom as expressed in the chapter on Human Rights. One member expressed it thus: Article 19(1) of the Draft provides that every person shall have the right to freedom of thought, conscience and belief. I am a Muslim and according to my religion I can only swear an oath by invoking the name of Allah. If your version of swearing an oath were to be law, it would be a violation of the requirements of my religion. This constitutes a violation of my religious right as protected under article 19(1). Irresistible logic. Similar expressions were voiced though not with the same logic. The remarkable thing is that the view that the name of God be invoked was shared by a cross-section of Eritrean public opinion, cutting across religion, age, gender, social background and educational level, both inside

Eritrea and among Eritreans in the Diaspora.
The debate in the Council of the Commission took place
on March 12-13. As expected, the Chairman made introductory statements commenting on the public debates and the
changes proposed as a result of those debates which had
themselves been discussed at length by the Executive
Committee of the Commission earlier in the year, following
the end of the public debates. The members of the Council
of the Commission were also invited to introduce any
changes, if they so wished, on their own initiative, reflecting
the evolution of their views as a result of their experience of
the public debates and their reflection on the outcome of
those debates. A number of such views were expressed by
some prominent members of the Council, particularly by the
lawyers, to good effect.

The opinions of the members of external Board of
Advisors were also thoroughly reviewed by the members of
the Executive Committee which found several points helpful.
Among the changes introduced as a result of the debate within the Executive Committee of the Commission as well as
based on the reflections of the members of the Council, none
is more important than the changes made in article 26(3) of
the Draft, changes that expanded the areas which cannot be
limited under the limitation Clause of the constitution.
Accordingly, articles 15, 16, and 17(5), (7), (8) were added
to the previous list of rights that cannot be limited.

Another change introduced in this respect concerns article 19(4) which was in the original Draft and which is now
substituted by article 19(1). This is an interesting change
which was made following a lengthy debate within the
Executive Committee and which will be discussed in chapter
8 below.

The final Draft which came out of the Council's debates
was then submitted to the President for final disposal in

accordance with Proclamation No. 55/1994, as will be discussed in the following sections.

Ratification and Promulgation.

The Ratifying Entity

Ratification as concept and process is not new to any people with a long history of organized life. What may be new is the form of ratification and the ratifying entity. In Eritrea, Proclamation No. 92/1996 which came out in late 1996, established the Constituent Assembly to ratify the constitution. Before discussing the function of ratification and its application in the Eritrean situation, we will note the composition of the Constituent Assembly as required by the law.

Composition

According to Proclamation No. 92/1996, the composition of the Constituent Assembly is as follows:

   a. members of the National Assembly;
   b. Members of the six Regional Assemblies; and
   c. 75 representatives elected from among Eritreans residing abroad.[14]

The Constituent Assembly elects its own Chairman[15] who has the powers and responsibilities to convene and preside over its meetings.[16] The quorum required for holding Constituent Assembly meetings is three-quarters, and decisions are made by an absolute majority of the members.[17]

The composition of the Constituent Assembly is an interesting combination of national representation, seen in comparative perspective with the practice of other countries. For instance, in Namibia, the first Parliament, elected on the eve of independence, turned itself into a Constituent

Assembly. In Ethiopia and Uganda, the respective Constituent Assemblies were formed by special national elections. There are two novel features in the Eritrean case: (1) the representation: of Eritreans living abroad, and (2) national representation via the Regional Assemblies. An additional novel feature is the fact that these two national groups would form the Constituent Assembly together with the members of the National Assembly.

How were these three groups themselves formed?

To take the National Assembly first, this was a transitional Parliament comprising 75 members of the Peoples Front for Democracy and Justice (PFDJ) and 75 others representing the Regional Assemblies. The 75 members of the PFDJ were all members of the Central Council of the Front, elected at its last Congress in January 1994.

The 75 representatives of the Regional Assemblies were elected by their respective Assemblies. Thus in terms of the law establishing the Constituent Assembly, its component representing the Regional Assemblies would be the total number of all the members of the Regional Assemblies, minus the 75 people who were the members of the National Assembly.

As for the election of the representatives of Eritreans living abroad, there was no law requiring such an election. The issue of the role of Eritreans living abroad in the constitution making process is related, in part, to the critical supportive role they played in the history of the armed struggle, and continue to play today, albeit in a somewhat subdued manner. As already pointed out, they played a significant role in the debates on the Draft constitution, during which several among them raised the question of their role in future elections to national legislative institutions. It is not surprising, therefore, that the law establishing the Constituent Assembly should require their participation in the ratification process.

In view of the fact that the election of these Eritreans was not required and regulated by law, how were they elected? This question was answered by the issuance of election guidelines in the form of circulars sent by the Ministry of Regional Administration through the various consular offices abroad. What follows reflects the essence of the guidelines issued for electing the representatives from abroad.

The 75 seats assigned to Eritreans abroad were distributed in accordance with the number of the residents, divided into Ethiopia, Sudan, the Arabian peninsula, Europe and North America (comprising the USA and Canada). To take North America as an example, 8 seats were allocated, six for the USA and 2 for Canada. The circular giving the guidelines required the election in North America to take place by the end of March 1997 in time for the elected representatives to arrive in Asmara to take part in the Constituent meeting in mid-May. Voters were required to be Eritrean citizens in possession of the appropriate ID, while candidates were required, additionally, to be persons who have paid the dues—a form of a special tax—required by the government.

The election was conducted by secret ballot. The consular office of the Eritrean embassy was given the responsibility of organizing the election. The consular office appointed election agents in the various sub-regions to perform the duties of running the election. In the USA, the election took place in six sub-regions: Washington DC and New York serving for the East and mid-Atlantic sub-region, Dallas serving for the South, Auckland serving for the West, Minneapolis for the mid-west and Seattle serving for the North-West. Canada was divided into two sub-regions, East and central. Toronto served for the East and Saskatoon for the central region.

Two rounds of elections were held, first in several city centers where a large number of Eritreans resided, and second in the main cities of the sub-region such as Washington DC. In the United States of America, elections took place in thirty-seven such centers.

Ballot papers and other related forms had been sent ahead of time to the various agents in the sub-regions and to city centers. Election committees were formed in several cities to ensure open and fair elections. All the necessary publicity was made informing Eritreans about the election and of the prerequisites, including the need to come with their IDs and of the need of registration. On election day, an election committee with a chairman and two members were chosen, followed by the designation of a sufficient number of officers to help count the ballots. The number of candidates to be nominated was fixed at the meeting and nominations were made. After the nomination was closed, the candidates introduced themselves and, as required, explained why they thought they deserved to be elected members of the Constituent Assembly. The electors wrote the names of the their preferred candidates on the ballot paper. The ballot papers were then counted with the help of the persons assigned for the task and the results announced by the chairman of the election committee. Thus at the first round of elections several candidates who received the highest number were chosen to go to the sub-regional centers to elect those who would be members of the Constituent Assembly. That election was held on March 15, 1997 in the six centers mentioned above (and in two centers in Canada).

Function

Why is it necessary to have a Constituent Assembly approve the Draft, after it had been approved by the National Assembly? This is a question which was asked by many members of the public during the public debate on the draft constitution. The ready-made, technical answer was: because the law establishing the Constitutional Commission requires it.

But, like all technical answers, it faced the question: why did the law require it, in the first place? Well, why did the law require it in the first place?

The Preamble to the constitution begins with the words "We the people of Eritrea...", and closes with the words "(we)...approve and solemnly ratify officially, through the Constituent Assembly, this Constitution as the fundamental law of our Sovereign and Independent State of Eritrea." As these words indicate the questions raised above are connected to the issue of legitimacy with its theoretical as well as practical significance. The underlying assumption of the concept of legitimacy, a central concept in political theory and discourse, is that government is established by and on behalf of the governed. The origin and ramification of this concept will be discussed in more detail in chapter nine below. In the present instance, it is sufficient to say that the nation as a whole must be represented in the creation of its fundamental Charter, the Constitution. The election of an entity to perform this supreme act of legitimization is a common method which the Eritrean National Assembly adopted in passing Proclamation No. 55/1994, requiring the formation of such an entity.

It is noteworthy that Proclamation No.55/1994 did not specifically give such a legitimizing entity the designation of "Constituent Assembly". The law, in defining the mission of the Constitutional Commission, provided that the mission shall be (among other things): "to present to the National Assembly a Draft Constitution for a final public discussion, and at the conclusion of such public discussion, to prepare a final draft and submit it to the National Assembly for approval and for eventual submission *to a democratically formed representative body*." This formulation implies flexibility in terms of the manner of establishing the legitimizing entity; flexibility, without sacrificing the essence of a principle is important, particularly in transitional situations. The formulation did, nonetheless, cause raising some sensitive eyebrows (!), as concerned citizens among the literate public wondered about the shape and form of the entity and the manner of its formation. As we have already seen, the answer came in the form of Proclamation No.92/1996.

This law is sub-titled: A proclamation to Establish the Constituent Assembly and, in what might appear to be an answer to the question in the minds of many, the penultimate paragraph of the law says: "Whereas in order to finalize this process, it is imperative that a Constituent Assembly be established to ratify the Draft Constitution on behalf of the people of Eritrea..."

The law gives the Constituent Assembly the power to ratify the Draft, "...having conducted debates thereon and making all necessary amendments..."[18]. It also gives it power "to take, or cause to be taken, all the necessary legal steps for the coming into force and effect of the Constitution."[19]

Some questions arise. In view of the extensive public debates that had been held on the Draft over reasonably long period, debates in which members of the Constituent Assembly may be presumed to have participated as citizens in their various communities earlier in the constitution making process, might it not involve unnecessary duplication of efforts and waste of time to hold yet another meeting on the same Draft? And what about the cost involved? The answer to these questions is, again, connected with the idea of legitimacy, that it is necessary for representatives of the nation to be formally convened and to consider, in conference, the basic law that stipulates the ties that bind them and the fundamental rules that define their commitment to a common purpose as a united people. To borrow the anthropological concept of ritual, there is also an element of celebration involved; a rough definition of ritual is: turning what is inevitable into something pleasurable. But the essential point is national representation in the formal approval of a basic national Charter. If more time, effort and money is expended for such an event, therefore, it would be time, effort, and money well spent.

There is also the possibility that some of the provisions of the Draft might be reviewed and amended as a result of the debates held in the Constituent Assembly. The law does require such a debate, after all. The occasion affords the nation's representatives a final chance to reexamine some issues and, if need be, revise them. This, at any rate, is the theory behind the requirement of ratification. In nations where there is a clear-cut division along class lines, class interest would obviously figure prominently in the debate; the same would be true where ethnic division involves the exclusion of some groups from participation in national politics or denies them access to essential resources. Indeed, one of the reasons that impelled the Constitutional Commission to organize large-scale national consultation over a long period is to address the issue of inclusion. The law establishing the Commission is clear on this issue, for it enjoins the Commission to organize and manage "a wide-ranging and all-embracing national debate and education through public seminars...etc."[20]

It is worth mentioning here, in parenthesis, that some Eritrean groups living in foreign countries, question the right of the government of the PFDJ(formerly EPLF) to appoint the Commission. This question concerns legitimacy of a special kind which needs to be mentioned here, since it has been raised by this group, irrespective of the validity, or lack of validity, of their case.[21]

First, the government is a government of a country recognized by the world community assembled at the United nations. The power that the government wields in the name of the nation came out of the "barrel of the gun" and was later given the cloak of legality, following a popular referendum. The power on which the government's authority to rule, and to appoint a commission, rests and its historical origin need hardly be the subject of controversy. It becomes necessary to state it, nonetheless, because the group that raised the question as already mentioned did not seem to apprehend it. Simply put, the story is that the world community accepted the Eritrean nation as a member, following the referendum of April 1993, as already noted. The referendum was held because the Eritrean nation was liberated by force of arms. The armed struggle that resulted in the liberation of Eritrea was led by the EPLF(now the PFDJ). It is also necessary to point out that, in accordance with international law and practice, the United Nations would have accepted Eritrea into membership even without the referendum. The legitimacy of the Front that liberated Eritrea was not in question by anyone except the Ethiopian military government which it fought and defeated.

Since this subject has been raised in connection with the concept of legitimacy, it is worth pointing out that the legitimacy of the EPLF is based not merely on the fact that it was an armed political organization that defeated the enemy, but also because its members are people who spent the best parts of their lives in the mountains and trenches, and who created a social infra-structure that benefited the people and thus secured their wholehearted support. The original legitimacy emotionally invested by the Eritrean people on its freedom fighters (of which the members of the former ELF formed a part until 1981), was reinforced by the social policy and practice of the EPLF, as well as the good behavior for which its fighters were generally known by the civilian population, and was finally crowned with military victory and the referendum that followed the victory. In short, the original legitimacy derived from initiative and sacrifice, reinforced by service was ultimately cemented by success in the achievement of victory.

And, as Ronald Reagan used to say, no one quarrels with success, no one that is, except people who do not have respect
for the facts on the ground. The government of the EPLF
(now PFDJ) could, and did, legitimately appoint a
Constitutional Commission to draft the future Constitutional
of Eritrea. It had the right and the duty to do so.

The Eritrean experience of ratification resembles, in all
its essentials, to those of Ethiopia and Uganda. But it is more
interesting to compare Eritrea's experience with that of the
United States in this respect. The similarity lies in the fact
that, in both instances, a new nation was being created. But
there was a critical difference in that the ratification process
was more difficult and protracted in the United States. The
complexity of the ratification process in the case of the
United States is to be understood in the context of its
history.[22]

Ratification and Promulgation.

Ratification.
The final act of approval of the draft constitution performed
by the Constituent Assembly led to the constitution's promulgation. Needless to say, beginning from the point when the
constitution comes into force and effect the country is governed by the constitution. Accordingly all necessary steps
must be taken to avoid a gap or conflict between the pre-
existing regime[23] of law and the successor regime.

As was noted above, the law establishing the Constituent
Assembly authorized it to take, or cause to be taken, all the
necessary legal steps for the coming into force and effect of
the constitution. This was done in order to facilitate smooth
transition from the existing government to a new government, (to be) formed following an election on the basis of the

new constitution.

There are two ways of effecting such transition in the practice of constitution making. One way is to write it in the constitution itself, invariably under a section titled "Transitional Provisions", with details providing for the manner and/or timing of the transfer of power from the old to the newly elected government. The other way is to do it by enacting an enabling law that facilitates a smooth transfer of power. Constitutions of countries that have a legacy of numerous laws, like the constitution of the new republic of South Africa, follow the first method. We will call it the South African model; the South African Constitution is one of the world's most detailed constitution. Eritrea followed the second method, Eritrea's constitution being one of the world's shortest.

The theory behind the preoccupation with instantaneous transfer of power and its legal underpinning is the notion that power does not like a vacuum. In European history of the monarchy, for example, when the king died the announcement read (or rather shouted) "the king is dead, long live the king", thus at once asserting continuity and reassuring citizens. The modern equivalent of this monarchical proclamation of continuity and legality is the ritual of investiture following an election because parliaments replaced kings in the political evolution. Aside from the ritual, however, somebody must have the responsibility of ensuring lawful transfer of power and that there is no gap between the promulgation of the constitution and the investiture of the new government elected on the basis of the new constitution.

The Eritrean Constituent Assembly is charged with ensuring, either directly or through the creation of an entity, that all necessary steps are taken to implement the requirements of the constitution, including the election of a government. The latter would require the passage of an electoral law and establishment of an Electoral Commission to organize such an election.

It would also include passing a law authorizing the existing government to continue in power, pending the election of a government on the basis of the new constitution.

Under what we called the South African model, transitional arrangements are provided for in great detail in 18 long Articles of the Constitution. These Articles cover definitions of all the principal governmental authorities from the legislative, executive, and judicial authorities to specification of pensions of political office bearers, with cross-references to existing laws. The following provision is an example:

"Transitional arrangement: Local government
245. (1) Until elections have been held in terms of the Local Government Transition Act, 1993, local government shall not be restructured otherwise than in accordance with the Act.

(2) Restructuring of local government which takes place as a result of legislation enacted by a competent authority after the elections referred to in subsection(1) have been held, shall be effected in accordance with the principles embodied in Chapter 10 and the Constitution as a whole.

(3) (a) For the purpose of the first election of members of a local government after the commencement of this Constitution, the area of jurisdiction of such local government shall be divided into wards in accordance with the Act referred to in subsection(1).

(b) Forty percent of the members of the local government shall be elected according to the system of proportional representation applicable to an election of the National Assembly and regulate specifically by or under the Act referred to in subsection (1), and sixty percent of the mem-

> bers shall be elected on the basis that each such
> member shall represent a ward as contemplated
> in paragraph(b):
> Provided.............etc.

The proviso makes further references to other laws and stipulates more conditions. It is a complex provision on a complex subject written in the constitution of a country with a complex political and social history and present condition. The South African constitution makers, therefore, decided to write a detailed constitution, thus conceivably sparing the judiciary much headache. Whether such detailed provisions help or hinder better resolution of conflicts in the future remains to be seen.

The Eritrean constitution-makers preferred a more concise constitution with flexibility built into it as better way of facilitating constitutional development and handling future disputes, thus giving the principal institutions of government, and especially the Judiciary enormous power. Moreover, the issue of transitional provisions was left to be dealt without reference made to it in the constitution. This choice makes for flexibility but, as noted above, requires legal steps that ensure the smooth transfer of power and help avoid confusion or conflicts in the law. For, once the new Constitution is in effect, everything should be in accord with it. For example, Article 32(1) provides that all legislative power is vested in the National Assembly. This provision, along with all the other provisions of the constitution came into effect on May 24, 1997. But there is no National Assembly elected under the new constitution. For such a National Assembly to be in office it has to be elected. For it to be elected, there has to be an election law, and an election law must be passed by an entity with legislative power. Under the constitution, the only entity with legislative power is the National Assembly, and as yet there is no such National Assembly.

It is a vicious circle. It was in anticipation of this conundrum that Proclamation No. 92/1996 provided that, in addition to ratification of the constitution, the Constituent Assembly shall have power: "...to take, *or cause to be taken,* all the necessary legal steps for the coming into force and effect of the Constitution". The legal imperative ("legal steps" that the Constituent Assembly must take) requires, as noted above, the passage of a law providing that, until a new government is formed on the basis of the constitution, the existing government shall continue in office, exercising governmental power. There can be no power vacuum, not only for theoretical reasons which may seem esoteric, but above all, for practical reasons.

Again, as noted before, another step that the Constituent Assembly has to take is the enactment of laws that create institutions necessary for the "coming into force and effect" of the Constitution. One such institution is the Electoral Commission that must organize and manage the election of the National Assembly. The Transitional Parliament that came out of the Constituent Assembly authorized the appointment of a drafting committee to draft an electoral law.[24]

Thus the vicious circle is broken. The rest will be up to the institutions created by the Constitution, notably the National Assembly, to implement the requirements of the constitution. Among the weighty functions of the National Assembly will figure, for example, the type of laws that were cited above from the South African constitution. Obviously, these could not be entrusted to the Constituent Assembly whose function should be essentially to bridge any possible gap between the requirements of the constitution, on the one hand, and contingency situations not covered by the constitution, on the other, and thus avoid any possible conflict or confusion in the law.

What changes did the Constituent Assembly introduce into the Draft Constitution?

There was only one substantive change that the Constituent Assembly made in the Draft. It concerns the privileges and immunities of the members of the National Assembly. Whereas the Draft provided for immunity covering the period when the National Assembly is in Session, the changed Article extends the privilege throughout the five years of the parliamentary term. The change reinforces the importance of the National Assembly as a key national institution. But if the law on parliament's Session provides for a few months out of the year, the immunity would include several months of the year during which the members of the National Assembly will not be doing the business of Parliament. This would be problematic because it could conceivably lead to abuse.

Promulgation.

The promulgation of a constitution, as of any piece of law, is the moment when the law comes into effect. During the final phase of Eritrea's constitution making process, the Executive Committee of the Commission considered the various alternatives in terms of the effective date of the constitution—the date of its ratification, the date of its publication in the official gazette of laws, some future date specified in the instrument of its ratification, or silence on the subject, leaving to the government to set a date. In consultation with the appropriate authorities of the government and the governing party, the Commission decided to leave the date open so that the government can "clear the decks" by reviewing and, if need be, repealing, laws that conflict with the constitution. The expectation of the Commission was that the constitution would come into force in the Summer or Autumn of 1998.

As is now well known this did not come to pass. War

broke out between Ethiopia and Eritrea in May 1998 and lasted for two years. Critics of the government charge that the government dragged its feet in implementing the constitution, and that war gave it an excuse to postpone its implementation. We leave this for historians to puzzle out and note that the Eritrean National Assembly passed a resolution for general elections to be held at the end of 2001. The election did not take place. The current government and its leader have not been able or willing to answer why this violation of people's expectations.

Notes

1. See Edward McWhinney, *Constitution-making, Principle, Process, Practice*, University of Toronto Press, 1981. P.122.
2. Ibid. The quote is from McWhinney
3. Quoted in Russell. F. Moore, *Modern Constitutions*. 1957. P.12. See also M. Morabiti and D. Bourmond, *Histoire Constitutionel et Polititque de la France 3rd Edition Montechristian* pp. 56-86.
4. Proposals P.13
5. Minutes of Executive Committee Meetings. The first draft was first written in English, then translated to Tigrigna and Arabic. The original English draft was then brought in line with the final version following the discussion and changes made thereon.
6. See Article 7(2) which went through several drafts.
7. See Article 12 of the Constitution.
8. In light of subsequent events, the author and other Eritreans have been sadly forced to revise their optimism concerning President Isaias' motives.
9. See chapter eleven below.
10. Chapter five below
11. Art. 4(4), Proclamation N. 55/1994.
12. Art. 5, Procl. No. 55/1994
13. As the Epilogue at the end of this book explains, the demand of the "G-15" that President Isaias mend his ways and desist from acting alone without consulting his colleagues is based, in part, on a history of collective decision-making during the liberation war.
14. Art. 2(1).
15. Art. 2(2).
16. Art. 4.
17. Art.5.
18. Art. 3(1).

19. Art. (3).
20. Procl. No. 55/1994.
21. Some members of the former Eritrean Liberation Front (ELF) raised this question at meetings held in North America and Europe.
22. In chapter 5 (tiltled "The Fight for Ratification") of his biography on Chief Justice John Marshall, Jean Edward Smith (1996), records the great legislative battles fought on the ratification of the constitution of the United States in what, at the time, was a state of the union, Virginia, in the aftermath of the Philadelphia convention's approval of the constitution in the Summer of 1787. Virginia was critical because some of the most articulate of the federal form of government were in Virginia, including Patrick Henry, the greatest orator and lawyer of his time. If the Virginia Legislature refused to ratify the constitution it was feared by the federalist forces, including Alexander Hamilton and John Marshall, it would be doomed to failure. Marshall's biographer credits him with a crucial role in helping secure the Virginia legislature's support. In the context of the larger national debate on the constitution by federalists and anti-federalists, a matter of special interest to the present discussion was the procedural battles that Marshall waged. His biographer writes:

"In October 1787, when the House of Delegates (the Virginia Legislature) passed Marshall's resolution calling for a ratification, both sides immediately began jockeying for position. The newspapers filled with articles pro and con; prospective delegates began to issue personal manifestos; and in New York, Madison, Hamilton, and John Jay commenced publication of their remarkable essays defending and explaining the Constitution, The *Federalist* papers. As a counterpoise to the nationalist drumbeat, George Mason issued his *Objections to the Constitution;* Richard Henry Lee published what is generally regarded as the most incisive critique of national power, *Letters from the Federal Farmer,* Patrick Henry kept up a steady fusillade against the proposed Constitution in public meetings throughout Virginia. In the House of Delegates, the maneuvering was intense. On November 30, 1787, the committee of the whole house reported a series of resolutions to defray the expenses of convention delegates. The resolutions included a motion offered by Patrick Henry to provide funds to send representatives to a second federal convention in the event the Virginia convention should judge it expedient to propose amendments to the Constitution. Henry and his supporters carried that motion in the committee of the whole with sixteen votes to spare. As Randolph wrote to Madison, 'the current sets violently against the Constitution.' Once again, Marshall went to work to fashion a compromise with Henry, and the final bill, passed on December 13, 1787, made no reference to a second federal convention..."[Smith, p.117]

23. For the political fallout that followed the frustration of this process see Epilogue.

24. The Election Committee met only once and inexplicably disappeared. See Epilogue below.

95

PART TWO
Text Analysis and Commentaries

Five

Preamble and General Provisions

There is no Freedom without Law (JOHN LOCKE)

The Preamble and the General Provisions of the Constitution are best treated together in one chapter. Apart from their brevity, the generality of the themes they cover justifies such joint treatment. I must begin, nonetheless, by noting their difference. It consists of the fact that, whereas the articles in the General Provisions, together with the articles of the other chapters, belong in the domain of the legal imperative which means that they are, generally speaking, enforceable, the Preamble, by contrast, does not necessarily have such legal effect, as will be explained in more detail below.

The Preamble.

I will first consider the essential contents of the Preamble, then examine the legal significance of its words in historical perspective, in the political and socio-economic context of Eritrea.

The Contents of the Preamble

The size of a Preamble differs from constitution to constitution. For example, the Preamble to the Constitution of the United States of America is one of the shortest. Ordaining and establishing the Constitution for the American people and their posterity, a single paragraph of 52 words, concisely outlines the purpose of establishing the constitution as being "to form a more perfect Union, establish Justice, insure domestic Tranquillity, provide for the common defense, promote the general Welfare, and secure the Blessings of Liberty." One scholar of constitutional law and government uses it as a title for a two volume treatise on the US constitution, its source, evolution and durability. It is also noteworthy that Judge Richard Matsch, the judge who tried the case of the People v. Terry Nichols, referred to the Preamble to the Constitution, when sentencing him. Nichols was tried and convicted for his role in the Oklahoma City bombing of 1996 that killed 168 people. The judge told Nichols that he was convicted of "a crime against the Constitution." Then in an unusual recitation of the Preamble he said, "the Preamble talks about establishing justice and ensuring the domestic tranquility." He reminded Nichols that he had helped destroy a building that housed federal agencies such as the Secret Service and Customs, whose employees were performing the function of ensuring domestic tranquility." He cited more from the Preamble and finally told Nichols that he had been proven an enemy of the Constitution. Why did the judge go to such lengths to cite the entire Preamble when reference to articles of the appropriate Penal Code could have sufficed? It was an unusual procedure in an unusual case; Nichols joined others who plotted to undermine the constituted government. The crime aimed at the foundation of the republic, so that foundation, i.e.,the Constitution was cited.

The clarity and precision of the Preamble to the US

Constitution is admirable, but it may be safely assumed that if the Constitution were drafted two hundred years later it would be somewhat longer, enlarging on some of the key objectives and adding more, as a function of the demands of modern life and the more extensive role played by modern governments, including the government of the United States.

While declaring the purpose of the constitution is one function of preambles, they must also indicate who is establishing the constitution and the government that is to be formed under it. For example, the founding fathers of the US republic, in Convention assembled in 1787, were faced with the dilemma of stating in whose name they were making the constitution. The Preamble to the Articles of Confederation—the loose arrangement that existed previously—had named all the participating states. The problem facing the Convention of 1787 was how the new constitution could enumerate the participating states without knowing which would actually ratify the document. The founding fathers solved this problem by a bold move, an imaginative leap of faith in themselves and in the future of democracy in the new nation.

The Preamble began with the words, "We the People of the United States..."

Similarly, the Preamble to the Constitution of Uganda begins: WE THE PEOPLE OF UGANDA, and the Constitution of Eritrea begins with the same words but adds the words "united in a common struggle for our rights and common destiny."

The Preamble to the Constitution of Eritrea represents, both in terms of size and content, a trend of modern progressive constitutions.

First, it gives a sense of the history of struggle of the Eritrean people—the justice of their cause and the sacrifice it exacted—and the imperative of cherishing, preserving and

101

developing the freedom, unity, peace, stability and security achieved by such struggle and sacrifice, and building a strong and prosperous Eritrea on the basis of these values. The Preamble commends the legacies of the long armed struggle, in particular the values of unity, equality, love for truth and justice, self-reliance and steadfastness to be the core of the national values. At the same time, the Preamble insists that these be related to the "traditional community-based" values of mutual "assistance and fraternity, love for family, mutual respect and consideration", and respect for the elders of the community.

A crucial feature of the text of the Constitution is presaged in the sixth paragraph of the Preamble. It asserts that the "recognition, protection and securing of the rights and freedoms of citizens, human dignity, equality without any discrimination, based on religion, sex, or ethnic origin" will

"guarantee the equal development of the citizens;"
"lay down the ground work for satisfying the material and spiritual needs of citizens;" and
"usher in a democratic order that is responsive to the needs and interests of citizens, guarantees their participation and brings about economic development, social progress and harmony."

The penultimate paragraph is unique in constitutional Preambles simply because the topic it covers reflects a unique historical phenomenon. The subject concerns the heroic participation of Eritrean women in the country's protracted armed struggle for independence. Without the participation of Eritrean women, the independence struggle would not have succeeded. True for numerical reasons only—the fact that one third of the fighting forces were composed of women—this was also true for cultural and psychological reasons. The women component of the EPLF army added what can best be described as a cementing element to the struggle, a quality of cohesiveness going beyond traditional army *esprit de corps*.

Apart from the exemplary deeds women performed in all of the activities of the struggle, in combat duties as well as in the social infrastructure of life behind the guerrilla line, women provided an emotional support to their male comrades-at-arms. Their massive presence created a better milieu and motivation which helped inestimably in sustaining the protracted struggle. This fact has been expressed in songs and poems written by the fighters which, when broadcast or disseminated, added to the cohesiveness of the liberation army. They also reinforced the popular support, including a spirit of resistance among the Eritrean public in the areas under enemy occupation, as the clandestine radio broadcasts were assiduously listened too and secretly discussed. In the battle for "the hearts and minds" of the Eritrean public under enemy occupation in which the strategy of dilution and eventual elimination of Eritrean cultural identity figured prominently, the role of the EPLF's radio, the "Voice of the Masses," was critical, and the radio projected a strong image of Eritrean women fighters, not just as singers or nurses, but as unit commanders, inspiring a generation of young Eritreans everywhere. Accordingly, the sixth paragraph of the Preamble unequivocally states that "the values and ideals generated by such struggle will serve as an unshakable foundation for our commitment and struggle to create a society in which women and men shall interact on the bases of mutual respect, fraternity and equality."

The rest of the Preamble records the covenant entered into between the people and the government they formed by their free will.

The Legal Effect of the Preamble.

As already noted, the Preamble neither confers an automatically enforceable legal right, nor imposes a corresponding duty, unlike the articles of the rest of the Constitution. Nevertheless, the Preamble has a compelling explanatory power which can be summoned in support of a given position in the application of the Constitution through interpretation, as was noted before in reference to Terry Nichols case.

General Provisions.

The General Provisions Chapter of the Constitution (Chapter One) comprises five articles:

Article 1: The State of Eritrea and its Territory;
Article 2: Supremacy of the Constitution;
Article 3: Citizenship;
Article 4: National Symbols and Language;
Article 5: Gender Reference.

The State of Eritrea

First, a word of explanation on the name-"The State of Eritrea." The designation of the name of a country is a function of several factors, principally historical and political. For example, "Ghana" replaced the previous, colonially given name, of "The Gold Coast" which the leadership of the independence movement, under Nkrumah, rejected. The ancient empire known as Ghana included parts of present day Ghana but extended far beyond its present border. This historico-geographical fact did not bother Nkrumah and his colleagues, who were determined to adopt a name with historical significance at a time when the renaissance of African history and culture, together with the need for African unity, was on the African liberationist agenda. Eritrea was a name given to the country by the Italian colonial government when it established the colony in 1890. The acceptance of the name by the new government of Eritrea reflects a general trend in postcolonial African history of adopting the colonially given name. Indeed, the boundaries of the African states were defined by colonial history; if you accept the territories, why reject the name? The logic behind this question operated in the majority of cases to retain the colonially given names. Eritrea was no exception; Ghana was, thus, one of the few exceptions to the main trend, Zimbabwe and Malawi being other examples.

In Eritrea's case, the adoption of the name went beyond following the general trend; the struggle for independence was deeply connected with the colonially defined Eritrean identity. To change the name in midstream—in the course of the struggle—would have been politically indefensible and self-defeating. Nor was such a change ever raised as an issue by, or among, Eritreans. The emotional attachment that developed in association with the name Eritrea in the course of the quest for national independence was such that any suggestion for a name change would have been ridiculed and dismissed. This is obviously an integral part of the political process involved in nation building or state formation.

Why "The State of Eritrea? Why not simply Eritrea, or the Republic of Eritrea? After all, Eritrea did become a State upon attaining sovereign independence and joining the family of nation states, following the referendum of April 1993. Why add the word "State" to a sovereign entity that had gained the attributes of a State?

The answer to these questions lies in the geographical location and recent history of Eritrea—in the linguistic affinity existing and affectional bonds forged with Eritrea and some neighboring countries in the course of the struggle for independence. In classical and popular Tigrigna, a major Eritrean language, the word *menghisti*, stands for state as well as government. In the new, official Tigrigna, however, *Hagher* has come to stand for state. **The state of Eritrea** in Tigrigna is thus *Haghere Eritra.* The Arabic equivalent of state is **Dawla,** and the state of Kuwait, for example, is *Dawlat'al Kuwait.* The state of Eritrea (dawlat'al Eritrea in Arabic), having been adopted as such at the Third Congress of the EPLF, in February 1994, has come to stay, the logic of the above-posed questions notwithstanding.

A Secular State?

In the Proposals submitted for public debate, the Constitutional Commission was categorical in its recommendation that the future constitution should incorporate, as part of its basic features, "the principles of nationalism, unity, secularism, democracy, independence and self-reliance...," among other principles.[1] Some foreign writers, while commending the idea of a secular democracy, made the obvious observation that this was "an entirely new idea in Eritrea."[2] Nor was such observation limited to foreign writers.

During public debate, many people were concerned with the possibility of a misunderstanding arising out of the use of the Tigrigna version of the concept of secularism. The Tigrigna word, *alemawinet,* conveyed a different, and potentially misleading sense, one that was associated with worldliness in the negative sense of the word. Many respected elders came to visit the Chairman of the Commission to urge abandonment of the term, or, if it was to be retained, there should be a better word.[3]

It is worth noting that in earlier English usage, the word secular was interchangeable with profane.[For example, the

106

renowned scientist, Sir Isaac Newton, is reported to have said: "I find sure marks of authenticity in the Bible than in any profane (secular) history whatsoever."]

Viewed in historical perspective, in the context of the earlier, documented, history of the EPLF's adoption of radical Left politics and language, such concerns expressed by responsible elders, particularly religious and community leaders, was perfectly understandable. But was the concern a justifiable one, in view of the evolution of EPLF politics, and given the iron-clad guarantee of religious freedom granted in the Constitution? Some thoughtful citizens have answered this question with anther question: was it necessary to write the need for secularism into the Constitution? Couldn't secularism be dealt with by other laws and by administrative policy and action? It was a good question. In reviewing the issue in the post public debate phase of its work, the Commission gave it extensive consideration, debating it internally in its own meetings and holding various consultations.

These consultations and the inspiring reflections that they involved helped the Commission to rethink its position on the issue. The Commission used the opportunity to ask itself some probing questions related to religion, state and society in a country like Eritrea. That there must be separation between the state on the one hand and church and mosque on the other was a matter beyond dispute among the vast majority of Eritreans including the leaders of the two main religions. A theocratic state was neither desirable nor practicable; it would be a prescription for disaster.[4] But the debate on secularism, even after a history of its provenance and its practical values were explained, still left lingering doubts about the value of mentioning it in the constitution. Would it not send the wrong signal to the effect that the government is anti-religion? Did the Constitution need to seem to drive a wedge between the sacred and the secular, even while recognizing the critical importance of the government having to be secular? The Commission recognized the dialectical relation between the sacred and the worldly, between spiritual and material well-being, and the Preamble to the Constitution reflects this recognition. Indeed, such a dialectical relation was an essential, timeless and creative aspect of Eritrean society.

The state and religion may have had to be separated but, to borrow the language of domestic relations, they could not be divorced from each other. There was too much at stake for the state not to be concerned with matters religious and for religion to be aloof from all politics. Although the golden medium of their relationship was not amenable to a cut-and-dry formula it was a dialectic and had to be worked out in the manner of all dialectics—with patience, caution and acumen.

With these considerations in mind, the Commission decided to leave out mention of secularism in the Constitution.

Eritrea's Territory

The country, Eritrea, consists of all its territories, including the islands, territorial waters and airspace, delineated by recognized boundaries.

A cardinal principle underlying the state system recognized in international law is the sovereignty of states defined by boundaries. Many such boundaries are the subject of treaties entered into between neighboring states, while some are the result of historical evolution sanctioned by custom and use.

In the case of post colonial Africa, the state system and the borders defining it emerged out of colonial history, as already noted. The African states are successor states to their former colonizers and are, for good or ill, bound by the treaties signed by the latter.[5]

Eritrea's territories, as defined in the opening paragraph of this section, comprises the mainland, the islands, territorial waters and airspace, inherited from the former colonial powers and recognized under international law. Its boundary with Ethiopia was delineated and recognized under Italo-Ethiopian treaties.[6]

National Government and Regional Administration

The national government of Eritrea is divided into three branches—the legislature, the executive and the judiciary. In explaining the adoption of this time-honored division of governmental power, the Constitutional Commission of Eritrea stated in its 1995 Proposals:

"Separation of power, and the principle of checks and balance, is an important, historically evolved principle which developed with the expansion and strengthening of government power. According to this principle, government power is distributed between the legislative, executive and judicial bodies, each checking the other and balancing power, yet all three working in harmony. Regardless of the type of government we choose, this principle is fundamental.[7]

The division of power into three branches of government was adopted as a crucial doctrine not only as a function of efficiency, which goes with division of labor, but above all, as a principle of accountability operating through a system of checks and balances. Montesquieu originally proposed this as a theory in his penetrating study, *L'Esprit des Lois*.[8] The American Constitution makers adopted it as a basic constitutional principle by writing it into their constitution, in 1789. From then on, this arrangement has been universally accepted as an essential principle of government by all constitutions, save those of the few surviving absolute monarchies or sheikdoms.

In this division of labor the legislative body is given the power of issuing laws as well as that of acting as watchdog over the executive branch. The function of all three branches will be described in more detail in subsequent chapters. At this point an outline will be given by way of introduction.

The Legislature.
By definition, the Legislature must be a representative body, representing the nation as a whole in whose name it issues laws, imposes taxes and other charges, among other functions. In order to be a proper representative body the legislature has to be elected by the people. The election of members of the legislature and the electoral system on the basis of which they are elected is, therefore, a crucial element of a constitutional system of government.

The Constitution of Eritrea provides for this crucial element in various ways, incorporating basic principles and leaving details to be dealt with by Acts of Parliament. In the General Provisions, the constitution requires the state to be established "by democratic procedures to represent people's sovereignty..."9

The Constitution also provides that "sovereign power is vested in the people, and shall be exercised pursuant to the provisions of this constitution.10

The question of what type of electoral system best fulfills the requirements of a truly representative government has been the subject of debate since the dawn of the era of representative democracy in modern times. In the village democracy familiar to most Eritreans, the traditional practice of members of the community openly calling upon certain individuals with proven qualities of leadership to perform certain leadership duties is the most direct and, therefore, the best kind of representation. This tradition must be preserved with some necessary changes; it is still the way by which village communities run their village affairs today. But, valuable as it is for local needs, village democracy cannot possibly accommodate the requirements of a modern nation with its need for adequate and proper representation at the national level.

National representation assumes, first and foremost, national consciousness. The people's representatives at the national level must be representatives of the whole nation first, and after that, of their local constituencies. The interest of the nation comes first—its unity, territorial integrity, stability and development. National representation also assumes a certain amount of specialization of function which the demands of modern government impose on those who come forward to serve. In other words, a certain minimum level of education and adequate knowledge of public affairs is required of members of the national legislature who are going to be at the center of public life.

The Constitution provides for the establishment of strong institutions, capable of accommodating people's participation and of serving as foundation of a viable democratic and popular order.[11] The Commission's Proposals had declared that the legislative body "must have the ability to collect essential information on the country and its surrounding areas in order to reach appropriate decisions; should utilize research and studies and show willingness to accept expert advice; be open to people's views; and above all, be an effective body that actually participates in leading the country and holding the executive body accountable.[12]

It is a tall order, but that is "the nature of the beast." It is a job for the tough and the competent. It is also, needless to say, a job for honest members of the public who are imbued with the spirit of service. Those who lack such qualities need

111

not apply, as is said in advertising. In the prevailing Eritrean public service ethos, proper qualification comes first and foremost, as evidenced by the systematic purging of the civil service undertaken by the government in 1994-96, in which no one was spared, if he or she did not qualify, not even veteran fighters. Painful as it may have been, this was seen by many as auguring well for the development of the country.

The president of Eritrea, Mr. Isaias Afwerki, has expressed concern that, given the paucity of adequately trained manpower, it is unrealistic to expect optimal performance from the members of the legislature of their legislative and other constitutional functions at the earlier stage of the country's constitutional system of government.[13]

The president has also pointed out that, even in the most developed constitutional governments such as that of the United States of America, legislators depend on a vast array of legislative aides and supporting staff of researchers and advisors in order to discharge their duties properly.

The point is well taken, of course, but it does not, indeed cannot, mean that legislators can suspend or abdicate their responsibilities in any sense. Nor can such a meaning be attributed to the cautionary remarks of the president which were meant presumably to state the constraints facing the nation at the moment. What it does mean is that the best available people must be chosen for candidacy to Parliament and that they should be supported by adequate administrative and research staff.

The Executive.

Again, by way of introduction in the context of the General Provisions of the constitution, I will pose some critical questions and leave the answers to the chapter on the Executive. In this respect also, I cannot do better than to quote from a section of the Commission's Proposals which sums up the subject matter as follows:

One of the most controversial issues in constitutional debates is the question: How can an executive body effectively carry out its responsibilities while obeying the rule of law and respecting the bounds of its power? This question arises because historically, executive bodies have shown a persistent tendency to accumulate power into their own hands.

Thus, it is essential to examine important questions such as: How can we develop an effective executive body with delineated powers, which is accountable and functions openly? What is the appropriate and workable balance between effectiveness and power limitation? Such questions are vital, especially in the current stage of nation-building, since a strong leadership is essential for development, the establishment of an appropriate executive body is fundamental.[14]

The Judiciary.
At this point only the essence of the judicial principle need be mentioned, leaving the rest of the discussion on the subject to later sections. The centrality of the Judiciary in a constitutional system under which the rule of law reigns supreme is critical. But a judicial system in which the judges are independent also assumes that the judges must be independent, competent and accountable to the provisions of the constitution and other laws. The judicial system must be free from corruption and discrimination on any basis. Indeed the Constitution so provides.[15]

Upon hearing the emphasis given to this principle, many Eritrean commentators express disbelief and find it hard to agree to a suspension of their disbelief, wondering, instead, whether this constitutional requirement is feasible, or even desirable, in view of the inherited judicial system and the reputation of judges. Despite the fact that the judiciary has been injected with new blood, as it were, of the generation of liberation fighters who are expected to be incorruptible, ill repute dies hard.

This is a matter of grave concern, one that needs to be addressed by every one concerned with the public good and the demands of justice. The Ministry of Justice and the budding School of Law at the University of Asmara are beginning to play a leading role in addressing the issue. It concerns legal education, to begin with and, so far, two sets of law graduates have joined the judicial service in various capacities and at different levels. The Law School has thus initiated a critical service, yet with a long way to go before it can fulfill the requirements of a properly functioning judicial system. At one level, a crash course has been devised to meet the immediate needs; this has already produced some results, but even in this respect, it will be a long way before the demands can be met adequately.

The university authorities must work on this as a matter of priority, not as a matter that must yield to other "priorities". There is no higher priority than a properly functioning justice system, contrary to some misguided opinions in this respect, for there is no aspect of life, which it does not touch directly, or affect indirectly.

Another question concerns the inordinate growth of litigation. The Courts are cluttered with cases, many of which were opened during the rule of the Dergue. Assaulting the culture of the Eritrean people, the Dergue sowed dissent and discord among people whose way of life had been characterized, by and large, by harmony and solidarity. Clearly, the Ethiopian regime found a potent weapon of division. The scars of this discord in Eritrean society, notably among family members and close relatives, are visible in the bitterness involved and litigious mania exhibited in numerous court cases, long after the overthrow of the Dergue and the inauguration of a new era.

Clearly, this problem has also to be specially addressed. It is, in fact, one of the questions that the Minister of Justice has raised in public address.

The constitution has addressed the issue as follows: "The state shall encourage the equitable out-of court settlement of disputes, through conciliation, mediation or arbitration."[16]

This is in tune with traditional practice, which is one of the salutary features of our system of customary laws. The settlement of cases out of court may not appeal to some private interest groups, including some members of the legal "profession" who enjoy an undeserved monopoly over the practice of law, but the demands of justice should not spare any interest group. Indeed, any proper adjustment of the system must begin by addressing the problems caused by, or associated with, a defective legal profession which at the moment is not a profession so much as a business. There is neither properly organized Bar with a system of professional ethics nor, with some rare exceptions, a sense of engagement with the public good, nor the scholarly curiosity and sense of adventure of ideas that should characterize and sustain the professional life. Crass material pursuit seems to be the order of the day, again with a notable exception.

Clearly then, in addition to legal education, there is a need for the establishment of a system of ethics governing the legal profession under which those who fall short of certain standards of conduct are weeded out.

Regional Administration.

The constitution of Eritrea provides for a unitary state " divided into units of regional and local government" whose functions and powers are to be determined by an Act of Parliament.[17]

In the constitutional debates organized by the Commis-

115

sion, the subject of the nature of the relationship between the central government and the regions and localities was one of the issues which was discussed extensively. It was one of the major issues selected as a subject for research and subsequent expert comments, and was debated during the international symposium held in Asmara in January, 1995. It was also included in the set of Proposals submitted for public debate during the third phase of the Commission's life.

The Commission's recommendation in the form of the Proposal was as follows:

> Eritrea should have a unitary government. This is consistent with our goal of building a unified and strong nation. And the existence of local government is essential to develop people's initiative and participation.
>
> The extent of decentralization is determined by the extent of the devolution of power from the central to the local bodies. We must handle this issue in a way that a balance is maintained between centralization and decentralization which can work in the conditions of our country and develop over time and with practice. Generally speaking, we need to realize that decentralization is something that naturally develops alongside regional(or local) economic and cultural development, and is not created, or even accelerated, by policy decisions alone.
>
> A workable decentralization is not possible without the establishment of appropriate local government administrations. We should understand that this is a process that develops in stages. The details of the administrative structure, which is dynamic, are better left to codification by the legislative body.[18]

In all of the debate, very few insisted on including detailed provisions on regional or local government in the Constitution. The argument and pleas of the Commission were found to be persuasive. In the meantime the transitional law on regional administration was revised along with structure and size of the regions. This revision was the subject of controversy among members of the public including, notably the inhabitants of regions whose area had been collapsed and joined with other areas and their administrative capital moved far away from them. Other complaint centered on the abolition of historic names like Hamasien, Seraie, Akele Guzai, Senhit Semhar etc.[19]

Supremacy of the Constitution.

The fundamental principle implied in the supremacy clause of the constitution contains the following main points:-

1. The constitution is the legal expression of the sovereignty of the people which is one of the pillars of a constitutional, democratic order.
2. The constitution is the source of all governmental power and of the rights of citizens.
3. The constitution is the supreme law of the country and the source of all laws of the state, and any law, act, or order which is contrary to its letter and spirit shall be null and void.

And in consequence of all of the above-mentioned principles, all organs of the state, all public and private associations and enterprises and all citizens are bound by, and must be loyal to, the constitution and ensure its observance.[20]

There are at least two areas of law, which may be potential sources of contest in the application of the supremacy principle. In the making of a constitution, clarity on both of

117

them helps to avoid future contests or, at least, their proper resolution, in the event of their occurrence. One potential source of conflict is international law. The other is traditional, or customary, law.

International Law.
The status of international treaties, to which a state is signatory, in relation to a national constitution has been, and still is, a subject of dispute. Some states place treaties on an equal footing with their constitutions.[21]

The majority of states, however, prefer giving treaties equal status with their other laws making them subordinate to the constitution.[22]

Let us consider the advantages and disadvantages of the two options. First, the supremacy option. In an ideal world in which nations abide by the rules of international law this option would commend itself without any doubt. The weight of international law would strengthen the national constitution and make its observance all the more certain. To the extent that greater observance of constitutional principles and rules would ensure more peace and stability, it would thus also create, or reinforce, the right political and social environment for orderly and sustainable development. Moreover, as it would promote a uniformity of laws globally, it would help promote a better world order in which the regular flow of commerce—of goods and services—would facilitate better international relations and development.

But this is not an ideal world; far from it. To begin with, there are serious theoretical hurdles that have to be crossed. National sovereignty is the cornerstone on which the edifice of the international state system is based. Placing a national constitution, on which national sovereignty rests, on equal footing with international treaties would negate such sovereignty by putting a limit on it. It is, theoretically speaking, contradiction in terms.

This theoretical objection may be answered by pointing out that nations place such limits on their sovereignty, in any case, by signing treaties—so why make a fuss over the equation of such treaty with the constitution? Also, in this era of globalization, the question of sovereignty, as classically conceived, has been eroded by the development of communications and related technology and the emergence of the global power of multinational corporations, over the last couple of decades. In today's reality, sovereignty, in its classical sense, has been overtaken by such developments and consigned to the realm of legal fiction, at best. The theory of sovereignty without limits is thus indefensible on practical grounds and in historical terms.

So, why do the majority of states, the most powerful among them included, resist the appeal of the first option—of placing international treaties on equal footing with the constitutions? It would seem that, despite the obvious advantages of the first option, the idea of national sovereignty has an undeniable emotional power and that such emotional power has domestic, political implications that are still too important to ignore or override, even with the best will in the world and the good intentions of national leaders.

The Eritrean constitution makers considered the two options and decided to be silent on the issue. Better leave it to historical events to dictate the best course of action. The option of silence has the advantage of enabling us, it was argued, to respond to events and thus avoid compromising the advantages of both approaches. For example, if the second option were to be adopted, it would operate to derogate from the value of any given international treaty that should ideally enjoy the same status as the constitution. On the other hand, Eritreans would not be faulted for being stingy about their own sovereignty, considering the heavy price paid to achieve it, and so recently.

Traditional Law.

The second source of potential conflict lies in the area of traditional law which may have a religious or secular base.

Ever since the advent of European colonial rule, Eritrea, like the rest of colonial Africa, had two systems of law—Italian colonial law and " indigenous" law. The first system of law pertained to public law covering criminal law and procedure, administrative law and constitutional law. The other was related to the various customary laws of the different ethnic groups who were brought under Italian, colonial rule. The short period of British rule (1941-1952) did not alter the situation that much; indeed much of the inherited law of Italian, colonial origin was retained and the customary system of law left intact.

Paradoxically, it was under the Ethiopian occupation that a systematic attempt was made to impose alien systems of civil and criminal law, much of it of European origin.[23]

It is not known to what extent, and in what areas, this systematic attempt succeeded in undermining the customary laws of any of the people of Eritrea. It may be safely assumed, however, that much of it is still intact.

It was on the basis of this assumption that the Constitutional Commission established a Board of Advisors to assist it in determining: (1) whether there are aspects of customary laws that are worth preserving as valuable assets that can serve overall national objectives; and (2) what aspects may be actually or potentially in conflict with the future constitution. The Commission made it clear, from the very beginning, that once the constitution was promulgated, all preexisting laws, customary or otherwise, would have to be in accord with the constitution, and that if they are not they would be null and void.

On the whole, the public understood and welcomed this point. Some elements in the religious community expressed fear, at first, that this might mean abolition of religiously-based laws such as Islamic (Sharia) law. Such fear was dispelled as the public discourse on the subject progressed and more clarification was given on it.

The supremacy of the constitution is thus one of those questions on which there is general consensus in principle. It will be a matter for future development through judicial interpretation and education as well as social action to secure proper adjustments in those areas of customary law and practice that tend to die hard, particularly in the areas of family law where women are often at a disadvantage. An example of matters which were considered for inclusion in the Constitution but were left for future judicial interpretation concerns family and succession laws practiced hitherto in Eritrea. It was thought wiser to leave it for courts to take judicial notice of, and apply, such laws in so far as the two parties to the controversy request for their application.

Suppose a woman partner to a marriage who, under a given customary rule (or Sharia law), is entitled to a smaller portion in the division of family property. She is customarily bound by an agreement in which she agrees to receive such a smaller portion. In such a case, the woman's consent to abide by the customary (or Sharia) rule would be the operative principle, which means that in the absence of such consent the rule would not apply.

Faced with a dilemma of the need to change an unjust customary practice, on the one hand, and of the potential social fallout that such a change might produce, on the other, involving a complaint that such a change violates a religiously derived principle, the Eritrean constitution makers chose to leave the matter for future judicial interpretation. Some might find this an unfortunate postponement of an inevitable, fundamental social question, but in engineering social change with the help of the law a proper balance and flexibility must be built in, with justifiable expectation that what the law maker considers the higher value would ultimately prevail. It would ultimately prevail, as noted above, through education and social action.

What if the woman relents and wishes to break the agreement? What a court of law would do if it were to be petitioned to recognize a breach of this kind of agreement will be one of those fascinating and important decisions that remain to be see in the future.

Citizenship.
The constitution of Eritrea contains the basic principles concerning citizenship, leaving the details to an Act of Parliament. It provides for two categories of citizenship: citizenship by birth, and citizenship by acquisition.

All persons born of an Eritrean father or mother are Eritrean citizens by birth. No person who is a citizen by birth may be denied or deprived of his/her citizenship.[24]

The acquisition of citizenship by foreigners shall be prescribed by an Act of Parliament together with other details.[25]

Presumably this will include the conditions for granting dual citizenship, given the fact that a great number of Eritreans live in the Diaspora, particularly in Europe and the North American continent and the overall benefits that would accrue to all concerned.

No Eritrean citizen shall be banished or extradited.[26]

National Symbols and Languages.
National Symbols.
This is concerned with the Flag, the National Anthem and Coat of Arms.

The Flag adopted at the Third Congress of the EPLF has been retained; it shall have green, red and blue colors with golden olive leaves located at the center. Other details are left to an Act of Parliament.[27]

Left to be determined by law are also the National Anthem and Coat of Arms.

None of these matters occasioned any dispute during the national debate over the constitution, unlike the issue of language.

Language.

The constitution guarantees the equality of all Eritrean languages.[28]

The language question was among the issues that was debated extensively by members of the public throughout the constitutional debate. There were mainly two opposed positions taken which may be summarized as follows:

> 1) The case for a national language was argued on the basis of the need of any nation to have one language of communication, or two at most. Such a common language, it was maintained, is an essential prerequisite for nation building, particularly in developing countries. Not to provide constitutionally for such an obvious need, apart from the practical problems it would create, would be to encourage the development of centrifugal tendencies (ethnic nationalism) and thus diminish national consciousness. And it would require more resources to cater for the needs or demands of the speakers of the different languages which would be unavoidable if all the languages are given equal status in the constitution. Is this desirable or feasible? Can a nation like Eritrea afford it?
>
> The logical and practical thing to do, some maintained, would be to constitutionalize the practice of the last quarter century, namely make Tigrigna and Arabic the official, or at least the work-

ing, languages of the nation. In the same vein others proposed that only Tigrigna be the official language. Still others maintained that, since Tigrigna and Tigre are the languages spoken by the majority of the population (over 80 per cent), they should be made official languages. After all, argued the latter, only a small fraction of the Eritrean people spoke Arabic, contrary to a mistaken belief held by a some that Arabic is widely spoken in the country.[29]

2) The Opposed Argument

The recommendation of the Constitutional Commission which was eventually adopted was simply that the equality of all the languages of the country be recognized and guaranteed by the constitution which was later adopted as reflected in Article 4(3) of the constitution. The Commission's Proposals stated the argument as follows:

"Objectively speaking, there is no compelling reason why the issue of languages should be a political issue. The people of Eritrea speak different languages. In Eritrea, it is necessary that equality of both written and unwritten languages be respected, all the people be able to speak in the language that is easiest for them, and everyone learn more than one language.

We think that the belief in the equality of all Eritrea languages, and a commitment to develop all of our languages, should be the starting point.

We must handle the issue of language in a way that serves and strengthens our basic goal of building a unified and strong nation. The equality of all Eritrean languages, the cultural and psychological importance of starting education with the mother tongue, the need for a common medium of instruction from intermediate school level, the right of every citizen to use in government activities any language he/she chooses, are all important considerations. Although the issue of language is not a constitutional issue, and thus in theory a constitution can be silent about it, in Eritrea's condition, the issue should be raised in the constitution. And the stand we take on this issue should serve nation-building, and enhance understanding and unity among Eritreans.

Thus, in our constitution, emphasis should be placed on equality of all languages, and the right of every citizen to use the language of his/her choice, without the designation of any official or working language."[30]

The overwhelming majority of Eritreans who took part in the public debates were persuaded by this argument, and the Commission felt justified in writing the essence of the argument into the constitution, as noted above.

What of the points regarding the potential effect of this language policy on the development of national consciousness, and about the implied financial cost?

As to the first point, the constitution makers of Eritrea started with the presumption that recognition of their languages would have the opposite effect on the various ethnic groups, i.e., of reinforcing their national consciousness, rather than diminishing it. This presumption rests on logic supported by the recent history of the country. This is quite apart from the fact that a fundamental principle is at issue here—the principle of equality. Denial of this principle has been a major reason for the revolts of various ethnic groups in the recent history of neighboring Ethiopia. The post-

Dergue government decided to make explicit recognition of minority languages and include a provision in the new constitution as an important aspect of the professed democratization objective.[31]

The issue of cost is an arguable one, of course, but surely, there is no worthier subject than the encouragement and support of the development of the languages and cultures of a nation. It forms part of the national treasure and the state has the responsibility of providing financial and other forms of support to the best of its ability. Given the recognition, in principle, granted them and their languages and cultures, the different groups within the nation can be reasonably expected to appreciate a rational decision by the government, even if such a decision should fall short of expectations due to lack of resources at any given moment.

What is always needed—what should never be absent— is trust, trust that the government is committed to certain basic principles, and that it would do whatever it can to accommodate and give satisfaction to all concerned. In the case of Eritrea, such trust between the people and their government, beginning from the days of the armed struggle, was the *sine qua non* of the success of the enterprise. It was developed and maintained during the years of struggle in far more difficult circumstances when equality of languages was not only declared as a policy but was practiced and produced good results in terms of national consciousness. Children were educated in their mother tongues up to the sixth grade. And they were taught English, Tigrigna and Arabic in upper grades, together with mathematics, science and other subjects that are normally taught elsewhere.

As for the medium of communication among Eritreans, this has been determined by need, by what might be called, for lack of a better term, the laws of the market. English has already become the language of communication in business and commerce, in government offices as well as among the business community. Tigrigna and Arabic were used, and are being used, as sort of working languages, although they have not been designated as such, because to do so would derogate from the basic principle of equality of languages. In the daily radio broadcasts, Tigrigna and Arabic are joined by three other languages: Tigre, Afar and Kunama, the language spoken by the smallest ethnic group in the country. For the rest, it is left for future events to determine.

Gender Reference.
Article 5 of the constitution provides: "Without consideration to the wording of any provision in this Constitution with reference to gender, all of its articles shall apply equally to both genders."

Traditionally, laws, having been drafted by men, invariably used, and continue to use, the masculine gender. In this day and age the equality principle demands that there should be no doubt whatsoever that such a traditional way of writing laws is not intended. Accordingly, no discriminatory purpose can be implied by any authority in construing a text related to this issue. A more awkward way of dealing with this is to use the "he/she" formula in practically every article. Such a recommendation was at times heard during the debates.

The formula of Article 5 is obviously a better alternative. It should also be pointed out that the rights and duties provided for in the text of the constitution apply to both genders. A special plea was sometimes heard in meetings that there should be provisions in the constitution, specifically aimed at reinforcing the rights of women as traditionally oppressed members of the society, in order to send a clear message that the government and society will not tolerate any future discrimination. Such plea was met by the argument that in view of the fact that the constitutional provisions are inclusive of

127

men and women, such special provisions would be, in effect, demeaning to women and their equal rights with men.

The reference in the preamble to the historic role of women and the nation's commitment to the equality principle is sufficient in terms of sending a signal to would-be violators of women's equal rights. The rest is a matter of education and social action, as has been stated already in the discussion on the preamble.

Notes

1. See Proposals
2. See Charlie Cobb, Eritrea Wins the Peace, National Geographic June 1996, pp. 82-105
3. For example, the Chairman of the Asmara (Hamasien) Regional Council, Grazmatch Misghina Almedom, made verbal representations to the Commission's Chairman to the effect that the members of his Council as well as many other elders considered the word *alemawinet* has negative connotations and they strongly urged that it no be used.
4. The Mufti of Eritrean Muslims, in an interview conducted by Hidri, one of PFDJ's publications as well as in a communication to the author as Chairman of the Commission, stated that in a country like Eritrea, which is evenly divided between Christians and Muslims, separation of state and religion is an imperative.
5. The Organization of African Unity affirmed the colonial borders at the second Summit in Cairo in July 1964.
6. Ethiopia recognized the borders as the Algiers Accord of 2000 signed between Eritrea and Ethiopia confirmed. The subsequent verdict of the Hague Boundary Commission on the border dispute between the two countries handed down on February 13, 2002, recon-

firmed this recognition.
7. Proposals p.19.
8. Charles Montesquieu, *L'esprit des lois*, book 2, Ch.2, para 27 (1949).
9. Article 1(4).
10. Article 1(3).
11. See Article 7.
12. See Proposals p.20.
13. The President's subsequent action, as explained in more detail in the Epilogue below, casts doubt on the sincerity of this claim.
14. See the epigraph of chapter ten below.
15. Articles 10(3) and 48(2).
16. Article 10(4).
17. Article 1(5).
18. See Article 1(5). See also Proposals p. 27-28.
19. The resentment is still alive. Whether it will go away remains to be seen.
20. Article 2.
21. The Constitution of the Netherlands is an example.
22. The Constitution of France is an example.
23. The Civil Code was based on the French Civil Code and was drafted by noted jurist, Professor Rene David of the Sorbonne. The Penal Code was based on the Swiss Penal Code and was drafted by noted Swiss jurist Professor Jean Graven of the University of Geneve.
24. Article 3(1).
25. Article 3(2).
26. Article 3(3).
27. Article 4(1).
28. Article 4(3).
29. In a public seminar I gave in Addis Ababa in 1996, an Arabic speaking Eritrean asserted that the majority of Eritreans speak Arabic and that Tigre is a primitive lan-

guage. It is interesting that the man happened to be from the Tigre-speaking nationality. This feeling was shared by a certain minority among the earlier leadership of the Eritrean Liberation Front who, according to eye witness reports, ordered the burning of books written in Tigrigna and Tigre. The vast majority of Eritreans do not speak Arabic and do not therefore share this sentiment. In truth, the issue is not numerical but psychological. It has to do with the fact that Arabic is held in high regard by Muslims because it is the language of the Holy Qur'an.

30. Pages 28-29.

31. Indeed, the post-Dergue government of Ethiopia has made its policy on regional organization of the country on linguistic (ethnic) basis.

SIX

Objectives and Directive Principles of the Country

"...Have ye leisure, comfort, calm,
Shelter, food, love's gentle balm?
Or what is it ye buy so dear
With your pain and with your fear?

Sow seed,—but let no tyrant reap;
Find wealth,—let no impostor heap;
Weave robes,—let not the idle wear
Forge arms,—in your defense bear...."

(P. B. SHELLEY, SONG TO THE MEN OF ENGLAND)

* * *

"We have to evolve a constitution that...opens up every access of self-fulfillment equally to all citizens...We recognize the indissoluble unity of a nation's humanity with opportunity, resources, responsibility and fulfillment, with education and housing, a unity in freedom

of association and freedom of religious worship, with freedom to believe or not to believe, unity with employment and health, with access to justice under the law. Above all, we must enshrine the dynamic unities—the unities that ensure on the one hand, that diversities are recognized, but only within the framework of an indivisible humanity that does not permit the violation of its kind in the name of such diversities." (WOLE SOYINKA, "AMALGAMATION AND THE IMPERIAL WILL." 2000)

The general objectives and directive principles by which the country is to be guided are defined in chapter two of the constitution, comprising the following topics:

1. National Unity and Stability.
2. Democratic Principles.
3. Economic and Social Development
4. National Culture
5. Competent Justice System
6. Competent Civil Service
7. National Defense and Security.
8. Foreign Policy.

As the heading of each topic indicates, the subjects covered under this chapter pertain to the overall aims that the country is to follow, expressed broadly but succinctly, and the general principles that would guide the pursuit of these and related aims. Most of the aims and guiding principles are discussed as rights and duties in later chapters. The constitutional significance of the chapter on general objectives and directive principles is that it provides a road map to help the government and people of the country in the pursuit of certain basic social, economic and political objectives, particularly when occasions arise that raise questions as to what to do and how to do it. This is particularly true when contentious economic and social issues arise.

In what follows, we will discuss competent judicial system after national unity and stability and democratic principles; the rest will be discussed in the order in which they appear in the constitution.

National Unity and Stability

National unity and stability is a basic political value on which the continued existence of a nation depends, and from which, therefore, derive a nation's other major political and juridical values. Only people who have not experienced the dislocating effects of turbulence caused by a lack of unity and stability, or have a dim memory of such effects, can ever question this simple verity.

Indeed, it is so basic—so elementary—that it is hard to imagine anyone questioning it. And in Eritrea's case, as already mentioned, national unity and stability is one of the five major questions which the EPLF (renamed the PFDJ) set forth in its Charter as one on which there must be a national consensus.

The Constitutional Commission, on its part, from the outset seized on the initiative which had been taken by the Front in searching for the values and goals that constitution makers need to promote, nurture and protect. The constitution, according to the Commission, must be both an embodiment and a consequence of a people's attachment to such values and goals.[1]

During the public debate, the issue of national unity was discussed in connection with the requirements of plurality. The concept of unity-in-diversity encapsulates the goal of mediating between the need of unity, while at the same time guaranteeing diversity-tolerance of a diversity of views and of the existence and growth of different groups within a political community embraced within one nation.

To quote from the Commission's Proposals,

> "...The experience of our revolution provides incontrovertible evidence to prove that a diverse society can be a source of unity and strength rather than one of division and weakness. From our diverse society—cultural, ethnic, linguistic, and religious—it is necessary to build and develop a unified and strong national unity through equal participation and recognition, and acceptance of diversity but without abusing it...The essential question is whether diversity is the source of economic and social inequality or of political exclusion..."[2]

These general considerations have found expression in the constitution under Article 6. In the national endeavor to establish a united and prosperous Eritrea, government and people are to be guided by the principle of unity in diversity.[3]

The state is enjoined to foster democratic tolerance and national consensus "through participation of all citizens; ensure national stability and development by encouraging democratic dialogue and national consensus; and by laying a firm political, cultural and moral foundation by building a strong political, cultural and moral foundation of national unity and social harmony."[4]

And the state is required to ensure peace and stability by establishing appropriate institutions that encourage people's participation and by creating the necessary conditions to guarantee equitable economic and social progress.[5]

It is clear from the above that the constitution makers of Eritrea link the requirements of national unity and stability both with an inclusionary, pluralist political community in which citizens' participation is paramount, and with economic and social justice. In other words, if peace is indivisible, so is justice; and if political participation is the condition for healthy politics, a fair share in the "national cake" is a precondition for peace and harmony.

Democratic Principles

Democracy is the keystone of the entire edifice of the political system of a country in the modern era. That is political democracy, which is the basis of other expressions of the democratic principle—social and economic. In the age-old human struggle for freedom and decency, the idea of democracy—of people being masters of their own lives in one form or another—has played a central role. That struggle, which began and was expressed in different forms in different places at different times, is an ongoing process today, even in countries that claim monopoly over its origin and development. And, as the paramount political value of our epoch, democracy requires continued stewardship and vigilance. It is not an end that, once achieved, can be taken for granted; the human tendency to want to dominate and be in control, to the exclusion of others, is one of those givens that have to be constantly born in mind and monitored with vigilance.

Accordingly, in the task of constitution making, democracy and the principles and mechanisms of attaining and maintaining it, are crucial subjects that must be properly and adequately addressed. The Constitutional Commission considered this task the most important among its tasks. Article 4(1) of the Proclamation which established the Commission provided the initial enabling authority in that respect. It stipulates that:

135

The mission of the Commission shall be:

"(1) to draft a constitution on the basis of which a democratic order would be established, and which, as the basic law, shall be the ultimate point of reference of all the laws of the country, and the final arbiter of all basic issues in dispute".

In explaining the meaning of democracy, the Commission started with the simple Lincolnian definition of democracy as government of the people, by the people, for the people, pointing out that its underlying principle concerns the equality of citizens and their right to participate in running the affairs of their country, as well as their own (local) affairs. It further elaborated the basic point by linking democracy to human rights and the rule of law, and stressing the critical importance of a free Press, political parties and of popular and professional organizations for the development of democracy.[6]

The Commission marshaled its arguments, based on historical and theoretical research, including research of the contemporary scene in which Procedural Democracy—elections and the procedures linked to them—has been given due emphasis. "That there cannot be democracy without political pluralism and without the freedom of expression and freedom to form organizations is beyond dispute", the Commission proclaimed, " nor can it be doubted that election is a necessary requirement for democracy. But democracy in its profound sense, is not concerned with the legal right to participate only, but is principally concerned with an enabling environment that ensures concrete and meaningful participation in political processes."[7]

A legal right in the absence of an ability to enjoy it is meaningless. In short, political democracy without economic and social democracy and development "is like a structure without a foundation."[8] In this respect, historical research bears out the conclusion reached by the Commission that democracy is an outcome of economic and social development in which social and political struggles figure prominently. The historical lessons are stressed in order to avoid being condemned to repeat some of their unpleasant aspects. By way of inscribing in the constitution the essence of the guiding democratic principle, Article 7 of the constitution requires the state:

1. To guarantee its citizens broad and active participation in all political, economic, social and cultural life of the country.[9]
2. To establish appropriate institutions to encourage and develop people's initiative and participation in their communities.[10]
3. To guarantee all citizens, without distinction, an equal opportunity to participate in any position of leadership in the country.[11]
4. To create conditions necessary for developing a democratic political culture defined by free and critical thinking, tolerance and national consciousness.[12]

Article 7 also prohibits any act that violates the human rights of women or limits or otherwise thwarts their role and participation.[13]

It also requires the conduct of the affairs of government and all organizations and institutions to be accountable and transparent.[14]

Finally, it requires that the organization and operation of all political, public associations and movements be guided by the principles of national unity and democracy.[15]

137

Competent Justice System

A question may arise as to why a section on the judicial system was considered to be necessary in a chapter on national objectives and directive principles of a constitution. Such a question should be expected logically since the basic principle concerning justice can be summed up in the need for the independence and impartiality of judges, a principle that is amply covered in the chapter on the Judiciary. The answer to this question is simply that the Eritrean constitution makers considered the reality, as stated already, of a situation in which there is a defective inherited judicial system with a judiciary that has been, by and large, inadequate, leaving much room to be desired both in terms of competence and judicial integrity. Hence the careful wording of Article 10:

1. The judicial system of Eritrea shall be independent, competent and accountable pursuant to the provision of the constitution and laws enacted pursuant thereto.[16]
2. Courts shall work under a judicial system that is capable of producing quick and equitable judgments and that can easily be understood by and is accessible to all the people.[17]
3. The judges shall be free from corruption or discrimination and, in rendering their judgment, they shall make no distinction among persons.[18]
4. The state shall encourage the equitable out-of-court settlement of disputes, through conciliation, mediation and arbitration.[19]

The provisions of Article 10 of the constitution were drafted taking into account the current condition of the judicial service in the general historical and cultural context of the

138

country and the critical need of rectification and at the same time maintaining judicial independence. This major consideration reflects two seemingly contradictory positions: on the one hand to ensure that a judiciary operating in a defensive milieu and an inadequate capacity does not use its judicial independence to flout certain basic principles of justice and democracy. Hence, the requirement of accountability provided for under sub article1. Hence also, the requirements of producing fast and equitable judgments. (Justice delayed is justice denied, and equity is a crucial element in rendering judgments.). The requirement that there should be no distinction among persons links a democratic principle with a basic principle of justice.

At the same time, these requirements must in no way infringe on the fundamental principle of the independence of the Judiciary.

Economic and Social Development

Article 8 of the constitution provides a concise summary of the basic principles concerning a subject on which volumes have been written.

Almost from the beginning of its mandate, the Constitutional Commission of Eritrea considered the issue of whether a constitution should contain, and if so, to what degree of detail, provisions on economic development and social justice. Some modern constitutions contain detailed provisions covering these issues, most including them as basic human rights. And the Commission shared the belief that these are indeed basic human rights. "Social, economic and cultural rights are important and integral aspects of fundamental human rights", it declared, adding that human rights cannot be complete without them and that they include rights to education, health, balanced development, development of cultures and languages, etc.

However, as already noted, the Commission cautioned that care should be taken in not including in the constitution rights that cannot be implemented or enforced. Such rights can and should be listed as goals that can be realized as the resources of the country may permit. "It is better to present social, economic and cultural rights in general terms which can be interpreted and expanded as progress is made."[20]

Thus the constitution provides that the State shall:

1. Strive to create opportunities to ensure the fulfillment of citizens' rights to social justice and economic development and to fulfill their material and spiritual needs.[21]
2. work to bring about a balanced and sustainable development throughout the country, and shall use all available means to enable all citizens to improve their livelihood in a sustainable manner, through their participation.[22]
3. In the interest of present and future generations, the State shall be responsible for managing all land, water, air and natural resources and for ensuring their management in a balanced and sustainable manner; and for creating the right conditions to secure the participation of the people in safeguarding the environment.[23]

It is noteworthy that the state is charged with two further responsibilities in addition to securing citizens' rights to social justice and economic development. The state must secure an equitable or balanced development, balanced in terms of closing the gap between town and country, and equitable in terms of closing the gap between different sectors of society. Note the adjective "sustainable" which is fastened onto the concept of development. Sustainable development must also consider safeguarding the environment as an increasingly important consideration, one that has already entered the lexicon of general terms and conditions insisted upon, or even imposed by, "donors" of development assistance like the World Bank, US-AID, and their European and Canadian equivalents.

Another point worth noting is that the state carries sole responsibility in the task of bringing about balanced and sustainable development. The state also carries the responsibility of securing the participation of the people in safeguarding their environment. Although neither responsibility—sustainable development or safeguarding the environment—can be discharged without the optimal participation of the people, the fact remains, nevertheless, that the burden of duty lies with the State. It is a debatable point as to whether the people should also shoulder the responsibility for guardianship of the environment, and different constitutions have answered it differently. The majority limit the responsibility to the State, but almost all require popular participation as a prerequisite for successful environmental protection.[24]

National Culture

A national culture should be distinguished from the local (ethnic) cultures that were discussed in an earlier section, although there is a sense in which the two are linked in some respects because national culture can have roots in some of the dominant local cultures, or may be influenced by them in its development. On the other hand, a national culture can have a powerful impact on local cultures through the Media and the educational system. An example of traditional culture impinging on national culture is the community spirit in which group interests prevail over those of individuals, coupled with the sense of obligation that an individual has for members of his kinship group.

The constitution of Eritrea seeks to preserve some of the positive aspects of traditional culture and link them with the new national culture. Thus it imposes on the state three principal duties in connection with national culture:

- the responsibility of creating and maintaining the necessary conditions for the enrichment of national culture;
- the encouragement of the values of community concern and the love and respect of family; and
- the promotion of the development of arts, sport and science and technology as well as the creation of the enabling environment for individuals to work in an atmosphere of freedom and manifest their inventiveness and innovation.[25]

These duties are clear and self-explanatory and need no further comments, as such. But it would be useful to put the matter in perspective. National culture is considered as the expression of national identity and the unity and progress of the Eritrean people. It played a crucial role during the liberation struggle in cementing a united effort against a common foe, mobilizing popular support in that effort. During the struggle, the music and dance and folklore of the various ethnic groups was featured in regular performances and had the dual role of entertaining and edifying the fighters as well as promoting unity and pride among the component groups within the struggle and beyond. The EPLF radio, Voice of the Masses, played a crucial role in disseminating information and promoting national unity.

At the moment, the Ministry responsible for cultural

affairs is the Ministry of Education which took over this function from the Ministry of Information. During the liberation struggle, culture, information and education were under the umbrella of the department responsible for ideology and national guidance. In those times, considerations of rational and efficient use of scarce human resources required placing several different functions under one head. There was also, in those days, the imperative of ensuring ideological unity within the movement which was dictated by the necessities of war, a common phenomenon in all wars.

In addition to music and folklore, the liberation-spawned culture did also lay the foundation for a new and progressive outlook on social and political issues. In that sense, it may be fairly characterized as a new culture born in the white heat of struggle. The values of unity, equality, love of truth and justice, self-reliance, and steadfastness which are mentioned in the Preamble to the constitution form an important part of this new culture. To these should be added the values of community that was mentioned earlier. This latter can be problematic in that community values, be they traditional or modern, are destined to clash with the emerging culture that stresses individual enterprise and interest and at the center of which lies the idea of contract.

To what extent the core values listed above, which form a central part of the new culture, can be sustained and transferred to the younger generation who were not part of the struggle is a question uppermost in the minds of Eritrean leaders. The start of the National Youth Service in 1995, together with the national military service is an aspect of this concern and, judging by its first results, a cautious optimism on some satisfactory results was justified. In addition to the values already mentioned, those of discipline and love of hard work which was imbued during the struggle, were instilled in the minds of the youth with some commendable results in public works, in afforestation and other environmental friendly, productive efforts.

The work ethic which had been all but destroyed, among the urban youth, during the rule of the Dergue was reinstated with new vigor. Hard work and pride in one's occupation, once a distinguishing characteristic of Eritreans, had become rare commodities among the young of the present generation, as business enterprises engaged in the construction industry found out when looking for workers. Clearly, this had to change if the government's reconstruction and development efforts were to succeed. However, the stories coming out of the military service experience particularly after the 1998-2000 war with Ethiopia, have dampened the earlier enthusiasm. Disappointments and war defections have replaced that enthusiasm.

National Defense and Security

This is a topic which was among those researched rather systematically by the Constitutional Commission, and was one of the issues included in the Proposals for public debate. It was also, understandably, one of those which never failed to draw questions.

The place of the military forces in the constitution is an important question to be considered carefully, especially in developing countries where the incidence of military coups d'etat has caused problems of political development in many countries. As a matter of fundamental principle, there should be agreement on one point. The armed forces and security services should abide by the law and serve the country and protect the constitution. This should be rule number one to be assiduously inculcated in them from the start of their careers and sustained throughout their lives.

The question remains, nonetheless: What guarantees are there that, even assuming that this rule is taught to them at the military schools, that it would not be broken, that military coups would not occur? It is a question that haunts political leaders of all stripes. Exacerbated by one-party hegemonies and, in some instances, by ethnic strife, the military coup has become a significant part of the problem of politics in the developing countries, and particularly in Africa. It is worth stressing, though, that Africa does not have the monopoly of this problem.

Different tactics have been devised to meet the challenge of military coups and enormous human and financial resources have been deployed to prevent them. Some leaders have, indeed, developed ingenious ways of coping with the problem.[26]

But they could not avoid the occurrence; at best they could only postpone them, for they only addressed the symptom, not the cause of the problem. Generally speaking, a military coup is a symptom rather than the root cause of a nation's problems. A sure guarantee against military coups or, related political problems, that would endure can only emanate from the establishment of an appropriate political system with effective institutions. As will be discussed in later sections proper systems of legislative and executive control is the first among such means of control. The armed forces and security services themselves must be effective institutions: in their formation, training, system of ethics and their relationship with the rest of society. And they must have adequate compensation and other favorable terms and conditions of service.

The constitution of Eritrea takes all these concerns into account and the provisions of Article 12 reflect these concerns. First and foremost, the constitution provides that they owe allegiance to, and obey the constitution and the government established thereunder.[27]

145

Secondly, they are an integral part of civil society, and are required to be " productive and respectful of the people."[28]

In the case of Eritrea, the history of close relationship of the liberation army with the civilian population was not only a critical factor in the success of the struggle, but established an ethos of community service in the rank and file, and among the officer corps, of the armed forces who lived with, and worked for, the public in all fields of endeavor, including the productive life of working the farms in all stages and at all levels. This fact helped in instilling the work ethic among the liberation fighters and cemented their relationship with the ordinary citizen who in turn developed a special respect and affection for the liberation fighters.

Moreover, the defense of the nation became rooted in the people and on their active participation as a result of the history of the struggle, a fact which is now constitutionalized, and which was proven beyond any doubt during the war with Ethiopia of 1998-2000.[29]

Above all, the defense and security forces are subject and accountable to the law, must be cultivated (indoctrinated is another way of putting it) to be worthy of their calling and to pass on these traits as a lasting tradition to future generations of their members.[30]

In sum, if all goes well according to plan, and if the values summarized above, both resulting from the specific historical condition of Eritrea and adopted from other systems, are maintained, the homegrown armed forces of the country will be expected to be an exception and an inspiring example of a model force in a continent that is in dire need of such example. The same would go for the security services, because they are subject to the same requirements as the armed forces, in essential respects. All this will depend on the political wisdom of the leaders who must resist the temptation to use the armed and security services to narrow, selfish ends. If they fail this test, all the gains of the armed struggle will be lost.

The police and related security forces are subject to the same constitutional requirement of being subject to the rule of law. The difference lies in their specific functions and organization and these factors impinge in their mode of training and in the manner of discharging their responsibilities. The relevant laws that prescribe their functions and organization will, of course, provide for the manner of the execution of their duties as well as for the terms and conditions of their service. The rest is a matter of practice and growth with experience in which nothing should be taken for granted. As always in these matters, an effective system of control and oversight by the relevant organs of the government, as well as a vigilant public, aware of its constitutional rights and duties, will be an essential condition for ensuring that the police and other members of the security service carry out their duties properly.

Foreign Policy

Article 13 of the constitution, one of the shortest, provides that " the foreign policy of Eritrea is based on respect for State sovereignty and independence and on promoting the interest of regional and international peace, cooperation, and development." This provision represents, in concise form, what has become a standard provision in most constitutions of the world. Recognition of the independence and sovereignty of countries is a basic requirement of international law and its inclusion in a constitution is logical and proper. So is the requirement for the promotion of peace, cooperation and harmony and development at all levels—regional and international.

This latter requirement reflects the basic maxim of international relations that peace is indivisible.

The establishment of regional organizations like the Organization of African Unity (OAU), the Organization of American States (OAS) and similar regional bodies concerned with other parts of the world, and operating independently but with the help and under the umbrella of the United Nations, is a function of the theory of the indivisibility of peace and stability. The contemporary scene of regional conflicts everywhere and the corresponding responses of the international community, some adequate, some not, demonstrates the need for a correct understanding that peace is indeed indivisible.

It is necessary, again, to put this particular constitutional provision in historical perspective. Eritreans, of all people, are keenly aware of such need because of the history of their lonely fight for freedom. In view of that lonely fight, it would have been perfectly understandable for Eritreans to despair of the value of international organizations, particularly the OAU, which lent a deaf ear to their pleas for help. But despite that sad history there is a kind of "family obligation" on their part to be supportive members of the organization.[31]

To do otherwise would have been unconscionable, irresponsible and unworthy of a people and its heroic fighters who, in their hour of triumph, made magnanimity in victory a compelling code of behavior in their dealings with those who opposed them. The Eritrean attitude in this as in other matters supports the sentiment expressed in respect of Nelson Mandela that a heightened sense of responsibility and deepened conscience are qualities which long suffering instills in a people. It is one of the premiums that struggle and sacrifice bring.

Foreign policy is an extension of the domestic policy of a nation; its content is determined by domestic politics and the basic policy followed by the government of the nation. The tension between such policy and politics, on the one

148

hand, and the requirements of international law and politics on the other, is a subject of continued debate under conditions of evolving international relations. The changed, and continually changing, world order in which the bipolar regime has given way to a much more complex situation, with the United States of America now enjoying the status of sole Super Power, has inevitably raised questions regarding the proper role of international and regional organizations.

Under the circumstances of this evolving scene, the traditionally neglected functions of peace-keeping and peace-making have assumed greater significance. These functions were neglected principally due to the Super Power rivalry which dominated international relations for over forty years, following the end of World War II right up to the fall of the Soviet Union. And, as the experiences in Somalia, Rwanda, Liberia, former Yugoslavia, Chechnia, Lebanon and elsewhere demonstrate, we have a long way to go before peace-keeping and peace-making become easily enforceable functions and part of the generally accepted norms of international relations. Apart from the fact of the primacy of domestic politics, the availability of resources to be marshaled readily and effectively, are major constraints.

In view of the above, a principal consideration of the foreign policy of a nation like Eritrea becomes dependence on its own defense capability and the requisite organization and resources and combat-readiness of its defense forces and its people. This is unfortunate, especially for nations like Eritrea, facing the enormous task of reconstruction and development. It will test, to the maximum, as it has done already, the skills and statesmanship of the leaders concerned. A search for a common ground among the leaders of the region in defense and foreign policy issues will be an important part of the search for a solution in the common aims of peace, stability and development. Hence the constitutional provision stipulated in Article 13, requiring "cooperation, harmony and development."

Many scholars and policy makers have been asking whether the sovereign state could continue to serve as the sole setting for public policy and action with respect to the daunting problems of development facing nations such as those of the Horn of Africa. In spite of some important accords reached by African states, it remains the case that in most of them the movement of goods and services is severely limited, natural and human resources are inadequately pooled, complementary material resources are not jointly exploited, and there is no efficient division of labor in the provision of urgent public service.

As the Ethiopian foreign Minster observed, " It is now becoming increasingly obvious that closer cooperation among countries and their economic integration is not one of option among many that states have to ensure a better life for their respective peoples. It is the only option they have."[32] This statement reflects the views of both governments of Ethiopia and Eritrea of those halcyon days. Clearly, there are obstacles to overcome, including vested bureaucratic interests and institutional rigidities. The desired goal of regional cooperation leading to eventual integration will take time, a healing of the wounds caused by the recent war, and a lot of political will.

Notes

1. See keynote address of Commission Chairman, delivered at the opening of the International Symposium on the making of the Eritrean Constitution, January 3, 1995. Speech is on file.
2. Proposals p. 8.
3. Article 6(1).

4. Article 6(2).
5. Article 6(3).
6. Proposals p. 11.
7. Ibid.
8. Ibid.
9. Article 7(1).
10. Article 7(3).
11. Article 7(4)
12. Article 7(7).
13. Article 7(2).
14. Article 7(5).
15. Article 15(6).
16. Article 10(1).
17. Article 10(2).
18. Article 10(3).
19. Article 10(4).
20. Proposals pp. 26-27.
21. Article 8(10.
22. Article 8(2).
23. Article 8(3).
24. Cf. Article 20 of the Constitution of Nigeria, and section 24 of the Constitution of South Africa.
25. See Article 9.
26. The late dictator of Somalia, Mohamed Siyad Barre, habitually began receiving guests at night, beginning after dusk and lasting until after dawn. This species of "ministerial curfew" was designed to keep potential would-be coupmakers in attendance or under surveillance, because coups invariably take place at night, when the powers-that-be are asleep. The present writer had a couple of such audiences and was duly advised in advance by friends to have a good day's sleep, because there was no telling at what time the President would see you, even though you were required to come at a certain hour.

27. Article 12(1).
28. Article 12(2).
29. Article 12(4).
30. Article 12(3).
31. The role of the Organization of African Unity in conflict resolution has been marked with a mixed record of success and failure. Its recent role in helping mediate and end to the Eritrea-Ethiopia war of 1998-2000, with the active participation of the United Nations, the United States, and the European Union, is one of its best achievements.
32. A statement made at the July 1993 International Symposium held at Addis Ababa, titled "From Conflict to Concord—Regional Cooperation in the Horn of Africa." He made this declaration of faith on behalf of his government which was generally received with favor—cooperation is not one of the options we have—it is the only option. In view of the alliance of the governing parties of the two governments, this did not come as a surprise to many of us; the question was how soon and in what institutional forms would the cooperation begin. The 1998-2000 war disposed of those questions. But to optimists, there is still hope of putting this nightmarish experience behind and starting all over again and charting out a realistic strategy of regional cooperation.

Seven

Fundamental Human Rights
PART I: HISTORICAL/GLOBAL CONTEXT

*The sacred rights of mankind are not to be rampaged for,
among old parchments, or musty records. They are written, as
with a sun beam in the whole value of human nature, by the
hand of divinity itself; and can never be erased or obscured by
mortal power.* (ALEXANDER HAMILTON, 1775)

Historical Context

Written one year earlier, Hamilton's statement presaged that most eloquent of historic documents: the
American Declaration of Independence, 1776. The
latter has been called "the promise" and the Constitution which
followed thirteen years thereafter "the fulfillment".[1] Hamilton's
language reflects the mood of the Enlightenment, linking reason with God. The attribution of the "writing" of the "sacred
rights of mankind" to divine hand suggests a reference to the
Ten Commandments in the authorship of which Moses was, to

believers, merely an agent, a divinely chosen medium, as Mohammed was of the Holy Koran, albeit that the Ten Commandments imposed more duties than established rights.

To express the source of human rights in our own times with reference to the Eritrean experience, is impossible without articulating the immense sacrifice paid by the Eritrean people: their tenacity and resilience, their resolve to fight to the end in the face of overwhelming odds, and the "scared" blood of martyrs. A veteran Eritrean fighter expresses that resolve and sacrifice thus: "I have seen men and women pitted against steel, as if they were made of steel, and winning. I salute my martyred comrades in my remembrance of their vital humanity which stood up to fight, unbending to the will of the enemy, until the last drop of blood, the precious blood which was the source of their being."[2]

As this quote of a veteran illustrates, much as they honor and respect the international legal instruments of human rights, to Eritreans, the source of human rights is not so much the international conventions and covenants, but rather the "vital humanity." In other words, universal values have historical points of reference of time, place and particular circumstance even though "humanity" refers to values common to all humanity, independent of time and space, etc. A discussion of human rights in the abstract, outside the social and political setting, outside a historical context, would be an academic exercise, at best. The Constitutional Commission of Eritrea's approach to this question reflects a keen awareness of the significance of historical context when it wrote in its Proposals the following:

> Even though the enumeration of the well-known and universally accepted political rights is of equal importance, the more essential question here is our understanding of those rights. Rights are linked to the

specific conditions of every society and its culture, and are, therefore, relative in nature. Thus the interpretation of such rights should take into account the social, economic and political conditions of our country.[3]

On a superficial reading, this statement might appear to suggest an absence of a sufficient degree of commitment to human rights on the part of the Commission. The use of the word "relative" may itself connote some doubt or uncertainty on the subject. That this is not so is evident upon reading the chapter of the Constitution devoted to human rights, the longest chapter. The overall message of the Proposals and the Constitution itself should dispel any doubt or uncertainty as to the requisite commitment to human rights. The intention behind the statement is to relate abstract principles to historical reality.

The question of the relative versus the absolute is a perennially debated philosophical issue. The resolution of the debate is itself subject to the vagaries of time and circumstance. What is taken as an absolute value at one time and in one place may be disputed in another. For example, during a revolutionary period in the history of a nation, certain principles are couched and proclaimed in absolute terms. They would lose their mobilizing capacity were they to be couched in relative terms. The Declaration of Independence of the United States speaks of "self-evident truths" ("We hold these truths to be self-evident..."). The Declaration was a clarion call and a justification of Liberty against monarchical absolutism, and, as such, cannot admit of relativity. But the Declaration's inherent relativity becomes clear when it proclaims that "all men are created equal" as a "self-evident truth" at a time when slavery was an accepted institution and the Declaration's principal author, Thomas Jefferson, was himself a slave owner. Also, women had no vote until a century and a half later.

The Constitutional Commission of Eritrea researched the question of human rights and produced an Issue Paper which was the basis for the section on human rights in its Proposal.[4] The Commission's paper, in its section titled "Universalism Vs. Cultural Relativism," discusses the subject in relation to the changing circumstances and the influence of politics, both national and global, in the framing of people's attitudes to the subject, as the following passage illustrates:

> Before the end of the Cold War, universalism was shunned and cultural relativism was in vogue. The existence of two superpowers promoted cultural relativism. It was then argued, and it is still argued in some quarters, that human rights and freedoms are deeply influenced by culture—a society's collective programming made up of its beliefs and values. The African Charter on Human Rights places emphasis on African tradition. The articulation of several rights and duties of the Charter is influenced by such an emphasis...[5]

The paper goes on to point out that there is an opposed argument along the line of natural law and natural rights philosophies that human rights are universal and all states should conform to them. The paper cautions against the seductive appeal of cultural relativism which can be, and has been, used as a cover for gross violations of human rights by many "Third World" leaders. Although all societies cannot have exactly the same outlook on all human rights issues, there is a moral fabric in all societies that can be used as a basis for the promotion and safeguarding of universally accepted human rights.[6]

Universal Principles

One of the achievements of the post-World War II period has been the incremental growth and universal acceptance of human rights in all their varied forms. Following in the footsteps of the UN Charter, numerous international resolutions and declarations have been adopted by the UN General Assembly, beginning with the Universal Declaration of Human Rights of 1948 which marks a milestone in the evolution of the international law on human rights. That Declaration has provided the basic framework for the future development of different aspects of human rights and influenced the writing of the national constitution in this respect.

The Declaration becomes a universalizing agent, giving legitimacy to the protest movement of all oppressed groups rising in rebellion against unjust systems.[7.] This represents a crucial aspect of human progress. The controlling principles of human progress, once gained, tend to become universalized and more or less permanent, despite periodic regression, as happened in the Nazi holocaust and as is happening in some places in our own time. What is gained becomes part of the common heritage of humamankind. Human rights, and democracy as the paramount political value of our epoch, reinforce each other, progressively beating down the walls of resistance originating from the forces of tradition or political interests. It is a progress that is continuing, and which will be continually facing challenges of one kind or another.

A climax in the evolution of human rights was reached with the adoption in 1966 by the United Nations of the International Covenants on Civil and political rights, and on economic, social and cultural rights.[8]

Today, even dictatorial regimes pay lip service to human rights as enshrined in these international legal instruments and the majority of governments have ratified them and have included their essential elements in their national constitutions. The inclusion of these fundamental principles in national constitutions, especially in those of dictatorial regimes has been an illustration of "Might" paying homage to "Right," putting dictatorial regimes always on the defensive in the matter of human rights violations. In this day and age, no one can justify human rights violations, not even dictators. They can only deny them or cover them up, which raises the issues of monitoring and sanctioning human rights violations, and creating and sustaining the necessary mechanism to those ends.

Monitoring can be done through official, UN channels or through private bodies dedicated to the observance of human rights. Such means have been growing steadily in number and in the diversity of their activities as non-governmental organization (NGO's) many of which are affiliated to the UN

Sanctions on Human Rights Violations

The universal acceptance of human rights principles is a signal achievement in the course of human progress, and the work of the United Nations in this respect has been of crucial importance. Despite its weaknesses, its glacial pace, and the occasional setbacks in the fulfillment of its objectives, the UN work has achieved significant success in many fields, including the articulation of universal principles of human rights and their protection. Human rights as a set of universal values must be based on justice under law as the ultimate value on which a universal consensus rests.

But law needs machinery for its enforcement and procedures for sanctioning its breach. In this respect, national laws, including a constitution, are more effective than international law. National laws and their enforcement constitute a defining characteristic of sovereignty. Every breach of law can be sanctioned at the national level, because the ability to sanction is an essential part of the concept of law.[9]

At the level of international law, there has not been an equivalent appreciable system of sanctions, although some progress has been made in recent years. The machinery and procedures for the application of international sanction for breach of its rules falls far short of those existing at the national level. Indeed, this is one of the major problems of international law; state sovereignty is the basis of the international system which prohibits intervention in the internal affairs of a sovereign state.[10]

But there has been steady progress in attempts to address this problem. Individuals may complain to the United Nations of violation of their human rights under procedures provided for in the First Optimal Protocol to the International Covenant on Civil and Political Rights and, the Convention Against Torture. In addition, another procedure exists for dealing with the thousands of letters and reports received each year which fall outside the specific mechanisms established by the above-mentioned legal instruments. This procedure is commonly known as the 1503 procedure, named after the governing resolution (XLVIII) of the UN Economic and Social Council.

Complaints of violations of human rights that are dealt with under the 1503 procedure are summarized and sent confidentially to the 53-member Commission on Human Rights and its Sub-Commission on Prevention of Discrimination and Protection of Minorities, comprising 26 experts elected by the Commission. Copies of the complaints are also sent to the states against whom the complaints are lodged. The identities of the complainants are not disclosed unless they consent to disclosure. Any replies from the government are forwarded to the Commission and Sub-Commission.

The Sub-Commission reports to the Commission if it finds

that a "consistent pattern of gross and reliably attested violations" of human rights has been committed.[11] The Commission can, in turn, decide to carry out an investigation of the matter. This procedure is confidential and involves private meetings until a report, if any, is made by the Commission to the Economic and Social Council. Until such a report is written and made public, there may be delay and consequent frustration. This is one reason, among many, why the official UN system must be supplemented by the work of members of civil society.

There have been movements to relax the rule on nonintervention in the internal affairs of sovereign states in some instances. The nature and scale of crimes committed in the former Yugoslavia and Rwanda, for example, was such that there has been near-unanimity to bring the perpetrators of the crimes to justice. In ideal situations, the criminals would have been brought before national tribunals to face justice, but the national judicial officials were too weak, corrupt or terrorized to perform their duties.[12]

The weakness or corruption of the national judicial system in many parts of the world has been a cause for concern, and ensuring its capacity and integrity has been linked to the building of a democratic order in which transparency and accountability become essential conditions for good governance. As stated before, democracy and human rights go hand in hand and reinforce each other. The recent events in Haiti have illustrated this critical link.

Haiti also has provided an important lesson on the question of amnesty given to past offenders by a new government. Hence a more detailed reference to it. In September 1994, the Clinton Administration persuaded the military leaders of Haiti to relinquish power in return for a U.S. guaranteed safe conduct into exile and an amnesty for their past crimes. However, the newly reinstated President, Jean-Bertrand Aristide and the Haitian Parliament refused to honor the grant of amnesty.

Being determined to break the vicious cycle of impunity that had condemned Haiti to a succession of brutal regimes, Aristide ordered a full investigation of past crimes, but he found that the existing judicial and investigative system was too feeble to secure justice. Therefore, he invited a team of foreign experts to help. He also dismissed the military officers *en mass* and established a Truth Commission to record the crimes under the military rule[13]

In other parts of the world the trials of leaders of previous regimes are also being held. In Ethiopia, forty-four leaders of the Dergue regime have been detained since 1991 facing trial. South Africa filed murder charges against a number of former senior officials including a former minister, General Maagnus Malan, in connection with abuses committed in 1980's. South Africa also established a Truth Commission which granted officials immunity from prosecution. In South Korea, President Kim Youn Sam called for legislation to authorize prosecution of the country's former military leaders for the 1980 massacre of pro-democracy protesters in Kwangju.[14]

In Europe, the International Criminal Tribunal for the former Yugoslavia began its trial of 52 people charged of murder, torture, rape and other offences including genocide, war crimes and crimes against humanity committed in Bosnia and Croatia. In 2001, former Yugoslavia leader, later President of Serbia, Slobodan Milosovic was apprehended and charged with crime against humanity. The tribunal prosecutors have pledged to seek indictment against those for whom evidence of the commission of serious crimes can be found. The clamor for justice in Yugoslavia, particularly the capture and charge of Milosovic reflects an encouraging trend. Whether this trend can be extended beyond Europe will depend in large part on the major powers.

The concerted action and demand for justice in such cases is a true foundation for lasting peace. As the 1996 World Report on

Human Rights rightly observes, "only justice for today's killers can deter those who might resume their bloodshed tomorrow...And only justice can substitute an individualized assessment of guilt for the false assumption of collective ethnic guilt that divide the Bosnia, Croatian and Serbian communities."[15]

The Report might have added Rwanda and Liberia, among others, concerning "the false assumption of collective ethnic guilt " that divide the feuding communities. The International Tribunal for Rwanda has actually made little progress, due to financial and logistical reasons and the absence of an international commitment similar to that of Yugoslavia. This lack of the requisite commitment constitutes a squandered opportunity.

The Case for Concerted Efforts

Each year, the Commission on Human Rights and its Sub-Commission consider, in public session, the question of violation of human rights in various areas of the world. They provide a significant forum in which governments and NGOs present information on violations and often the errant governments are present to refute the complaint or present clarification.

The Commission can appoint a special council of experts and rapporteurs to investigate and report on serious cases of complaints of human rights violation. The Commission also studies human rights as a global phenomenon by the investigation of thematic human rights issues and violations which are not specific to a particular country. For example, the problem of enforced or involuntary disappearances has been examined since 1980 by a five-member Working Group set up by the Commission. The Group receives reports of cases of disappearance from all over the world and transmits them to the governments concerned to help families find missing relatives. The results of this work are debated in public sessions of the Commission on Human Rights. Similarly, a Working Group on Arbitrary Detention was established by the Commission in 1991. Also, special rapporteurs have been named to investigate reports of summary or arbitrary executions, torture and the sale of children, child pornography and child prostitution.[16]

Increasing the role of NGOs and civil society as a whole is of crucial importance in terms of providing information, and monitoring human rights violations. Human Rights Watch explains the significance of NGOs as follows:

> Often the best measure of government respect for human rights is the visible presence of people exercising those rights by forming organizations, assembling, speaking out publicly, and publishing independently. However, because this pluralism is antithetical to the monopoly on political space that dictators seek to maintain, civil society is a frequent target of their repression.[17]

The Report cities examples of such targeting from the recent actions of governments in Nigeria, Kenya, Peru, Cambodia, Azerbaijan, Armenia, Turkey, Saudi Arabia and Syria, among others.[18] It might have added Eritrea, had it been written in 2001 or 2002.

The work of Human Rights Watch itself in monitoring, investigating and reporting on human rights violations all over the world has gained universal acceptance and obtains the cooperation of the press corps and even individuals from within governments.[19] And there is growing cooperation between Human Rights Watch and local human rights groups. This trend is irreversible and its effectiveness has forced grudging admiration and cooperation of the UN system which is by its very nature bureaucratic, involving delays. The struggle continues.

163

Eritrea in the Global Context

Eritrea has taken its rightful place among the family of nations with all the implications of privileges and obligations that this membership entails. One obvious privilege is access to UN financial and technical assistance, and an example of an obligation relevant to the present discussions is strict observance of international agreements such as the 1966 covenants on several aspects of human rights.

The discussion of a nation's place in the global context assumes an acceptance by the nation of certain universal principles on which there is international consensus. The rule of law is one such principle, as is also democracy. Some regimes habitually flout the basic tenets of the rule of law, even though they are members of the United Nations and their constitutions enshrine the rule of law. The state of international law, with state sovereignty as the basic rule is such, however, that there are as yet no adequate sanctions that can be applied effectively, as the preceding section illustrated. But there is an encouraging development to that end, albeit incremental.

In Eritrea, there was a commitment to the rule of law and democracy even before independence, starting from the latter part of the armed struggle. The legitimacy of the armed struggle of the liberation fighters, which was originally derived from initiative and sacrifice, was reinforced by the submission of the gun to politics—to popular will and general interest of the public. Without this transition to democratic rule and the primacy of law, the movement would have been doomed to failure. The promise of this lesson seemed to be fulfilled in the post-independence period when the provisional government immediately translated its military victory into a government of law.[20]

What needs to be emphasized here is that a nation's observance of human rights and the rule of law, like charity, begins at home. Without a clear and emphatic commitment to the rule

164

of law and democracy at home, dependence on international rules on the subject would remain a distant, aim, at best. In Eritrea's case, the earlier promise is fulfilled in the new Constitution. What remains now is to translate the principles laid down in the Constitution into practice through the creation of appropriate institutions. In this dynamic process of the development of constitutionalism, the international standards set forth in the various Resolutions and Declarations have an important role as guidelines and points of reference. The obligations that membership in a community of nations bound by certain rules imposed will no doubt have a restraining effect. Eritreans should welcome such a role. And their government cannot escape its obligations.

Notes

1. This characterization was made by the Commission on the Bicentennial of the United States Constitution, July 1976. Washington DC.
2. This statement was made by veteran freedom fighter, Samuel Gebre Adonai, in a radio broadcast published in Hadas Eritrea. 1994.
3 .Proposals, p. 24
4. Issue Paper Number 5, Fundamental Human Rights and Freedoms, 1994.
5. Ibid, p.8
6. Ibid, p.9 et seq.
7. See paragraph 3 to the Preamble.
8. See International Covenant on Civil and Political Rights, December 16, 1966, 99 U.N.T.S/171, U.N. Docs. ST/HR/1/Rev.5m UN Sales No. E. 94. XIV. 1 (1994). See also International Covenant on Economic, Social and Cultural Rights, December 16, 1966. Article 1 of each of

THE MAKING OF THE ERITREAN CONSTITUTION

the covenants provides: "All peoples have the right to self-determination. By virtue of that right, they freely determine their political status and freely pursue their economic, social, and cultural development."

9. Cf. John Austin, Jurisprudence.
10. The recent assertiveness of international organizations seen in the prosecutions of Serb leaders, as well as the apprehension of former Chilean dictator, Agustino Pinochet, gives room for hope.
11. See Basic Facts About the UN 1992, pp. 168-169
12. See Human Rights Watch, World Report 1996, PXIII
13. Ibid.
14. Ibid.
15. Ibid. P. XV
16. Ibid.
17. Ibid p. XV.
18. Ibid.
19. Ibid.
20. See Proclamation 37/1993.

EIGHT
Fundamental Rights (and Duties)
PART II: TEXT COMMENTARIES

A people without a free press is not a free people. Unless people are free to express themselves without fear and trepidation, they cannot say they are truly free.
(VOICE OF ERITREA EDITORIAL, MARCH 1954) [1]

A hungry man is not a free man
—OLIVER WENDEL HOLMES

A Bill of Rights as the Anchor of Constitutionalism

Chapter 3 of the Constitution contains what is commonly known as a Bill of Rights which enshrines the people's fundamental human rights and freedoms. The chapter also contains sections on duties. An essential element of the Bill of Rights is that it is justiciable, which means that the rights contained in it are subject to the protection by the courts.

The Supreme Court, in particular, as will be seen in chapter eleven in more detail, has the jurisdiction of determining the constitutionality of any law enacted or any measure undertaken by the government, including laws or measures affecting the rights and freedoms listed in Bill of Rights. If in such testing the laws or actions contravene any of the provisions in the Bill of Rights, the court can strike down the law or declare the action null and void. This principle is the anchor of the constitutional system, of constitutionalism.

I will now examine chapter 3 article by article. Each article will be reproduced here and followed by commentaries.

Equality Under the Law

Article 14

1. All persons are equal under the law.
2. No person may be discriminated against on account of race, ethnic origin, language, color, gender, religion, disability, age, political view, or social or economic status or any other improper factors.
3. The National Assembly shall enact laws that can assist in eliminating inequalities existing in Eritrean society.

Commentary

Article 14(1) enshrines the fundamental principle of equal treatment of all members of society. The concept of equality is a basic tenet of human rights and democracy. Its human rights aspect may be traced to all traditions and spiritual teachings that stress the value of all creatures in the eyes of their Creator. Every human civilization that is worthy of the name contains this element, whether it is realized in actual practice or not, and to the extent that equality among members of any given political community is a way of life, as it is in most traditional African village communities, its origin lies in such spiritual source.

As a basic tenet of democracy, European political theory traces the concept of equality to the writings of Aristotle. Throughout history, it has been the focus of attention of critical thinkers whose sensitive minds have questioned its restriction to some members of their communities such as the free citizens of ancient Greece and Rome and the feudal classes of the pre-modern era. The French Revolution, which can be considered as the watershed of the modern era, dividing the feudal and modern eras, was the result of the mobilizing power of such philosophical ideas and the uprising of oppressed classes. In that momentous event, the revolutionaries proclaimed the dawn of the democratic era by asserting the slogan of *"liberatè, egalite, fraternite"* as the guiding principle of the new, post-feudal order.

Does the principle of equality admit of differences among individual members of society on any ground? Aristotle's notion of "distributive justice" recognizes that there can be reasonable grounds for differences based on differences of natural, mental endowments. On this Aristotelian base and the works of philosophers like Nietzche, Nazi theorists sought to propagate and justify differentiation based on the superiority of one race over others.

To counter such perversions, the provision contained in Article 14(2) is elevated to a constitutional principle as an application of equality guaranteed under 14(1). Today, it is a universally recognized legal norm that there can be no discrimination based on the ground of the factors enumerated in article 14(2), although discrimination against women and minorities continues in practice in many instances. Note that, in order to preclude any derogation or limitation from the generality of the equality provision, Article 14(2) adds the words "or on any other improper factors".

In accordance with the justifiability principle if any person suffers discrimination on these grounds he or she can have redress upon application to a competent court of law. A discrimination can be direct or indirect. An example of indirect discrimination would be an application of different standards of admission to any employment or profession used for men and women, such as height or strength standard for police. The notion of reasonableness may of course, be applicable here in that laws may be passed for example to enter into, or exit from, an employment. If such a standard of reasonableness is disputed by any affected person or class of persons, it will be determined by the court.

The equality clause is of particular significance in Eritrea, as in other societies at a similar stage of development, where there have been custom-bound discriminatory practices, especially as regards women. These customary practices are so widespread and deep-rooted that it will take a great deal of effort and determination by all concerned to uproot, and the role of the courts in this respect will be critical. This, indeed, is one of the purposes of Article 14(3), which puts in the hand of the Eritrean Parliament the responsibility of enacting laws that can provide a more concrete legal basis to help eliminate existing inequalities in the society.

Article 14(3) provides the basis for instituting what is commonly called affirmative action, aiming to redress a balance in favor of disadvantaged groups in society, such as women. Even before the ratification of the Constitution, the government of Eritrea provided for affirmative action in favor of a more equitable representation of "all citizens and women" in regional government. The law on the establishment of Regional Administration reserves a 30% of the seat for women in the Regional Assemblies while women are at the same time given an equal opportunity to compete for seats in the remaining 70%[2]. As far as the equal rights of women is concerned, as already noted, there is a firm commitment, as clearly articulated in the Preamble to the Constitution and in Article 7(2) of the Constitution which prohibits "any act that violates the human rights of women or limits or otherwise thwarts their role and participation..."

Right to Life and Liberty

Article 15
1. No person shall be deprived of life without due process of law.
2. No person shall be deprived of liberty without due process of law.

Commentary
There are essentially two types of constitutional provisions regarding life, one typified by the Constitution of the United States of America, and the other by the Constitution of South Africa. Eritrea's formulation is akin to that of the United States, which provides, inter alia: "No person....shall be deprived of life, liberty, or property, without due process of law...."[3]. The constitution of South Africa provides: "Every person shall have the right to life."[4]

The controversy over life concerns three questions: the death penalty, abortion and euthanasia. The provision of the South African constitution, which spells out the right to life in the broadest possible terms, is susceptible to an interpretation whereby it prohibits capital punishment, abortion and euthanasia. In contrast those of the American and Eritrean constitutions leave the question open to be determined by laws enacted pursuant to the constitution. Under such laws a person may be subject to the death penalty upon commission of crimes for which death is prescribed as the punishment. Under the present Penal Code of Eritrea a person may be punished by death for example for murder and treason under aggravating circumstances.[5] And

171

there are provisions prohibiting abortion and euthanasia.[6]

Article 15 speaks of due process of law. This is a crucial constitutional principle with a long history, but first articulated in those terms in the US constitution. Due process puts great emphasis on procedure as specified in laws on criminal procedure and similar legislation. More examples of the application of due process are apparent when considering other aspects of human rights, particularly in the criminal process. (See Article 17. below). Due process is principally designed to guard against abuse of power such as the police and security forces taking the law into their own hands in the treatment of people under their care or control. Due process is a precaution based on the accumulated experience of mankind in the relationship between those wielding power and ordinary citizens.

The right to life is so fundamental that it may not be suspended during a state of emergency (see article 27 below). In the formulation of the South African Constitution, the right to life seems to be an absolute right not to be limited under any circumstances. With respect to abortion and euthanasia, any determination on these questions on the bases of relevant laws must involve a balancing of circumstantial factors in the scale of values of the particular society. Is the protection of the life of an unborn child more compelling when weighed against the well being or free choice of the mother? Every society at any given time has its own policies and criteria for making the necessary determination. In the United States of America, as in other parts of the world, there are continual debates held between the "Right to Life" groups and the "Free Choice" groups, debates that at times take on acrimonious forms and occasionally erupt into violence and murder concerning the issue of abortion. With respect to euthanasia, there is also the notorious case of Dr. Kervokian, a Detroit physician who helps terminal patients to take their own lives.

Opinion is divided on the abortion issue depending on

whether one is a "free choice" or a "right to life" supporter. Most women tend to support the former, as an aspect of what they consider to be their right to "self-determination", while opponents stress the moral question of taking away an innocent life. At what stage in its development the fetus can be defined as a person and be subject to the right to life clause of the constitution is a medico-philosophical question which has itself become controversial. On a religious basis, Catholics and Muslims are aligned on the side of the "right to life" argument, as was demonstrated at the Cairo Summit on World Population in 1995.[7]

Where capital punishment is not prohibited, there is an unresolved controversy about whether it can unquestionably act as a deterrent to offenders. With the rise of crimes in the inner cities of the industrialized world, there is a growing demand for the reinstatement of capital punishment in countries like the United Kingdom and the United States of America. In South Africa, the Constitutional court gave a judgment for its abolition.[8] Whether this decision is to stay unchallenged remains to be seen.

Namibia's Constitution has the most emphatic provision prohibiting death penalty: "The right to life shall be respected and protected…" "No law may prescribe death as a competent sentence. No Court or Tribunal shall have the power to impose a sentence of death upon any person. No execution shall take place in Namibia."[9]

In Uganda, on the other hand, the Constitution provides: "No person shall be deprived of life intentionally except in execution of a sentence passed in a fair trial by a court of competent jurisdiction in respect of a criminal offense under the laws of Uganda and the conviction and the sentence have been confirmed by the highest appellate court."[10] On abortion the Ugandan constitution prohibits the termination of an unborn child "except as may be authorized by law."[11]

173

The Constitution of Ethiopia provides in a generic Article that "everyone has the inviolable and inalienable right to life, liberty and the security of the person."[12] The Article that follows further provides, "No person shall be deprived of his or her life except for grave crimes defined by law."[13] The competent courts of Ethiopia may be faced one day with the question whether the two provisions contradict each other and if so, which one shall prevail. Would the canon of interpretation that the latter article supersedes, or derogates from the former apply as an extension of the maxim: *lex posterior derogat lex anterior*? It would be a far-fetched application of the maxim.

When the Article on the right to life was debated at the meeting of the Eritrean Constitutional Commission which approved the Draft, the issue of capital punishment was raised and a few members strongly expressed their opposition to it. The remaining members of the Commission agreed with the provision of the Article, cited above, which permits the death sentence as already discussed.

Right to Human Dignity

Article 16

1. The dignity of all persons shall be inviolable.
2. No person shall be subjected to torture or to cruel, inhuman or degrading treatment or punishment.
3. No person shall be held in slavery or servitude nor shall any person be required to perform forced labor not authorized by law.

Commentary

It is trite to say that human dignity is a fundamental right. Like life itself, human dignity may not be suspended even under an emergency situation. (See Article 27 below.) What is the ambit of this right? Does it cover so called second and third generation rights, such as the right to economic security and employment? This is debatable. Certainly, Articles 16(2) and (3) specifically refer to first generation rights, i.e. protection from oppressive and degrading treatment. And protection from slavery or servitude is a fundamental right, which was gained with the triumph of democracy, as already discussed. Does the wording of Sub-Article 2 imply an extension of the right beyond protection against such treatment to include such rights as economic security? In other words, does inviolability of dignity demand that a person should not merely be free from oppressive or degrading treatment but free from want, hunger and other forms of human suffering?

The answer to these questions hinges on the matter of justifiability. Freedom from oppression and degrading treatment is a justiciable issue enforceable by a court of law. Are the other issues justiciable? The rights to employment, and a clean environment are not, as matters stand now, justiciable issues, but rather subject to policy decisions and available resources as stipulated under Article 21. (See below). Nonetheless, the provision of article 16(1), even as it stands, can cover a wide range of circumstances (including, for instance, freedom from sexual harassment) which may conceivably involve or amount to an infringement on dignity. Laws may be enacted, based on this provision, prohibiting certain activities as infringements on human dignity. Ideally, such laws should include denial of employment as infringement on social and economic rights. (see discussion on article 21 below).

Slavery, Servitude and Forced Labor

No one in his/her right mind would contemplate condoning the practice of slavery in any shape or form, in this day and age.

However, this universally condemned practice has reared its ugly head in some form in some neighboring countries, reminding humanity that it cannot take things for granted. Moreover, in some societies women are held under conditions and treated in ways that approximate servitude and that call for vigilance and sustained efforts to liberate them from such conditions. International conventions against servitude and all forms of discrimination provide the normative basis for such sustained efforts. National Constitutions must add the necessary muscle in order to implement the international conventions, by creating institutions and mechanisms of monitoring and redressing wrongs.

With forced labor, there are also international covenants that prohibit it and most national Constitutions are in accord with the international prohibitions. The question arises as to what constitutes forced labor. In the Eritrean condition, the practice of requiring the youth to do national service has made this question a contentious issue. To begin with, the Constitution provides that no person shall be required to perform forced labor *that is not authorized by law.* The key here is authorization by law. A prisoner sentenced to a term of years with hard labor is required by the criminal law and the judgment of a court based on such law to perform forced labor. Can a government require such service of its youth without the promulgation of law authorizing it to require such service? According to Article 16(3) of the Constitution, the answer is no.

Arrest, Detention and Fair Trial

Article 17

1. No person may be arrested or detained save pursuant to due process of law.

2. No person shall be tried or convicted for any act or omission which did not constitute a criminal offense at the time when it was committed.

3. Every person arrested or detained shall be informed of the ground for his arrest or detention and the right he has in connection with arrest or detention in a language he understands.

4. Every person who is held in detention shall be brought before a court of law within forty eight (48) hours of his arrest, and if this is not reasonably possible, as soon as possible thereafter, and no such persons shall be held in custody beyond such period without the authority if the court.

5. Every person shall have the right to petition a court of law for a Writ of *Habeas Corpus.* Where the arresting officer fails to bring the person arrested before the court and provide reason for his arrest, the court shall accept the petition and order the release of the prisoner.

6. Every person charged with an offence shall be entitled to fair, speedy and public hearing by a court of law; provided, however, that such a court may exclude the press and the public from all or any part of the trial for reasons of morals or national security, as may be necessary in a just and democratic society.

7. A person charged with an offence shall be presumed to be innocent, and shall not be punished, unless he is found guilty by a court of law.

8. Where an accused is convicted, he shall have the right to appeal. No person shall be liable to be tried again for any criminal offense on which judgment has been rendered.

Commentary

The rights enshrined in Article 17, which are justiciable, form an important part of what are called procedural human rights. They can only be limited in a specified manner as defined under the limitation and emergency clauses of the Constitution (see Articles 26 and 27 below). As the several Sub-Articles indicate, these rights are concerned with arrested, detained, accused and convicted persons. Whether expressly or by implication, these basic procedural rights afford arrested and detained persons the rights to be informed of the reason for their arrest or detention so that they can refute or otherwise answer, the charges and prepare to defend themselves. This assumes a related right, the right to inform their relatives and seek legal assistance and thus challenge the lawfulness of their arrest or detention.

Other assumed rights, which are left to laws on criminal process for detailed provisions, include the right to remain silent to avoid self-incrimination, which is related to the principle of the presumption of innocence [Article 17(6)], and the right to bail, unless the circumstances require denial of bail in the interest of justice. When too many criminals "get off easily" for their crime, there is the temptation to be restrictive, asking, "what about the rights of the victim of the crime?" A sage once said that it is better for the moral health and ultimate social good of the community that nine guilty persons go free rather than for an innocent man to be wrongly punished. The law is like a sanctuary and a sanctuary can be abused by undeserving persons, but in the end the sanctity of that refuge can best be preserved by erring on the side of a broadminded view which lays emphasis on doing justice to the innocent and waiting for (and working hard towards) the eventual capture and/or conviction of the guilty. In the ultimate analysis, the quality of a civilized community is judged by the manner of its treatment and the nature of the punishment it metes out to its members who are accused of crimes.

The same is true of the right to appear before a court immediately after arrest, to a public trial, to be properly informed of the charges and to challenge them, to be informed and tried in a language that one understands, and the right of appeal. Again, the principles of the non-retroactive application of offenses (Article 17(2)) is a fundamental principle expressed by the Latin maxim: *nullum crimen sine lege*. This principle also applies to sentences *nulla poena sine lege;* the punishment ordered in the sentence must be in accordance with rules existing and applicable at the time of the commission of the offense.

As already noted, the right to legal representation is an assumed right and one which practice has sanctioned. The right to obtain legal representation, when necessary at state expense, is another right sanctioned by existing practice and the interests of justice require that it must continue.[14]

Right to Privacy

Article 18

1. Every person shall have the right to privacy.
2. (a) No person shall be subject to body search, nor shall his premises be entered into or searched or his communications, correspondence, or other property be interfered with, without reasonable cause.
(b) No search warrant shall issue, save upon probable cause, supported by oath, and particularly describing the place to be searched, and the persons or things to be seized.[15]

Commentary

The rights enshrined in Article 18(1), as other fundamental rights, are subject to the limitation and emergency clauses of the Constitution and to the derivative limitations under certain conditions as prescribed in the criminal procedure code.[15] Being justiciable rights, any infringement of these rights can be subject to court scrutiny. Such scrutiny can reveal, inter alia, whether an infringement has occurred in terms of the limitation clauses of the Constitution. (See Article 26 of the Constitution and the discussion thereon, below.)

Respect for privacy is a universal human value, which predates modern constitutional systems. However, two factors may operate to cause its infringement: social and political. Socially, in African society at any rate, the emphasis on community interests has traditionally limited a strict application of the privacy principle. People make it their business to inquire into the affairs of their neighbors with the best of intentions. The form of their homesteads and other aspects of their social infrastructure tend to limit privacy, with the voluntary submission of individuals and families to group intervention, and all for a good cause. Traditional values of mutual concerns, of caring and sharing, are ingrained in the village community ethos. "It takes a whole village to raise a child" is a proverb that justly expresses this community ethos. But with the advent of "modernization," of individualism, the scale of values begins to tip towards more privacy.

Politically, the growth of the modern state, particularly in autocratic regimes brings with it a penchant for intervention in private affairs. This has to be offset by constitutional provisions in conformity with a new way of life. How to balance these competing interests is problematic, but the limitation clauses and their interpretation by the competent courts can provide the solution, as explained in greater detail below.

Freedom of Conscience, Religion, Expression of Opinion, Movement, Assembly and Association.

Article 19

1. Every person shall have the right to freedom of thought, conscience and belief.
2. Every person shall have the freedom of speech and expression, including freedom of the press and other media.
3. Every citizen shall have the right of access to information.
4. Every person shall have the freedom to practice any religion and to manifest such practice.
5. All persons shall have the right to assemble and to demonstrate peaceably together with others.
6. Every citizen shall have the right to form organizations for political, social, economic and cultural purposes.
7. Every citizen shall have the right to practice any lawful profession, or engage in any occupation or trade.
8. Every citizen shall have the right to move freely throughout Eritrea or reside and settle in any part thereof.
9. Every citizen shall have the right to leave and return to Eritrea and to be provided with passport or other travel documents.

Commentary

Article 19 makes a distinction between the rights to be enjoyed by every person (Sub Articles (1), (2), (4), and (5), and rights that are applicable to citizens only (Sub-Articles (3), (6), (8), and (9).

Freedom of thought, conscience, belief, freedom of reli-

181

gion and the right to practice it are fundamental rights which cannot be suspended in times of emergency, and they may not be limited under any circumstances or suspended in times of emergency. (See Article 26 below). There may be authorization by appropriate legislation to provide for religious observance and administrative and logistical arrangements on a fair and equitable basis. This should be understood not as placing limit on the rights, but as the facilitation of its enjoyment, as the need may arise.

Sub-Article 4 is related to religion, whereas Sub-Article 1 covers rights to freedom of thought, conscience and belief, which pertain to such matters as political belief. The right to freedom of speech and its allied freedom of the press as well as the right to assemble and demonstrate are a function of free and fair political activity. They are also all closely linked to principles of democracy and representative government, which will be discussed in chapter nine. These rights are the lifeblood of a free, democratic society and as such, they are among the most susceptible to dispute. And like other rights, they are subject to the limitation clause of the Constitution. Such limitation should be understood, nonetheless, to require strict compliance with the test of being "necessary" "in the national interest..." etc. Freedom of speech in particular is also subject to the law of defamation. Speech that is libelous is actionable at the instance of the person libeled.

There is also the right to practice one's chosen trade or profession and to that end of optimizing one's interest, both material and intellectual, by forming or joining and being part of an association which advances those interests. This right has economic as well as social and cultural aspects and, as such, can be the basis for the advancement not only of the interests of individuals and groups, but also through their activities, the general interests of the community.

Five categories of rights are reserved to citizens only. The first is the right of access to information. The second is the right to form organizations for political, social, economic, and cultural purposes. The third is the right to practice any lawful profession, or engage in any occupation or trade. The fourth is the right of free movement and establishment of residence in any part of Eritrea. Last, is the right to leave and return to the country and to be issued a passport or other travel documents. [Article 19, (3), (6), (7), (8), and (9).]

The right of access to information is an important right in and of itself for citizens in need of certain information affecting them or members of their families or friends. This right is also important as a critical means to help realize other fundamental rights, notably administrative redress. (See Article 24, below). The right of access to information is also crucial for the social and political health of the community as a whole by helping secure a more accountable government. Bureaucracies tend to over-emphasize secrecy and may resort to it in denial of the satisfaction of fundamental rights. This can have adverse effects on the well being of the community. Secrecy limits the number of minds that can be brought to bear upon a problem. People working in a closed circle can arrive at some wrong conclusions. Undue secrecy also tends to break the confidence of people in their government. A more open society can properly define and differentiate between matters that can and cannot be kept secret. Excessive secrecy also hampers intellectual creativity and the advancement of knowledge.

The right to form political parties and to join and participate in them is a fundamental democratic right that is too obvious to need detailed discussion. This enshrined right is aimed at ensuring freedom of political activity by parties and their members in a representative multi-party democracy. It should be read with Article 7 of the Constitution, which lays down the democratic principles that are the basis for this right. Article 7 sets forth the basic conditions that must be satisfied for the enjoyment of this right, and in particular Sub-Article 1 of Article 7, provides that "the organization and operation of all political and public associations and movements shall be guided by the principle of national unity and democracy".

Article 19 is the constitutional expression of the earlier commitment of the Eritrean struggle for independence to a democratic, multi party system which experience in Africa and elsewhere has shown to be the better guarantee for a sustainable democratic order than the one party system whose vaunted advantages have proved to be illusory.[16]

Right to Vote and to be a Candidate to an Elective Office

Article 20
Every citizen who fulfills the requirements of the electoral law shall have the right to vote and to seek elective office.

Commentary
The right to vote is a basic democratic right of a citizen. Through this right citizens who are eligible to vote, exercise, in their totality, their sovereignty and to have a voice in government through their elected representatives. Much else in political and economic life depends on this right. It was not in vain that the slogan "No taxation without representation" was used in the struggle of the American colonies waged against an irresponsible absolute monarch. Much of political (and constitutional) history hinges on this right in the progress towards representative democracy.

Economic, Social and Cultural Rights and Responsibilities

Article 21

1. Every citizen shall have the right of equal access to publicly funded social services. The state shall endeavor, within the limit of its resources, to make available to all citizens health, education, cultural and other social services.
2. The State shall secure, within available means, the social welfare of all citizens and particularly those disadvantaged.
3. Every citizen shall have the right to participate freely in any economic activity and to engage in any lawful business.
4. The state and society shall have the responsibility of identifying, preserving and developing, as need be, and bequeathing to succeeding generation historical and cultural heritage; and shall lay the necessary groundwork for the development of the arts, science, technology and sports, thus encouraging citizens to participate in such endeavors.
5. The National Assembly shall enact laws guaranteeing and securing the social welfare of citizens, the rights and conditions of labor and other rights and responsibilities listed in this Article.

Commentary

This Article and its provisions apply to citizens only. It draws a distinction between citizens and non-citizens in the enjoyment of economic, social and cultural rights. It charges the state and society with the responsibility of respecting national cultural heritage. In this connection, while all the other Sub-Articles enshrine rights, Sub-Article (4) charges the state and citizens alike with responsibilities.

As in the case with other rights, these rights can also be limited subject to the same criteria as prescribed under Article 26. Economic activity, for instance, though a fundamental right and the basis of development, may nevertheless be limited by consideration of the protection of the quality of life, which is connected with the protection of the environment and the rights of future generations and associated with sustainable and environmentally sensitive economic growth.

As always in these matters, there has to be a balancing of values and interests. Article 21 contains so-called second generation rights which are not necessarily justiciable. The issue of the place in the Constitution of economic and social rights is one of those that the Constitutional Commission researched and debated extensively from the beginning.

Economic and social rights are of more recent origin, compared to civil and political rights, but no less important. They are the essential bases for human dignity and the free development of the individual in society. To take education as an example, there is no question about its critical importance as a condition for personal growth and worth, not only in terms of material benefits but also in intellectual achievement. Similarly, the absence of adequate health care can render even an educated person incapable of making his or her due contribution in society. Moreover, a comprehensive approach to health is necessary, one that takes into account nutrition, clean water, proper and affordable housing and a safe and healthy environment. Such an approach should also pay special attention to mothers, children and the elderly.

All of these considerations point to the need to constitutionalize these issues, while also raising the practical question of what may or may not be delivered. The Constitution has to enshrine basic social and economic rights, as the Eritrean and other Constitutions have done. But, as the Commission's earlier research paper pointed out, a constitution "fitted with a list of well meaning rights is of little use if for whatever reason the chance that the right would be enforced is limited".[17] Hence the careful wording of Article 21(1): "...The State shall endeavor, within the limits of its resources, to make available to all citizens health, education, cultural and other social services." The nature and extent of the social services are to be commensurate with the ability of the State to provide them at any given stage. That is why it was observed earlier that these rights are not necessarily justiciable. The qualifying word "necessarily" is inserted in contemplation of the possibility of court intervention where, in the clear presence of available resources, decisions are made that may involve unfairness or unequal treatment of any aggrieved person or persons. This is going to be one of the issues that the National Assembly will be concerned with in its future legislative agenda and also one of the areas of constitutional development that should be watched with care and fascination by all concerned.[18]

Family

Article 22

1. The family is the natural and fundamental unit of society and is entitled to the protection and special care of the State and society.

2. Men and women of full legal age shall have the right, upon their consent, to marry and to found a family freely, without any discrimination and they shall have equal rights and duties as to all family matters.

3. Parents have the right and duty to bring up their children with care and affection; and, in turn, chil-

dren have the right and the duty to respect their parents and to sustain them in their old age.

Commentary

Three interrelated matters are contained in Article 22:

(a) The family as a basic unit of society and the need of its protection;

(b) the right of the partners to a marriage both in the act of marriage (their consent) and in their equal rights in all family matters;

(c) The mutual rights and duties of parents and their children.

The first point needs no further comment, beyond saying that the family is and has been a vital unit of traditional Eritrean Society. The breakdown of family values, the high divorce rate and related social pathology that are haunting industrial societies has confirmed Eritreans in their commitment to the preservation and sustenance of family values, both with respect to the "nuclear" family and the extended family. The latter is part and parcel of the traditional African socio-cultural landscape, not peculiar to Eritrea, and has functioned as the source of "social insurance" for its members. Even in the presence of State-sponsored social services, the cradle-to-grave family network of obligations will continue for a long time. It needs appropriate State support and societal encouragement. Article 22(1) provides the constitutional basis for such support and encouragement.

The rights of marriage partners can be problematic, viewed in the traditional context, where parentally arranged marriages, frequently involving girls who are under age, were the norm, and still continue in some parts of the country. But there has been a progressive movement away from arranged marriages in favor of marriage between consenting partners, particularly in urban areas. The constitution makes this the norm. Article 22(2) speaks of men and women of full legal age, leaving the definition of legal age to laws subordinate to it. Under the present law, the minimum age for marriage is 15, marriage of girls under 15 is prohibited, and the pressure on the traditional segment of the society to adjust accordingly has now found constitutional backing. The pressure will increase as it also involves another public policy: the need to give women equal rights to education, which, as stated earlier, is of paramount importance.

Lastly, there is the matter of the rights and duties of parents and their children (Article 22(3)). Traditionally, parents exercise great authority and control over their children with an implicit right of chastisement, including corporal punishment of errant children. Correspondingly, children respect and fear their parents. Religion and tradition are bound in this as in other matters. Traditional approaches to matters of parental authority and children's rights in Eritrean society, which is evenly divided between Christians and Muslims, draw their inspiration from religion, both Islam and Christianity.

While corrective chastisement administered with care and moderation and accompanied with wise counsel and love may be and is acceptable, the "modern" view on this is that there should be no punishment in the sense of beating. This view is gaining ground among young couples in urban areas in Eritrea but is by no means a widely held view. The subject occasionally gives rise to controversy, where teachers acting *in loco parentis* administer a beating. There is going to have to be some guideline issued with the authority of the Ministry of Education. The debate on the subject is not yet closed.

Meanwhile, Eritrea has signed the Convention on the Rights of the Child.[19] The Convention which stipulates the age of a child to be under 18, makes him or her subject to a number of rights which the signatory states are required to translate into national legislation and institutional support. The working of Article 22(3) encapsulates the rights enumerated in the Convention and is also to be the basis for legislative and institutional support of children's rights. However, in practice there may be situations engendering conflict between the demands of the Convention and those of particular societies that may wish to balance rights with duties. Article 22(3) speaks of both rights and duties and to see if a potential conflict may be resolved in the future will be interesting. On this point, too, the debate may just be beginning.

Right to Property

Article 23

1. Subject to the provisions of Sub-Article 2 of this Article, any citizen shall have the right, anywhere in Eritrea, to acquire and dispose of property, individually or in association with others, and to bequeath the same to his heirs or legatees.
2. All land and all natural resources below and above the surface of the territory of Eritrea belong to the State. The interests citizens shall have in land shall be determined by law.
3. The State may, in the national or public interest, take property, subject to the payment of just compensation and in accordance with due process of law.

Commentary

Property in general, and in terms of Article 23 of the Constitution, covers both movable and immovable property. Article 23 also includes tangible and intangible property, an example of the latter being stocks and shares in commercial entities. Sub-Article 1 restricts the right to acquire and dispose of property to citizens. This Sub-Article also provides for the right of group ownership further reinforcing the freedom of association provision protected under Article 19(7) which would be the constitutional basis for corporate development. Rights of property also extend to the heirs and legates.

Sub-Article 2 is the provision, which affects the vast majority of the population whose livelihood depends on land. Historically, the ownership of land fell into two main categories: (1) Community land inhabited and owned by village communities with kinship ties and claiming a common ancestor; (2) *Gulti* which belonged to feudal authorities or their retainers granted by a king or regional chieftain. Changing fortunes of local grandees and their overlords could, of course, cause a transformation of *gulti* into the *risti* (ownership) owned by other citizens with the result that there were, side by side, two types of land tenure systems: communally owned village land (*diesa*), on the one hand, and *Tsilimi* (private ownership) land, on the other. After 1977, the Ethiopian government declared all land to be State owned and abolished private ownership of both urban and rural land.

The new government of Eritrea issued a law declaring all land to be State owned, making provision for conditions under which citizens, both private and village communities can acquire use rights. The law also provides for incentive systems to encourage investment in development projects.[20] The law referred to in the second sentence of Sub-Article 2 determining the interests of citizens, is in fact already in existence. The law provides for the establishment of a machinery of administrative justice to adjudicate land disputes, including expropriation and compensation, in the terms of Sub-Article (3) of the Constitution. According to this Sub-Article, any expropriation

191

of property must be "in the national or public interest," and the compensation must be just and determined in accordance with due process of law. The provision of due process read together with the criterion of "national and public interest" is designed to ensure due care and fairness and to guard against arbitrary and hasty decisions by the concerned authorities. It is worth noting that the land question has been raised by opposition groups as one of the issues that needs to be revisited when the time comes for a review of the Constitution's application, when it is implemented.

Administrative Justice

Article 24

1. Any person with an administrative question shall have the right to be heard respectfully by the administrative officials concerned and to receive quick and equitable answers from them.
2. Any person with an administrative question, whose rights or interests are interfered with or threatened, shall have the right to seek due administrative redress.

Commentary

Administrative justice has been in operation for a long time, developing in line with the growth of administrative authorities in modern governments. In countries following the Common Law system such as England, redress has been had through the operation of Common Law procedural remedies such as the writ of *certiorari* and writ of *mandamus*.[21] Administrative tribunals have been established by law, ensuring uniformity and speed and a more effective rational approach under which they can hear complaints on a range of issues concerning administrative decisions. The ordinary courts can review decision of tribunals on appeals made on points of law. In France and several European countries, following Napoleon's rule, a uniform system of administrative law has also been in operation. Judges of the ordinary courts have been forbidden in France from interfering in matters of public administration. What in the United States goes under the term judicial review by the Supreme Court has been the jurisdiction of the *Conseil d'Etat,* which sits at the pinnacle of the hierarchy of administrative tribunals.[22]

In Eritrea, administrative law and practice is in a state of infancy. Ordinary courts customarily shy away from involvement in administrative justice. Since independence, however, there are some interesting developments in this field, spearheaded by administrative tribunals of the Commission on Land and Housing.

It is too early to judge whether they will dispense justice as required by the Constitution, or whether a uniform system of administrative justice will need to be instituted.

One aim of Article 24 is to ensure that administrative officials do their jobs properly and efficiently and with due regard to the respectful treatment of members of the public who have to deal with them (Art. 24(1)). Another aim is to provide redress for persons whose rights or interests are adversely affected or threatened by the action of administrative officials. The first aim seeks to make the bureaucracy responsive to the public and thus close or narrow the gap between an insensitive, unresponsive bureaucracy and the public which is prevalent in many African states. The second aims to provide a constitutional basis for principles and machineries for redress, whose details will be prescribed in future Acts of Parliament.

Duties of Citizens

Article 25:

All citizens have the duty to:

1. owe allegiance to Eritrea, strive for its development and promote its prosperity;
2. be ready to defend the country;
3. complete one's duty in national service;
4. advance national unity;
5. respect and defend the constitution;
6. respect the rights of others; and
7. Respect the rights and freedoms of others; and
8. comply with the requirements of the law.

Commentary

Rights without duties would mean anarchy, just as duties without rights would be slavery. People tend to insist on their rights but may not always comply with their duties. The list of duties contained in Article 25 are the most basic, so basic as to merit a place in the basic law of the country. Allegiance, defense of one's country, performing legally required national service, advancing national unity, and respecting the rights and freedoms of others should not be subject to dispute. What about respect and defense of the Constitution? This question occasioned a great deal of debate in the Commission. In the original draft, knowledge of the Constitution was included as a duty on the ground that it was the very basis for proper compliance with the other duties, but this was deleted following a lengthy debate. Another duty similarly deleted was respect for the rule of law. It had been included on the argument that the rule of law was the center-piece of a constitutional order and that civil society would be ill-equipped to appreciate its rights and duties without a good grounding in the knowledge of the main pillar of constitutional rule.

And how does one enforce such duties? Would they not be honored in their breach more than in their observance? The establishment of monitoring institutions, which might militate against certain basic rights was repellent. In a just and democratic society a culture of self enforcing habits would develop to cultivate a proper sense of duty which went beyond the realm of law, even though there were and would be laws that provide for sanctions against breaches of duties.

Limitations Upon Fundamental Rights and Freedoms

Article 26

1. The fundamental rights and freedoms guaranteed under this constitution may be limited only in so far as is [necessary] in the interests of national security, public safety or the economic well-being of the country, health or morals, for the prevention of public disorder or crime or for the protection of the rights and freedoms of others.

2. Any law providing for the limitation of the fundamental rights and freedoms guaranteed in this Constitution must:

   a. be consistent with the principles of democracy and justice

   b. be of general application and not negate the essential content of the right or freedom in question;

   c. specify the ascertainable extent of such limitation and identify the Article or Articles hereof on which authority to enact such limitation is claimed to rest.

3. The provisions of Sub-Article 1 of this Article shall

not be used to limit the fundamental rights and freedoms guaranteed under Articles 14(1) and (2); 15;
16; 17(2), (5), (7) and (8); and 19(1) of this
Constitution.

Commentary

Article 26 is a general limitations clause which rests on the
assumption that there is no absolute right that cannot be limited
under any circumstances. The Article sets forth criteria for the
courts to apply, when called upon to decide, when a limitation on
a fundamental right is valid and acceptable. In addition to the
general limitation that is permissible under Article 26, other limitations are also placed on some of the fundamental rights in terms
of specific provisions of certain Articles of the Constitution.

An example of such other specific limitation concerns
actions that a government may take to ensure the advancement
of women and disadvantaged groups in society which, on the
face of it, may be contrary to the equality guarantee clause of
the Constitution (Article 14). Other examples on which limitation is placed are the socio-economic rights which are recognized only in so far as is practicable to meet them, depending
on availability of resources, as discussed above (Article 21).
Similarly, the right to economic activity may be limited by
other policy considerations, and property may be expropriated
subject to criteria spelt out in Article 23(3).

Lastly, it should be noted that Sub-Article (1) of Article
26 lays down the criteria that must be satisfied in order for fundamental rights to be limited. This limitation may be placed
"only as far as is necessary in a just and democratic society"
required on the following grounds:

- in the interests of national security;
- public safety and economic well-being of the
  country;

- health or morals, for the prevention of public disorder or crime, or for the protection of the rights and freedoms of others.

A court must be satisfied that the measures taken are necessary in a just and democratic society. Both "just" and "democratic" are to be determined by discerning judges. The next step in the court's determination is to consider whether the measures satisfy one or a combination of the requirements listed above. The onus of proving that the measures are necessary is on the authorities who take them.

The US Constitution has no provision similar to Article 26 of the Eritrean Constitution. But the US Courts have developed guiding principles. The Canadian Constitution is also helpful in this respect, placing fundamental rights subject to "such reasonable limits prescribed by law as can be demonstrably justified in a free and democratic society."[23] The South African Constitution also provides that a fundamental right may be limited by "a law of general application" provided that such a limitation is "reasonable" and "justifiable in an open and democratic society based on freedom and equality."[24] The German constitution contains similar provisions,[25] as does the European Convention of the Protection of Human Rights and Fundamental Freedoms.[26] The Constitution of Namibia agrees.[27] The Constitution of Uganda deals with this subject from a different angle. It provides:

(1) In the enjoyment of the rights and freedoms prescribed in this Chapter (chapter 4), no person shall prejudice the fundamental or other human rights and freedoms of others or the public interest.
(2) Public interest under this Article shall not permit:
    (a) political persecution;
    (b) detention without trial;

(c) any limitation of the enjoyment of the rights
and freedoms prescribed by this Chapter
beyond *what is acceptable and demonstrably
justifiable in a free and democratic society, or
what is provided in this Constitution.*[28]

The criteria set forth in the Ugandan Constitution hinge
on public interest and the contention that there shall be no
political persecution and detention without trial in the name of
public security. In contrast to the Eritrean Constitution, national interest is not included together with a "public interest". It
will be interesting to see whether the Ugandan Courts will
decide that "national interest" is co-terminus with "public
interest." The Eritrean constitution-makers preferred to use
both terms on the assumption that they can be subject to different meanings.

Of further interest are the italicized words in 2(c) above:
"what is acceptable and demonstrably justifiable in a free and
democratic society..." Whether "what is acceptable and demonstrably justifiable" is stricter than what is "reasonable" is debatable. The government counsel who is required to prove that a
certain measure is demonstrably justifiable may have a more difficult time than one who is required to show that it is reasonable. But, in the final analysis, this distinction will turn on the
subjective determination of the judges involved.

Non-Derogable Rights and Freedoms.

The provisions of Sub-Article 3 of Article 26 single out rights
that may not be limited on the grounds specified under Sub-Article 1. The principle behind these rights, known as non-derogable rights, applies in the Constitutions of most
countries, with some variation. For example, Article 44 of the

Constitution of Uganda provides:

"Notwithstanding anything in this Constitution, there shall be no derogation from the enjoyment of the following rights and freedoms:

    (a) freedom from torture, cruel, inhuman or degrading treatment or punishment;
    (b) freedom from slavery or servitude;
    (c) the right to fair hearing;
    (d) the right to an order of *habeas corpus.*

The equivalent Article in the Constitution of the Federal Republic of Nigeria (Article 45) is more complicated. The Nigerian Constitution permits the restriction on and derogation from fundamental rights when it is "reasonably justifiable in a democratic society—

    (a) in the interest of defense, public safety, public order, public morality or public health; or
    (b) for the purpose of protecting the rights and freedoms of other persons." [Article 45(1)]

Rights that may be subject to restriction or derogation on the bases of the above-mentioned criteria are specifically listed in the Article. They are: rights to privacy and family (Article 37), rights to freedom of thought, conscience and religion (Article 38), rights to freedom of expression and the press (Article 39), right to peaceful assembly and association (40), and right to freedom of movement (Article 41).

Article 45(2) provides that measures taken, during periods of emergency, that involve risk to life must be reasonably justifiable for the purpose of dealing with a situation that exists during the period of emergency. The right to life is one of the few non-derogable rights under the Nigerian Constitution

THE MAKING OF THE ERITREAN CONSTITUTION

(See Article 33). Article 45(2) prohibits any derogation from the provisions of Article 33 of the Constitution, "except in respect of death resulting from acts of war..." The same Sub-Article also prohibits any derogation from the right declared in Article 36(8) [No person shall be held to be guilty of a criminal offence on account of any act or omission that did not, at the time it took place, constitute such an offence..."]

Comparing the three constitutions on the issue of derogation of rights, the Eritrean Constitution's inclusion of freedom of thought, conscience and belief is remarkable. This inclusion was among the issues that the Executive Committee of the Commission spent a great deal of time debating.

Emergency

Article 27

1. At a time when public safety or the security or stability of the State is threatened by war, external invasion, civil disorder or natural disaster, the President may by a proclamation published in the Official Gazette declare that a state of emergency exists in Eritrea or any part thereof.

2. A declaration under Sub-Article (1) hereof shall not become effective unless approved by a resolution passed by a two-thirds majority votes of all members of the National Assembly. A declaration made when the National Assembly is in session shall be be presented within two days after its publication, or otherwise, the National Assembly shall be summoned to meet and consider the declaration within thirty days of its publication.

3. A declaration approved by the National Assembly

pursuant to Sub-Article (2) of this Article shall continue to be in force for a period of six months after such approval. The National Assembly may, by a resolution of two-thirds majority vote of all its members, extend its approval of the declaration for a period of three months at a time.

4. The National Assembly may, at any time, by resolution revoke a declaration approved by it pursuant to the provisions of this Article.

5. A declaration of a state of emergency or any measures undertaken or laws enacted pursuant to it shall not:

   a. suspend Articles 14(1) and (2); 16; 17(2); and 19(1) of the Constitution;

   b. grant pardon or amnesty to any person or persons who, acting under the authority of the State, have committed illegal acts;

   c. introduce martial law when there is no external invasion or civil disorder.

Commentary

A distinction must be made between suspension of fundamental rights on the grounds of state of emergency on the one hand, and the limitation of fundamental rights (as explained above) on the other. The first is based on the necessity of the defense of the State when threatened by actual war or impending invasion, civil disorder or natural disaster, whereas a limitation of rights is based on the principle that no right is absolute. The similarity of language that justifies the suspension of rights ("national security and public safety") in Article 26(4) and "public safety or the security or stability of the state" in Article 27(1) should not cause confusion between the two. During a state of emergency the justification for the suspension of rights is national self-defense.[29]

Even in a state of emergency, however, there are limits. Even in circumstances giving ground for suspension of fundamental human rights, in a constitutional order the arbitrary or irresponsible exercise of power should not be admissible, as it would be irreconcilable with the Rule of Law and due process principles. The exercise of emergency powers must be proportionate to the threat which causes the suspension of the fundamental rights. It must be guided by necessity to meet the threat. When called upon to review such exercise of emergency powers, in cases of dispute over whether there is unnecessary excess, the courts would have to weigh the means employed with the nature and extent of the threat.

Moreover, the limits prescribed in Sub-Article (5) of Article 27 are important.

the right of equality under the law shall not be suspended;
the guarantee against discrimination shall not be suspended on any ground;
the right to human dignity shall not be suspended;
there shall be no retroactively applying criminal offenses or penalties;
the right to freedom of thought , conscience and belief shall not be suspended;
no pardon or amnesty shall be granted to any person who commits illegal acts under the authority of the State
a declaration of a state of emergency shall not introduce martial law "when there is no external invasion or civil disorder."

Again, the non-derogable rights to freedom of thought, conscience and belief are not to be affected by a declaration of a state of emergency.

Enforcement of Fundamental Rights and Freedoms

Article 28

1. The National Assembly or any subordinate legislative authority shall not make any law, and the Executive and the agencies of government shall not take any action that abolishes or abridges the fundamental rights and freedoms conferred by this Constitution unless authorized by this Constitution. Any law or any action in violation thereof shall be null and void.

2. Any aggrieved person who claim that a fundamental right or freedom guaranteed by this Constitution has been denied or violated shall be entitled to petition a competent court for redress. Where it ascertains that such fundamental right or freedom has been denied or violated, the court shall have the power to make all such orders as shall be necessary to secure for such petitioner the enjoyment of such fundamental right or freedom, and where such applicants suffer damage, to include an award of monetary compensation.

Commentary

Who enforces fundamental rights and freedoms? And who defends them or ensures that their violation is sanctioned? The answer to these questions is given by the Constitution itself.

First, and foremost, the citizens have the duty to observe them and to act as watchdog for their observance. (See Article 25 on duties of citizens, both Sub-Article (5) and (6)). The supremacy clause of the Constitution (Article 2) is, of course, the foundation. Sub-Article(3) of that clause bears repetition here: "This Constitution is the supreme law of the country and

203

the source of all laws of the State, and all laws, orders and acts contrary to its letter and spirit shall be null and void".

The provisions of Article 28 flow from the supremacy clause. No State authority can make any law or take any action which contravenes the provisions of the Constitution, including any abolition or abridgment of the fundamental rights conferred by it, and such law or action shall be null and void. The question, then, is: who is entitled to declare them null and void, or to take any measures to rectify the consequences of such unconstitutional measures?

Sub-Article (2) supplies the answer which is also sanctioned by tradition and the development of constitutional law in other jurisdictions. The answer is: the courts of law. If upon complaint by an aggrieved person that his or her fundamental right or freedom has been violated and a court ascertains the complaints to be well-founded, a court is empowered by the Sub-Article to rectify the wrong and to order, at its discretion, an award of monetary compensation in favour of the complainant, where, it determines such an award is justifiable.

The experience of other jurisdictions shows that such disputes invariably arise in the area of limitation of rights. This naturally involves interpretation of the constitution. And, as some Canadian scholars have opined, "in interpreting a constitutional instrument courts have to strike a balance between allowing the democratic process of an elected Parliament to take its natural course while ensuring that the framework of values as contained in the instrument continue to form the broad context within which social, political and economic activity takes place".[30] The South African constitution provides more detailed provisions on the subject of constitutional interpretation (See Article 232(4)). The Eritrean constitution leaves entirely to the courts the creative task of giving content of the provisions of the Constitution. This policy option is preferred on the ground that constitutional development is a dynamically evolving matter which will be influenced by changing values in a given historical context. This policy decision is confirmed by the history of the Supreme Court of the United States, as well as the English Courts and the courts of other countries.

Residual Rights

Article 29
The rights enumerated in this Chapter shall not preclude other rights which ensue from the spirit of this Constitution and the principles of a society based on social justice, democracy and the Rule of Law.

Commentary
Again, we begin with a question which must occur to the discerning reader. The question arises in view of the fact that the Constitution is the source of all rights and is framed as comprehensively as possible, in regard to the enshrinement of rights as well as other constitutional issues. What other rights can there be, other than the ones conferred by the Constitution? An allied question is: Would Article 29 on residual rights not open the door for claims of entitlement based on customs and traditions that may be in contravention to the provisions of the Constitution?

First of all, to begin with the last question, we go back to the supremacy clause. The provisions of the Constitution, as the supreme law, prevail over all others laws or practices, be they based on customs, traditions or any other source. What other source of rights can there be, then, that the Eritrean constitution makers saw the necessity of including Article 29 in the Constitution? Note the phrasing of this Article: it speaks of other rights not enumerated in the Constitution "which ensue from the spirit of this Constitution and *the principles of a society based on social justice, democracy and the Rule of Law.*"

The italicized words are the key to an understanding of what has generically been called residual rights. If any claims are pressed that the courts find to be contrary (a) to the spirit of the Constitution, (b) to social justice, (c) to democracy, and (d) to the Rule of law, they would not be entertained. Customs that are not contrary to these values, and are on the contrary an enlargement or a refinement of them, would be entertained. Customs that negate the equality principle, for instance, such as customs that relegate women to a subordinate status, would not be acceptable. On the other hand the Preamble to the Constitution asks that traditional community-based values of mutual respect and assistance, fraternity, love of family, respect for elders be given careful consideration. In this, as in other matters, the role of the courts will be critical.

Notes

1. The text from which this quote comes was brought to my attention by Tekie Fessehatzion.
2. Procl. No. 86/1996 Art 10, Art 10(2)and (3)
3. Fifth Amendment to the US. Constitution
4. Article 9.
5. See. Arts 522 of the Transitional Penal Code.
6. There was the case of a doctor who was killed in his abortion clinic by a "Right to Life" zealot in Buffalo, New York.
7. Other than Catholics, a significant segment of the Christian evangelical movement also subscribe to "Right to Life."
8. See The State v. Makwanyene, 6BCLR 665, 1995.
9. Article 6.
10. Article 22(1).

11. Article 22(2)
12. Art. 14
13. Art 15
14. The practice of regular courts appointing attorneys to defend indigent defendants continues today. The fact that the "Special Court" denies this right has been the subject of continued criticism by members of the opposition groups and civil society organizations of Eritrea.
15. See Transitional Criminal Procedure Code of Eritrea.
16. See the Resolution of EPLF's Second and Third Congresses (1987 and 1994 respectively).
17. Issue Paper No. 6 Part I: Economic rights p.5.
18. For a very good discussion on this subject see Herman Schwartz, "Social Welfare Rights Should be Constitutionalized Rights," in *Tradition und Weltoffenkeist des Rechts Festschrift fur Helmut Steinberger*, Max Plank Institute, Heidelberg 2002.
19. The Convention was adopted by the U.N. General Assembly on November 20, 1989. The President of Eritrea singed the Instrument of Ratification on July 21, 1994.
20. Under the pre-existing land holding system, particularly in communal land, the periodic reallocation of land rights among the villagers had the effect of inhibiting any investment on the land thus creating obstacles to development. The new law allows investors to be granted leasehold concessions for development, provided such land lies outside that reserved for subsistence farming and housing of the village community.
21. See, for example, Griffith and Street, Administrative Law, London 1968.
22. Cf Paul - Marie Falane the Conseil d'Etat; in An Introduction to French Administrative Law: 11AP Educational Series No.21 pp97-109.
23. Article 1.

24. Section 33(1) (a). See on this Dion Basson, South Africa's Interim Constitution, Juta Aco. 1994 P.49.
25. Article 19(2).
26. Article 9.
27. Article 22.
28. Article 43,
29. The Latin maxim *Salus republicae supremma lex* (The well-being of the republic prevails over law) shows that this is a principle with a long history.
30. See Cachalia, Cheadle, Davis, Hayson Maduna and Marcus, Fundamental Rights in the New Constitution, 1994 p.9.

NINE

The Legislature:
Democracy and Representative Government

Democracy constitutes the social state; the dogma of popular sovereignty constitutes political right. The two things are not analogous. Democracy is a way of being for society, whereas popular sovereignty is a form of government. (ALEXIS DE TOCQUEVILLE)

1. The Democratic Idea and its Application.

Ours is the age of democracy. That democracy is the most desirable political system is now disputed by no one but a few extremists; even autocratic rulers pay lip service to it, as noted before.

It has taken over two hundred years of philosophical discourse and political struggle for the democratic idea to gain universal acceptance and reign supreme. But, as the quoted statement of de Tocqueville indicates, it is a malleable concept subject to different interpretations to advance different ends. From the philosophical discourse of revolutionary France

209

(1789-1794) to the first half of the 19th century, two basic elements emerged to define democracy's essential content which have been characterized as "political" and "sociological." De Tocquivelle draws a distinction between democracy (as a "social state") and popular sovereignty (as "a form of government"), but even he qualifies this dichotomy by saying "popular sovereignty and democracy are perfectly correlative terms: the one presents the theoretical idea, while the other presents its practical realization."[1]

How relevant, to our discussion on parliamentary democracy and representative government, is this semantic difference of the political and sociological aspects of democracy? And what is the practical import of reference to the history and evolution of the idea of democracy?

The first thing to note here is that, before the explosion of the revolutionary discourse of the late 18th century France and early 19th century Europe, the word "democracy" was generally used to designate an obsolete type of political system. A study of pre-Revolutionary France's dictionaries reviewed by Rosanvallon confirms this conclusion[2]

It took the authoritative works of Montesquieu's *Espirt de Lois*, and Rousseau's *Contrat Social* to rescue the idea of democracy from its associations with the archaic, and to advance it to represent the twin principles of self-government and legitimation. Montesquieu notes that it is "a fundamental law in democracies, that the people should have the sole power to enact laws."[3]

Earlier definitions of democracy "as a form of government in which offices are distributed by lot found their place even in the works of Montesquieu and Rousseau. The former explains this in terms of fairness and motivation. "Suffrage by lot", he writes, "is natural to democracy.....the suffrage by lot is a method that offends no one, but animates each citizen with the pleasing hope of serving his country". Rousseau repeats these formulations, adding that suffrage by lot does no harm to equality.[4]

The second thing to note is that neither of these two great thinkers nor others in their time imagined that democracy, thus defined, could be applicable to the modern world. It was an ideal type that would work "if there were a people of gods," as Rousseau observed. The historical significance of their writings lies in the revolutionary implication of the idea of democracy. The idea of democracy eventually yielded to that of popular sovereignty *(la volonté général)*. Popular sovereignty, in turn, yields to representative government. For Rousseau, the great revolution of modern times lies in the process of institution building from the popular base. It was revolutionary in that it implied, and eventually led to, the destruction of the *ancien régime*, the feudal order, and its replacement by elected representatives, the *Etat Genereau*.[5]

The third point to note concerns the practical application of the idea of democracy, or what may be called the problems of democracy. As a method of government, democracy was criticized by the earlier writers, including the 18th century philosophers. The main line of argument of such criticism was that it tends to lead to instability and the consequent abuse of its principles. The French *Encyclopidistes* denounced it in those terms.[6] But even in pre-revolutionary France there were a few men of vision whose writings presaged what later would be the basic principle of modern government. The Marquis d'Argenson was one such writer who distinguished "false" democracy and "legitimate" democracy—the first being fraught with danger, the second designating representative government. "In true democracy", he wrote, "one acts through deputies, who are authorized by election; the mission of those elected by the people and the authority that such officials carry constitute the public power".[7]

It should be remembered that the English Revolution of

1688 had already instituted a measure of representative government, albeit qualified by the fact that the English House of Commons only embraced, at the time, the middle class of land owners and rising bourgeoisie. Locke's Second Treatise on Civil Government, which puts property ownership at the center of political rights, was the gospel of the ascendant class of English property owners, and was a major source of inspiration of the American Declaration of Independence of 1776 and the constitution of 1789. It is ironic that it took France, the home of revolutionary philosophical ideas, a longer time to settle the question of parliamentary democracy and representative government. Democracy's pejorative connotation—anarchy and disunity—held sway in the minds of Frenchmen even of the generation of 1789. As an example, the proposals for a member-by-member voting in the Etat General proved to be controversial.[8] Rosanvallon writes that during the debate over the right to vote that took place from 1789 to 1791 the word "democracy" was not used a single time which he also confirms by an examination of the dictionaries dating from that era.[9]

The transition from a pejorative conception of the idea of democracy to an acceptable one came with the ascendancy of popularly elected representative government. At first, many of the French writers of the revolutionary era made a distinction between the two, as de Tocqueville did later, but only for tactical reasons, it would seem. "Moderate" revolutionaries like Sieyes and Brissot associated democracy with its ancient (Greek) source and used the word "republic" in a sense which was synonymous with what later came to be democracy. Rosanvallan observes: "in dissociating 'republic' from 'direct democracy', he, (Brissot) wished in effect to recast the republican idea by freeing it from the accusations of bad motives and anarchism that its detractors were leveling against it."[10]

It was Sieyes, however, who clearly articulated the idea of representative government implied by recognizing its positive function of the democratic ideal. He wrote: "there are two ways of bringing the citizens together for the purpose of making laws directly: the citizens may exercise their right to make laws directly, or they may entrust it to representatives, *who are much more capable than the citizen of knowing the general interest,*"[11] Note the insertion of the criterion of capability. Viewed in the context of the size of the country and, eventually also, the technicalities that must be mastered in a more complex polity, representative government as the best institutional expression of democracy became an irresistible idea. The resurgence of democracy later was connected with a phase of the political struggle in which the people played a central part. Democracy and representative government hitherto viewed as technically distinct, now became one in tracing power to a popular source, both resting on people's sovereignty.

In the Constitution of Eritrea, as noted already, the principles of democracy and the people's sovereignty is clearly defined. Article 1(3) provides that in the State of Eritrea, "sovereign power is vested in the people, and shall be exercised pursuant to the provisions of this constitution.

The equal participation of citizens "in all areas of human endeavor" is guaranteed under Article 7, which charges the State to create the necessary conditions and institutions to realize the democratic ideal. Electoral laws constitute one such condition to enable citizens to exercise their sovereign power through duly elected representatives.

In concluding this section, it is worth reiterating that representative democracy is a more complex form of self-government by the people, indirectly through representatives whom they elect periodically. This contrasts with the more direct, "participatory" form of self-government that is associated with the *polis* of Athens, but which was, and still is, practiced in village communities throughout Africa. *The baitos* of Eritrea perform the same functions as the Athenian *polis* of old.[12] With the advent of the modern state, embracing different communities which were brought together under colonial rule, the *baitos* of Eritrea have been aggregated and transformed into the national assembly *(Hagerawi Baito)*. The election of the members of this national *baito* cannot be done by drawing lots or putting a laurel (Qosli) on the head of the chosen one. A more complex mechanism, reflecting the complex requirements of the times, has to be utilised. Hence the significance of modern electoral systems which will be considered in the next section.

2. Electoral Systems and Democracy

An Electoral System constitutes the meeting point between what de Tocqucville and others divided, for analytical reasons, into popular sovereignty and representative government. It deals with how the citizens' voting rights—the primary expression of their sovereignty—are translated into parliamentary seats. In these parliamentary seats resides legislative power with its associated power of control of the purse and of monitoring of executive power which will be discussed in a later section. As one scholar put it, "the electoral system is the most fundamental element of representative democracy."[13] Hence the decision of the Constitutional Commission of Eritrea to include Electoral Systems as one of the issues to be researched, as already mentioned.[14]

Elections express the principle of government by the consent of the governed and should therefore be designed and organized in a way that would enable the governed to choose the best available candidate to represent them. An Electoral System must be designed, in other words, in such a way as to enable every citizen to participate freely and fully in the election of representatives. To that end the Commission's Issue paper identified four general purposes that must be served by elections:

1. reflection of the main opinions of the electorate;
2. establishment of majority rule;
3. election of suitable representatives; and
4. establishment of strong and stable government.

An Electoral System should be devised to fulfill these purposes.

Implicit in these general purposes, is another feature of elections, i.e., that the elections should take place at regular intervals and for specified terms of office. In the case of Eritrea, the term of office of five years has been specified in the Constitution (see below), whereas the time of elections together with other details is left to be specified in the electoral laws. The fixed term of office, or mandate, enables citizens to review the performance of their elected representatives and to pronounce judgment at the next election either by re-electing them or terminating their mandate and choosing other candidates. Election time has thus tremendous juridical as well as political significance. For electors and candidates alike, it is a day of judgment on which the quality of representative government depends.

Electoral Systems

There are different types of Electoral Systems whose variety reflects national political and demographic factors. Most typically, however, they may be divided into two broad categories: the majority system and the proportional representation (PR) system.

Majority System. This system, also known as "first-past-the post" is a system in which one person is elected by a relative majority, that is to say, the person obtaining the most votes, from among competing candidates, is declared elected. Experience in many countries over the years has shown that this system failed to fulfill the purposes listed above, particularly in terms of reflecting the views or interests of the majority of the electing citizens.

The following example of voting results of four candidates participating in an elections under this system illustrates the failure of the system in terms of reflecting the majority of electors:-

Candidates	Votes Obtained
A	7,000
B	4,000
C	3,500
D	2,500

The failure of the majority system to represent majority views is shown in this example, in that candidate A would be declared elected with a 7,000 vote, whereas the combined vote for candidates B,C and D is 10,000. Given a second chance, it is conceivable that the voters might prefer candidate B or C.

A study of the election history of several countries shows that attempts were made to remedy this inherent weakness of this system. One solution is to provide for second ballot, or more, to give people an opportunity to re-cast their votes in favor of one or the other of the candidates who received less votes on the first count. the most frequent practice has been to have the two top vote-getters submit to a second ballot. This and similar attempts at modifying the majority system imply financial cost and voter fatigue. The alternative is Proportional Representation.

The Proportional Representation System

For a number of years now, proportional representation (PR) has been advanced as a better electoral formula, particularly for countries with multi-ethnic composition which is the case in most countries in Africa. The principal argument in favor of PR is that it protects minorities or facilitates the representation of their voice in national politics. There have been some instructive studies conducted recently on Southern African elections which demonstrate the superiority of PR.[15]

The comparative advantage of PR over the majority system should be analyzed in relation to party politics. The primary consideration is that parties should obtain seats in the Parliament in proportion to their support in the electorate which is possible under PR more than under the majority system.[16] The simplest arrangement is one in which the number of seats in a constituency is divided into the total votes cast in an election, so that each party obtains its share of seats in relation to the votes it obtains at the polls. For example, in a constituency where 150,000 votes are cast and it is entitled to five seats in Parliament, each party will be entitled to one seat for every 30,000 votes it gets at the polls.

Different varieties of this formula have been used in an attempt to have a more equitable representation. Opinions differ as to the value of PR, some even arguing that it is not suitable to "agrarian" societies.[17] The principal criticism of PR is that it weakens the link between the individual members of Parliament and their constituencies. This prevents the development of what has been called the "vertical' dimension of democracy (i.e. the representational relationship between elites and the " common people" with a common political interest) and reduces the prospects for the consolidation of democratic rule.[18]

These arguments will be among those to be considered and weighed carefully at the time when the Eritrean Parliament debates the Bill on the electoral laws stipulated in Article 29(2) of the Constitution. At least that was the expectation of the constitution makers.

In these (future) deliberations the principal objective should be a fair and equitable representation of the whole population in Parliament. As already mentioned, the Commission's proposals state that whatever the system chosen it must be capable of ensuring fair and adequate representation of the whole population. The Proposals recommended that since electoral systems may be changed from time to time to suit the demands of changing circumstances, a provision on electoral systems should be left to laws to be issued under the Constitution, rather than be included in it.[19] Accordingly, Article 30(2) provides that the National Assembly shall enact an electoral law "which shall prescribe for and ensure the representation and participation of the Eritrean people".

The Constitution also provides for the establishment of an Electoral commission.[20] The Constitution is fastidious about the operational independence of the Electoral Commission because the integrity of the electoral process must be maintained scrupulously. It provides that the Commission must operate independently, without interference, in order to "ensure that 'free and fair elections are held.'" The Commission is empowered to manage the implementation of the elections, "decide on issues raised in the course of the electoral process, and formulate and implement civic educational programs relating to elections and other democratic procedures".[21]

The Electoral Commissioners are to be appointed by the President with the approval of the National Assembly.[22] The details on the powers and duties and organization of the Electoral Commission is left to a law to be enacted by Parliament.[23]

3. Composition, Mandate, Powers and Duties of Parliament

Composition and Mandate

The Eritrean Parliament consists of a one Chamber (uni-cameral) National Assembly. It is composed of representatives of the people elected by direct and secret ballot by all citizens who are qualified to vote.[24] Any Eritrean citizen, of 18 years of age or more, has the right to vote.[25] The qualifications and election of members of Parliament and the conditions for vacating their seats shall be determined by law.

Members of Parliament (MP), though elected from particular electoral districts, are representatives of the Eritrean people as a whole. In discharging their duties as MPs, they are governed "by the objectives and principles of the Constitution, the interest of the people and the country and their conscience".[26]

Parliamentary mandate lasts for a term of five years from the day of the first session held, following a general election. Exceptionally, where there exists a state of war or a state of emergency in terms of Article 27 of the Constitution, which would prevent a normal general election from being held, Parliament may, by a resolution supported by not less than two-thirds vote of all its members, extend its term for a period not exceeding six months.[27]

From the foregoing, the following topics require further comments:

- The Uni-cameral nature of Parliament
- Universal, direct and secret voting (suffrage).
- National character of the MP's duties and principles that guide the discharge of such duties.

To start with the first topic first, the question arises: why a unicameral Parliament? What were the reasons that led the Eritrean constitution-makers to choose this, in preference over a two-chamber (bi-cameral) Parliament? The question was part of the 23 issues that the Commission grappled with at the start of its work and was, accordingly, a subject of research. The team that researched the subject submitted a report with a divided opinion: a majority proposing a one-chamber Parliament, and a minority view cogently arguing in favor of a two-chamber Parliament.

The arguments advanced in support of a two-Chamber

Parliament outlined three principal advantages: (a) it ensures wider representation of a nation, especially one with a multi-ethnic composition; (b) it can guarantee the issuing of better laws and policies, because it ensures more deliberation and ampler time frame: (c) it can help in the resolution of tension that may arise out of controversies between the Executive and Legislative branches. The proponents of this minority view recognized two drawbacks of a two-chamber Parliament: that it may involve delay and more expenses.

The majority view argued: (a) that a single-chamber parliament better reflects the sovereignty of the people and enacts laws without undue concerns over the special interests in society, be they based on ethnicity or class; (b) it is speedy, and (c) is less costly. The supporters of the majority view were aware of the drawbacks of potential haste and the tension that may arise between the Executive and Legislative branches, but argued that the advantages outweigh these drawbacks, and that constitutional provisions can be devised to overcome them. For a nation like Eritrea, a dynamic leadership is required, one that reflects unified representation of the people in one chamber, even in the context of a (future) multi-party system. Whatever merit the two chamber system may have in other situations, the historical and socio-political circumstance of Eritrea is such that there is no need to constitutionalize divisions that have been resolved particularly due to the recent history of a 30-year armed struggle against a common enemy. The "objective" conditions of a country must determine the type of system constitution-makers adopt.

The Commission accepted these arguments and decided to adopt the one-chamber parliament. In making such a choice the Commission added a further point: whatever groups in society might have merited representation in a second chamber, can be accommodated through the careful drawing up of electoral laws and procedures. In this respect, the Commission considered, but ultimately rejected, the practice followed in some countries under which the head of state appoints to the Parliament members of certain groups in society, such as elders or chieftains, or professional people. In the considered opinion of the Commission, such people can and should enter parliament through the electoral process.

As for the topic of universal, direct and secret voting, a detailed discussion is not necessary beyond stressing the significance of these requirements for parliamentary democracy. Universal adult suffrage is an electoral category which historically marks the triumph of the right of the common man against the prior system of suffrage which had been limited to the privileged class. In England, known as the home of parliamentary government, this right was not won until the Reform Act of 1832, and even after that, it was limited by the requirements of property ownership, a requirement that took several decades to be eliminated. Moreover, it took a long drawn-out battle of the suffragette movement in England until the 1920's before the vote could be extended to women, in England, and until the 1960's in Switzerland.

The requirement of direct voting is to be distinguished from indirect vote. Indirect vote is vote which is exercised indirectly through community or clan leaders, or through elected members of local assemblies. In other words the citizen does not elect his representative directly himself. This is a rare political phenomenon nowadays. Then there is the secrecy principle which ensures that the elector casts his or her vote in an enclosed space out of sight of anybody. This is also obviously an essential requirement designed to enable the voter to exercise his or her right without fear or pressure of any kind. The electoral law must make provisions to facilitate this and other requirements to ensure a free and fair election. The practice of having election observers to witness the electoral process helps guarantee free and fair elections.

Finally, there is the requirement that MPs must discharge their duties by thinking of themselves first foremost as representatives of the whole nation. This does not mean that they forget all about their constituencies; on the contrary, they must also represent the views and interests of their constituents and maintain regular contact with them. Article 38(1) of the Constitution provides: MPs "shall have the duty to maintain the high honor of their office and to consider themselves as humble servants of the people."

Powers and Duties of Parliament

The MPs collectively constitute the Legislature. Following their election, and by virtue of the elections the representatives of the people are collectively vested with government authority. In terms of the Constitution of Eritrea the members of the National Assembly (MPs) who are elected directly by the voters, as noted before, collectively embody the democratic idea of representative government. In this section of the chapter we will see in what way this democratic idea is translated into legislative power.

The power of the National Assembly may be divided into four main categories: (a) legislation, *strictu sensu*, (b) oversight of executive or administrative matters; (c)hearing citizens, (d) approval of appointments and (e) impeachment .

(a) Legislation

To begin with, the National Assembly (Parliament) must be bound by the principles enumerated in the Constitution and is by duty bound (constitutionally) to strive to fulfill the objectives therein stated[28] And pursuant to the Constitution, it has the power "to enact laws and pass resolutions for the peace, stability, development and social justice of Eritrea."[29] Only Parliament is the sole legislative authority of the State and any matter that is legislative in nature (law) must issue out of Parliament or by delegation from Parliament. Such delegation must itself come under the authority of law passed by parliament. The Constitution puts it this way: "Unless authorized by a law, no person or organization shall have the power to make decisions having the force of law".[30]

This being the principle, it must be noted, however, that the Executive branch of government impinges on the legislative power of Parliament in two respects. First, it has the power of initiative and the near-monopoly over expertise in the researching and preparation of draft law which it then presents to Parliament for its deliberation and enactment. Even in countries with immense resources, like the United States, where Congress (Parliament) commands a good deal of human and financial resources to conduct its own research and prepare draft laws, the comparatively greater resource at the command of the Executive branch gives it greater advantage in this respect. In countries like Eritrea, there is an overwhelming advantage in favor of the Executive branch.

In theory, however, and in terms of constitutional principle, Parliament can reject all drafts prepared by the Executive. In practice this occurs rarely for political and pragmatic reasons of national interest. A government in a parliamentary system enjoys a majority of votes in Parliament and can rely on such majority to ensure the passage of draft laws that it submits. Can the government of a party in power always rely on its members? The answer is that it almost always can, but that in some instances, members may "vote their conscience," as the saying goes. This may occur in matters involving moral issues such capital punishment, abortion or other questions concerning human rights. The experience of other parliamentary systems shows that the "party whips" (who enforce party discipline in parliament) normally release their members from their obligation to "toe the party line".

In presidential systems like that of the United States, the

223

doctrine of Separation of Powers holds sway to a great extend. Even though there are party whips in Congress, there is less strict control over party members, even in matters of a political nature. In practice, of course party loyalty and respect for the President (the leader of the party) and his power of persuasion may cause party alignment over nearly all such issues. If a member insists in "voting his conscience," greater pressure may be exerted or some bargaining may be struck, including promises of satisfying some demands of the particular member in respect of favors done for his constituency. Votes may then be obtained in exchange for particular favors, which is in the nature of the give-and-take of politics.

The other area in which Executive power impinges on the Legislature is delegated legislation. The laws that Parliament passes concern major issues. Constitutions of the countries of Europe such as that of France delineate the areas on which Parliament only can legislate. These are sometimes termed "the domain of law", or matters within the sphere of legislation and are listed in the constitution.[31]

In almost all cases laws passed by Parliament contain "an enabling clause" under which Parliament delegates its legislative authority to a Minister or another member of the Executive. In the hierarchy of laws of a country, beginning from the Constitution, the higher law contains basic principles or major policy issues which lay down the framework of powers and duties or rights and obligations. The lower down we go in the hierarchy the more detailed the provisions become, from minute details on organization of municipal government, for example, to the circulars that a minister issues as guidelines for his employees.

In the Constitution of Eritrea, the "sphere of legislation" under which only Parliament has authority include the following:

- Approval of the national budget and enactment of tax law.[32]
- Ratification, by law, of international agreements.[33]
- Authorization of the government to borrow money "pursuant to law."[34]
- approval of state of peace, war or national emergency.[35]

As stated above there is an "omnibus" clause which gives power to parliament to pass laws or resolutions "for the peace, stability, development and social justice of Eritrea." Theoretically, Parliament can take initiative, or cause initiatives to be taken, to research, study and pass laws concerning the matters of national stability, development and social justice. Almost any subject can be covered by these topics. In practice, of course, it will be the Executive branch of the government which will take the initiative, as already noted.

(b) and (c) Parliamentary Oversight and Audience of Citizens' Complaints.

Article 32(7) and (12) of the Constitution gives power to Parliament "to oversee the execution of laws", and to discharge its oversight authority...with "power to enact such laws and to establish such standing and ad hoc committees as it deems necessary."

The power of Parliament to oversee the work of the Executive rests on the principle of popular sovereignty which Parliament represents by virtue of its election by the people. The electoral process involves, as we saw, **investiture** of (legislative) authority collectively on those who are elected to represent the people. It also involves a **legitimation** process under which the voting public transfers legitimacy to Parliament based on its (voting public's) sovereignty. This legitimation extends to the initiation, monitoring and control of government policy.

There is thus an organic link between the various categories under which Parliament seeks to exercise its power. Hence the combining of (b) and (c) under this sub-section of the chapter. The initial impetus that sets the machinery of inquiry, monitoring or control may come from an individual initiative of an MP or a Committee of Parliament, or it may be based on the complaints of citizens either as affected individuals or groups, or as concerned subjects. This process, and the parliamentary power on which it is based, makes for a healthy inter-action between government and citizens. Through its power of oversight, normally exercised through parliamentary committees, The Legislature operationalizes the principle of government accountability thus accomplishing two basic and related purposes: keeping the members of the Executive branch "on leash" and addressing citizens' grievances.

How this task is performed is a question related to the matter of parliamentary process which will be discussed in the next section. But we should note here that there are several ways in which citizens' grievances may be aired and addressed. There may be a variety of public fora organized in pursuance of the citizens rights of freedom of association, opinion and conscience, notably the right to use the Press and other Media to those ends. Practices develop which may become constitutional conventions under which rights are exercised, balanced by responsibilities. It takes time before such conventions become accepted part of the constitutional process, and the parliamentary immunity of MPs (see below) plays a crucial role in the development, nurturing and maintenance of such conventions which give life and force to the text of the constitution.

(d) Approval of Appointments

The power of appointment is one of the powers reserved to the Executive branch, notably to the President. But there are certain offices of the state which are regarded as so important that the appointment of people who fill them are made to be subject to parliamentary approval. The Constitution of Eritrea has singled out the following office holders to be subject to such parliamentary approval:-

- All Ministers
- All Commissioners[36]
- Auditor-General[36]
- Head of the Bank of Eritrea (Governor)[36]
- Chief Justice[36]
- Justices of the Supreme Court[37]

The scope of the constitutionally required parliamentary approval of the appointment of office-holders varies from country to country. In some jurisdictions, it involves all diplomatic appointments at ambassadorial level, high court judges, and junior ministers. This is the case in United States, for instance, which includes the appointment of all federal judges. In other systems such as that in France, parliamentary approval is limited to cabinet ministers who are judged collectively as members of the government of the day. The parliamentary "judgment" is rendered, not so much on the basis of the individual minister's merit as such, as on the program or general policy submitted by the Prime Minister and his Cabinet.[38] The same is true in Britain.

Parliamentary approval of Presidential appointment of office-holders under the Eritrean Constitution is appropriately limited to those listed above. All are high positions of crucial importance to the nation covering various aspects of its life. The case of the ministers needs no explanation as they collectively represent executive authority. The approval of this appointment is the first "line of defense" in Parliament's role in the system of checks and balances. The case of Commissioners is similar to that of ministers; apart from the fact of their non membership of the Cabinet, they perform functions that are as important as those of ministers. To take the example of the Commissioner of Elections, he/she is, as we saw, the repository of the trust of the nation in election matters who is entrusted with guaranteeing the integrity of the electoral process. Such an office-holder must necessarily be appointed with the approval of Parliament. The same is true with the Auditor-General, the Governor of the Bank and the Chief Justice and Justices of the Supreme Court.

(e) Impeachment Power.
Among the powers and duties of the National Assembly nothing is more momentous than the power to impeach the President on the grounds specified under Article 41(6) (a) and (b), or to remove him under Article 41(6)(c). [For a details discussion, see Chapter Ten, below]

4. Parliamentary Process

Parliamentary life is defined by parliamentary process. The process itself is measured by rules of procedure governing the internal institutions that comprise Parliament and the dynamics of their operation, as well as their relationship with the Executive branch of government. For the purpose of analysis and exposition, we will leave to the next section the question of parliamentary privileges and immunities, although these latter impinge on the quality of the institutional life of Parliament, including the behavior or performances of its members.

In terms of the Eritrean constitution, Parliament may pass laws or resolutions and "undertake all such measures as are necessary to discharge its constitutional responsibilities."[39] The internal institutions—standing and *ad hoc* committees—that

Parliament creates and the rules on procedure that it lays down, are designed to enable it to discharge its constitutional responsibility and to exercise its powers. The Constitution provides the basis for the accomplishment of these tasks and for the resolution of any potential conflicts that may arise in Parliament's performance of its duties or the exercise of its power.

Parliamentary Rules of Procedures

This is laid down, in broad outline under Article 3 of the Constitution, under which the National Assembly is required to have regular session and is authorized to determine the timing and duration of its regular session.[40] The National Assembly issues "rules and regulations concerning its organization, tasks, operations and internal processes and those of the standing and *ad hoc* committees, including the code of ethics of its members".[41]

Voting procedure is so important that it is made the subject of constitutional provision. The Constitution thus provides as follows:

> "Except as otherwise prescribed by this Constitution, any question proposed for decision by the National Assembly shall be determined by a majority vote of those present and voting, and in case of a tie of votes, the Chairperson may exercise a casting vote."[42]

The exceptions to the voting procedure referred to in this provision should be noted. But first, a word of explanation of the phrase "a majority of those present and voting." This is sometimes called a simple, or relative majority. It must be distinguished from "an absolute majority" which is required under Article 41 of the Constitution, for example, for the election of the President.[43] The rule of the constitution, then, is that, unless otherwise provided, all questions in Parliament are determined by a relative majority, i.e., by majority vote of those present and voting.

The question may arise: How many of the MPs must be present in Parliament, before matters can be debated and/or submitted for voting? Is there an irreducible minimum, and if so how is it determined? What if only 20 out of 120 MPs are present? Or even 30 or 40? What are the criteria for determining a minimum? These are obviously among the questions, which Parliament itself will answer in its internal rules and regulations.

An exception to the relative majority rule is, as we saw, the absolute majority rule which requires the presence of all members, as already noted. Parliament may add more issues to the rank of those to be determined by an absolute majority, as in the case of the election of the President. There is another exception, where a higher proportion of vote is required, constitutionally. The best example concerns the amendment of the Constitution. Different Constitutions require different percentages for this purpose.

The Constitution of Eritrea lays down a two step procedure for constitutional amendment, following a proposal tabled for such an amendment. The initial proposal for amendment of any provision of the Constitution may be tabled by the President or 50 percent of all the members of the National Assembly.[44]

The amendment proposal will then be debated by all the members of the National Assembly, and if three-quarters of all the members vote in favor of the amendment, the matter will be put on record and await final disposal by Parliament the following year. A one year period must elapse before the matter is taken up again. If, a year later, four-fifth of all the members accept the amendment passed by a three-fourth majority the previous year, then the amendment will pass and on the effective date become a part of the Constitution.[45]

Parliament may be convened for emergency meeting at the request of the President, its chairman or one-third of all its members.[46] The most common occurrence in respect of emergency meeting, as illustrated by the experience of other countries, is one where the President convenes Parliament in terms of the circumstances stipulated in Article 27 of the Constitution of Eritrea. Very rarely, the Chairman or members may request such a meeting particularly in the event of political crises facing the nation in which the President is either unable or unwilling to call a meeting.

Another point to be noted here in relation to parliamentary rules of procedure which has been included in the Constitution concerns the approval of a draft law passed by Parliament. The Constitution's provision is simple: "Any draft law approved by the National Assembly", it says, "shall be transmitted to the President who, within thirty days period, shall sign and have it published in the Official Gazette.[47]

During the research and subsequent discussion phases of the Constitutional Commission's work this question was among those many others that were hotly debated. It was debated in relation to the larger question: what form of government would be suitable for Eritrea?

The approval procedure of a draft law and related rules in presidential systems is different from that under parliamentary system. In a presidential system with a strict separation of powers, the president may reject a parliamentary draft law. When that occurs, rules must be devised constitutionally to resolve the conflict. Under the US Constitution, a presidential veto of a draft law passed by Congress (Parliament) will "kill" the draft unless Congress overrides the veto by a two-thirds majority.[48] In parliamentary systems, with a single chamber, all that is required is a majority of votes in the chamber supporting the party in power. But this may be complicated where, in a parliament elected under proportional representation, there are a number of parties whose total votes may outnumber those of the principal party. Moreover, in a two-chamber parliament

231

the process may be further complicated by a split in the votes which may necessitate a joint session of both-chambers to settle the split.

In the Eritrean situation, which is a parliamentary system with an executive president, a draft passed by Parliament cannot be questioned or returned for review, but must be published as law. This is the constitutional requirement. This requirement should be understood in the context of our earlier discussion of the Executive's initiative in preparing law. In the vast majority of cases, it is the Executive that drafts laws.

Notes

1. Quoted in Pierre Rosanvallon, The History of the Word "Democracy" in France, Journal of Democracy, Vol. 6 No.4. pp. 140-154, at p.150.
2. Ibid. pp. 140-141.
3. Ibid. p. 141.
4. It is remarkable that the village democracy of "primitive" societies in Africa depends on drawing lots or calling on some individuals with generally recognized leadership qualities to hold "office", as noted before. European colonial authorities never deigned to compare this with those of Ancient Greece or Rome.
5. Cf. Marcel Morabiti and Daniel Bourmond, op.cit.
6. The Chevalier des Jancourt, who edited the article on democracy for the Encyclopedia in fact bases his critique on Montesquieu's *Esprit de Lois, as cited in* Rosanvallon, op.cit. p. 142.
7. D'argenson, *Consideration sur le gouvernements ancient et present de la France* (1765). Quoted in Rosanvallon - Ibid pp.142-143.
8. Cf. Morabiti and Bourmond op.cit: pp. 49-61.
9. Op. Cit. PP 143-144.
10. Ibid.
11. Ibid.
12. Historically, the idea of democracy existed in much of Eritrea. Even at times when conquering kings ruled over their land, Eritreans administered their affairs through periodically elected representatives. For instance, the village baito in highland Eritrea, was and is still the center of the life of the communities. In imperial Ethiopia, by contrast, the sovereignty of the kings was a deeply ingrained doctrine; so much so that a Sorbonne-educated Ethiopian lawyer and Minister tried to impress upon the UN Com-

missioner on Eritrea that UN Resolution 390(V) had granted the Ethiopian Emperor the right to appoint a Governor-General for Eritrea on the presumption that only a sovereign Emperor can make appointments. The idea of sovereignty of the people was alien to this mentality. Cf. Tekie, op cit p.26.

13. See Andrew Reynolds, South African and Malawian Parliamentary Election under Alternative Electoral System Formula, in Timothy Sisk and Andrew Reynolds, eds. Elections and Conflict Resolution in Africa, Washington DC US Institute for Peace 1996.

14. Ibid.

15. See, for example, Joel Barkan, "Elections in Agrarian Societies," *Journal of Democracy*, Oct. 1995 - pp. 106-116.

16. Ibid. P.107.

17. Ibid.

18. Ibid.

19. See Proposals p. 24.

20. Article 58(1).

21. Article 58(1).

22. Article 58(2).

23. Article 58(3).

24. Article 31.

25. Article 30(1).

26. Article 31(4).

27. Article 31(5).

28. Article 2.

29. Article 32(1)(a).

30. Article 32(1)(b).

31. Cf. Article 34 of the Constitution of France.

32. Article 32(3).

33. Article 32(4).

34. Article 32(5).

35. Article 32(6).

36. Article 42(7).
37. Ibid.
38. See Article 49 of the French Constitution.
39. Article 32(12).
40. Article 36(1).
41. 36(5).
42. Article 36(4).
43. Article 41(1). Note that the President may be removed from office by a two-thirds majority under Article 41(6).
44. Article 59(1).
45. Article 59 (2)(a) and (b).
46. Article 36(2).
47. Article 33.
48. Article I. Section 7.

TEN

The Executive

A government must be strong, of course, if it is to govern effectively. But if government is to be controlled, as it must be, it ought to be harnessed, like a horse. So, do not forget the lugam (harness) when you write the constitution. (AN ERITREAN ELDER, SPRING 1994)

"The pessimism of the intellect is a good corrective to the optimism of the will" (ANTONIO GRAMSCI)

The Central Place of the Executive.

In all governments, the executive occupies a central place, whether the system is republican or monarchical, parliamentary or presidential. Indeed, in earlier times, not only was power concentrated in the hands of the monarch but sovereignty was vested in him. Political advance, viewed in historical perspective, has been marked by the progressive transfer of power from king to commoners and from the executive to the legislature accompanied by principles of checks and balance.

The doctrine of separation of powers, conceived by an exiled French philosopher, crossed the Atlantic to be fashioned by the American revolutionaries into a central constitutional principle. In the US constitutional system, the central feature in the distribution of power is the independence provided for the three branches of government. But this independence is not absolute; the three institutions share powers such as the power of appointment, treaty ratification, and the enactment of laws. The system provides a balance of interests wherein one branch has a voice in some of the work of another.

The first epigraph of this chapter, quoting the words of an Eritrean elder, bears remarkable similarity to the words of Federalist no. 51 which argues that "the great security against gradual concentration of the several powers in the same department, consists in giving to those who administer each department the necessary constitutional means and personal motives to resist encroachments of the others." Again, Federalist no. 49 observes that the constitutional arrangement gives a blend of powers with "the several departments being perfectly coordinated by the terms of their common commission."

In practice, however, these arrangements have not been perfectly coordinated. There have been conflicts among the three branches, almost from the beginning concerning a range of issues, some of which will be cited as examples in later parts of this chapter.

Implicit in the Eritrean elder's admonition in the epigraph, are the two primary considerations with regard to the powers of the executive. The first concerns the need to give sufficient power to enable the executive to perform its constitutional functions. The second concerns the need to control the executive which different systems have handled differently. Let us now see how chapter five of the Eritrean Constitution answers these two questions.

238

The President: Head of State and Government

Article 39

1. The President of Eritrea is the Head of the State and the Government and the Commander-in-Chief of the of Eritrean Defense Forces.
2. The executive authority is vested in the President, which he shall exercise, in consultation with the Cabinet, pursuant to the provisions of this Constitution.
3. The President shall ensure respect of the Constitution; the integrity and dignity of the State; the efficient management of the public service; and the interests and safety of all citizens, including the enjoyment of their fundamental rights and freedoms recognized under this Constitution.

Commentary
a. Head of State
The executive has a dual function, the one representing the nation as a whole, the other heading the government of the day. In principle, the Head of State's role is to be above politics, but to live with the outcome of the political process and mediate in situations of conflict that may have far-reaching implications to the integrity of the republic. In the constitutions of some countries the two functions are performed by two different people. In such a case the head of state—be he/she king/queen, or president—performs ceremonial and mediation and custodial functions. For example in the constitution of Ireland the President is custodian of the Constitution. The President has the right to check legislation to see that it conforms with the Constitution, with the assistance of the Council of State, and to determine to send the Bill to the Supreme Court for decision in

THE MAKING OF THE ERITREAN CONSTITUTION

case of doubt.

Executive power is vested in a chief executive—usually called prime minister—who is head of the governing party and of the government of the day. Examples of this type are the United Kingdom, Ireland, Israel, Sweden, Germany, Ethiopia and Lesotho. In the case of countries, including Eritrea, with a single executive, also known among political scientists as monocephalous, in contradistinction from the bicephalous (dual) executive, the chief executive is both head of the government and of the nation.

The President of Eritrea, in his capacity as Head of State, performs the tasks traditionally performed by a Head of State, including the following:

- Once every year, deliver a speech in the National Assembly on the state of the country and the policies of his government;[1]
- Sign and publish in the Official Gazette of draft laws approved by the National Assembly;[2]
- Accredit ambassadors and diplomatic representatives;[3]
- Pardon, grant amnesty or reprieve offenders; [fn. Art 42(12)[4]
- Confer medals or other honors on citizens, residents and friends of Eritrea in consultation with relevant persons and institutions.[5]

b. Head of Government
In his capacity as Head of the Government, the President of Eritrea performs the following functions:

- Subject to the provisions of Article 27 of the Constitution, declare state of emergency, and when the defense of the country requires, state of war;[6]

240

- Summon the National Assembly to an emergency meeting and present his views to it;[7]
- Ensure the execution of laws and resolutions of the National Assembly;[8]
- Negotiate and sign international agreements and delegate such power;[9]
- Appoints with the approval of the National Assembly, ministers, commissioners, the Auditor-General, head of the National Bank, the Chief Justice of the Supreme Court and any other person or persons who are required by the Constitution or other laws to be appointed by the president;[10]
- Appoints justices of the Supreme Court upon proposal of the Judicial Service Commission;[11]
- Appoints judges of the lower courts upon proposal of the Judicial Service Commission;[12]
- Appoints high ranking members of the Armed and Security Forces;[13]
- Establishes and dissolves such government ministries and departments necessary or expedient for the good governance of Eritrea, in consultation with the Civil Service Administration;[14]
- Presides over meetings of the Cabinet and coordinate its activities;[15]
- Presents legislative proposals to the National Assembly;[16]
- Pursuant to the Constitution, removes any person appointed by him.[17]

It should be noted from the above that the two functions are not arranged into two separate groups in the Constitution; rather they are interspersed throughout Article 42. This is due to the vesting of the two functions in one person.[18] This combined function makes for simplicity and efficiency. In the dual executive system, there may be tensions between the head of state and the government leader; indeed, in some African experience, the tension blew up into open conflict and constitutional crisis.[19]

One of the aims of constitutional law is to determine the scope and limit of the powers and responsibilities of the central organs of government. We look to the Constitution as the primary source of such scope and limit. To find out how—how effectively—the functions are performed, however, we have to go beyond the formal provisions of the Constitution. The dynamics of executive power is a function of many things. The constitutional provision is the starting point. Next comes the political culture of the society concerned, including generally accepted conventions of dealing with conflict between different branches of the government.

Last, but not least, comes political leadership. In a divided executive, the head of state is invariably a conciliatory figure, an elder statesman of national reputation, whose prestige and wisdom is, in theory, expected to exert influence in helping resolve conflicts and in focussing attention on the common interest, as distinct from sectarian interest. In the event that the Head of State belongs to a party other than that of the government leader, conflict may occur that can hamper government business.[20]

The Eritrean constitution makers considered the option of a dual executive, as it also considered a bicameral legislature, but decided against it for reasons similar to the ones discussed in chapter nine. First, the developmental needs of a country like Eritrea require a unified, dynamic executive. Looking ahead to a time when there will be multi-parties, it is conceivable, the constitution makers thought, the two executives could be locked in conflict representing diverse political views and interests. A second, and less grave reason has to do with duplication, delay and cost.

Qualification to be a Candidate to the Office of the President.

Article 40. Any member of the National Assembly who seeks to be a candidate to the office of the President of Eritrea shall be a citizen of Eritrea by birth.

Election and Term of Office of the President

Article 41

1. The President shall be elected from amongst the members of the National Assembly by an absolute majority vote of its members. A candidate for the office of the President must be nominated by at least 20 percent vote of all the members of the National Assembly.
2. The term of office of President shall be five years, equal to the term of office of the National Assembly that elects him.
3. No person shall be elected to hold office of the President for mor than two terms.
4. When the office of the President becomes vacant due to death or resignation of the incumbent or due to the reasons enumerated in Sub-Article 6 of this article, the Chairperson of the National assembly shall assume the office of the President. The Chairperson shall serve as acting President for not more than thirty days, pending the election of another President to serve the remaining term of his predecessor.
5. The term of office of the person elected to serve as President under Sub-Article 4 of this Article shall

not be considered as a full term for the purpose of Sub-Article 3 of this Article.

6. The President may be removed from office by two-thirds majority vote of all members of the National Assembly for the following reasons:

    a. Violation of the Constitution or grave violation of the law;

    b. Conducting himself in a manner which brings the authority or honor of the office of the President into ridicule, contempt and disrepute; and

    c. Being incapable of performing the functions of his office by reason of physical or mental incapacity.

7. The National Assembly shall determine the procedures for the election and removal of the President from office.

Commentary
We begin with Article 40—qualification to be President.

It should be noted that only citizenship is mentioned in Article 40. Unlike other Constitutions, the Eritrean constitution does not mention age or level of education.[21] A maximum age of 70 had been considered, during the debate on the Commission's Proposals, but was abandoned on the reasoning that it would deny the participation of experienced and talented citizens the opportunity to serve their nation. The door was also left open on minimum age on similar grounds.

As was noted in an earlier discussion, there are two types of Eritrean citizenship: citizenship by birth, and citizenship by acquisition.[22] Article 40 requires citizenship by birth for the office of President. And a person can be an Eritrean citizen by birth if he is born of an Eritrean father or mother. In a traditional society in which lineage is claimed through the male line, this was bound to provoke, and did provoke, intense debate during the constitution making process.[23] This issue is bound up with the question of women's equal rights to which the government and the governing party seem to be committed, equality that is now guaranteed by the Constitution.[24] However, even to people who are in principle committed to equality—or to some of them—the patriarchal patrilineal mentality impinged in their thinking and became a bone of contention. What if, they wondered, what if a man whose father is a citizen of a neighboring country is elected President and Eritrea goes to war with such a country?

What was involved in such debates was nothing less than a leap of faith demanded on Eritreans made by the constitution makers, and by the country as a whole, since its representatives ratified the Constitution, that guaranteed equal rights to women. Such equality must necessarily imply that an Eritrean who is a citizen by birth through his mother would be expected to be as good a citizen as one who is a citizen through his father. It is a revolutionary principle in a traditional society but, as it was repeatedly explained during the debates, women's equal rights was one of the signal achievements of the Eritrean revolution. This question is thus a logical application of the fruits of the revolution and, as such, constitutes a supreme test of the authenticity of the revolution.[25]

Article 41
Election to be President

Election is by an absolute majority vote of the National Assembly members. Originally a two-thirds majority was considered which was the case under the UN-given Constitution of 1952. In addition to the fact that the President comes out of the National Assembly, the majority required for his election was one of the few matter that the Constitutional Commission considered looking into the 1952 Constitution for comparative purposes. After lengthy debate, the Commission decided in favor of a simple majority.

The issue of vote required to elect a president was debated in the larger context of the choice of the mixed system that the Commission adopted. In the U.S. model of executive presidency, the President is elected by the citizens, whereas in the parliamentary—or Westminister model—the Prime Minister is the leader of the party which has majority seats in parliament. Eritrea has adopted a hybrid system which combines parts of the two systems. While the 1952 Constitution was not in any way an inspirational source of the constitution making process, the fact that it provided for a parliamentary system with an executive Chief Executive was something familiar. But more important, from the point of view of Eritrean experience as an inspirational source, was the structure of the EPLF "government" in the *maquis,* under which the Central Committee of the EPLF which was elected by a Congress, acted as the legislative body and the Political Bureau as the Cabinet, with the Secretary-General acting as the Chief Executive.

In terms of the new democratic Constitution, sometime in the not-too-distant future, multi-parties will emerge making politics "messy," if more interesting, a prospect anticipated by the constitution makers. In such eventuality, obtaining a two-thirds majority may be hard—even impossible—to obtain, which would be a prescription for constitutional crisis. No nation, especially a developing one, should be subjected to such crisis. Hence the decision to settle for a simple majority.

Nomination

Note that to be nominated for the Presidency, a candidate needs the vote of 20 percent of the members of the National Assembly. Under this requirement, in a National Assembly with 100 members, 20 members would be needed, which means that only five candidates can compete. The opposed considerations were, on the one hand, providing a large number of candidates the opportunity to compete and, on the other hand, maintaining the dignity and integrity of the process. If the nominating threshold were to be lower, say 5 percent, then theoretically, there can be 20 candidates which might trivialize the process. Experience in other countries shows, of course, that it would be the leaders of the various political parties or groupings that would be the candidates. If there are 20 parties, therefore, they would aggregate on the basis of ideology or interest and agree to submit a common candidate. All of which would encourage a politics of consensus and, one hopes of civility.

Term of Office
The two year term limit of five year each was one of the universally applauded provisions of the Constitution. The five year term runs parallel with that of the National Assembly, because the President comes out of the National Assembly of which he must be a member in order to qualify. The membership requirement means that the potential presidential candidate must stand for election to the National Assembly from one constituency.

The term limit provision serves a dual purpose:

a) The general, democratic objective of acting as check on undue concentration of power.[26]

b) The objective of orderly transfer of power for which the cultivation of future leaders is a prerequisite. Term limit will induce political parties to prepare alternative future leaders and thus spare the nation destructive and wasteful power struggle. The idea of term limit encourages incumbent Presidents to plan on serving in other capacities, depending on their interest and capabilities. The two African leaders who left office voluntarily—

247

Presidents Leopold Sedar Senghor and Julius K. Nyerere—were believers in the idea of life after the presidency.[27]

President Nelson Mandela left office at the end of his term, even though there is no term limit provision in the South African Constitution. It is conceivable that term limit and voluntary retirement by upright leaders will contribute to a healthy African politics. Certainly, in the Eritrean case, the domination of politics by one man has raised concerns and become the subject of daily conversations even among his closest colleagues.[28]

Vacancy and Succession
Vacancy may occur in the office of the President resulting from the death of the incumbent, his resignation or his removal by the National Assembly in terms of Articles 41(6) and 32(9) of the Constitution.

Death and resignation for health or other personal reasons do not invite comments for the simple reason that they do not pose vexatious constitutional problems. All that needs to happen is for the Chairman of the National Assembly to assume the Presidency for thirty days followed by an election, by the National Assembly, of a successor President to serve the remaining Presidential term.

Impeachment
The more vexatious problem concerns the removal of the President in consequence of impeachment in terms of Articles 41(6) and 32(9) of the Constitution. As was already noted, one of the most momentous powers of the National Assembly is the power of impeachment. The National Assembly has the power to impeach a President on the ground of two categories of wrongs: a)Violation of the Constitution and laws, and

248

b)behaviour considered incompatible with the Presidential office. [Physical and mental incapacity as cause for removal will be discussed in (c) below.]

a) Violation of the Constitution or grave violation of law

A President can violate the Constitution in a number of ways, including acting *ultra vires,* i.e., exercising power not vested in him by virtue of the Constitution. He may do this by arrogating to himself judicial or legislative power that is clearly the province of the judicial and legislative bodies. Such unconstitutional arrogation of power constitutes an act of violation in terms of the law. Can violation of the constitution extend to omission? Could a President be subject to impeachment for failure to act to perform his constitutional duties, such as, for example, failing to declare a state of emergency pursuant to Article 27 of the Constitution? The answer to these questions is provided by the Constitution itself, as we saw when discussing the powers and duties of the President. It may be stated as a general principle that where the power is mandatory (the President *shall* do such and such), he would be accountable for failure to act. In a case where the power is discretionary (the President *may* do such and such), he would not be accountable in law although it may conceivably cost him politically, depending on the nature of the issue and how his failure to act affected the country or important forces in society.

What about Grave Violation of the Law ? The question raises another question: What is grave violation of the law, and who determines it ? The US Constitution speaks of high crimes and misdemeanor as impeachable offences. In the Eritrean Constitution, the use of the phrase "grave violation of the law," on the one hand, leaves much room for discretion. On the other hand, the use of the word "grave" clearly implies that it would not be acceptable to hold a president answerable for petty offences such as traffic violations. That leads us to consider the second category of impeachable behaviour.

b) Behaviour Incompatible with the Office of President

The Constitution provides a parameter for defining behaviour that is incompatible with Presidential office. The President must not "conduct himself in a manner which brings the authority or honor of the office of the president *into ridicule, contempt and disrepute.* This is one of the universal formulae adopted in world constitutions that the Eritrean Constitutional Commission adopted. Nevertheless, in terms of defining the underlined words, in the event that impeachment proceedings are set in motion, different interpretations might be given by different cultures. Can a President who habitually lingers with the claret in a Pub be said to bring the office into ridicule, contempt and disrepute? If the answer is yes, would it make a difference if he drinks two or three bottles of Heineken in the Pub, habitually? What if the drinking is done in private among friends, but that it it is done habitually and in large quantities?

Apart from sectarian politics which would obviously exploit any behaviour of an opponent, the answer to these questions lie in cultural attitudes to drinking and related behaviour, as well as on the effect drinking would have on the performance of his constitutional duties. Although there are universal values shared by humankind in general, there are country-specific values that may determine what would or would not bring the office of President to ridicule, contempt or disrepute. What is disreputable in one country may even be laudable in another. An example of this was the attitude of Greek citizens to the late Constantin Caramalis when he, as a married man, carried on an affair with, and later married, an airline hostess young enough to be his grand daughter. Greeks not only approved his prowess but returned him to office with high votes. Whether the odyssey of President Clinton reflects a different cultural attitude in America in this matter, or whether it is a function of the "feeding frenzy" of the American Media, is a question on which the jury is still out.

With regard to who determines behavior incompatible with the office of President, the National Assembly is obviously the body that makes the preliminary determination. Sub-Article 7 of Article 41 of the Constitution gives the National Assembly the power to enact a law providing for the procedures for the election and removal of the President. It is conceivable that such a law may spell out guidelines on determining the criteria for judging behavior that is incompatible with the office of President.

c) Physical and Mental Incapacity

A President's mental incapacity, supported by a certificate issued by competent medical practitioner, is ground for the removal of a President. The type and degree of such mental incapacity can be controversial, of course. Medical science, including psychiatry, has developed criteria for determining mental illness. In the spectrum of "abnormal behavior," ranging from quirky unsocial behavior characteristic of many creative people, to schizophrenia, there may be types of behavior that medical science might not define as constituting incapacity within the meaning of Article 41(6)(c). The controlling phrase in the Eritrean Constitution is incapacity of the President to perform "the functions of his office." The functions of the Presidential office are as listed above. Actual experience of removal from office on grounds of mental incapacity is very rare, and there have been disturbing revelations of incapacity of Presidents who continued in office for political or other reasons.[29]

251

Powers and Duties of the President

Article 42

The provisions of Article 42 that were enumerated above may be grouped as follows:

1. The Power of Appointment;
2. Legislative Power;
3. Quasi-judicial Power;
4. Diplomatic Power;
5. Emergency Power

1. The Power of appointment

This is the most important power of the Executive branch of government, and of the President, in particular. It is critical as a means of the policy making and conduct of government policy as well as of administrative control over the machinery of government. It is also a major source of political patronage through which members of the President's party as well as friends and supporters are rewarded for their loyalty and support. In many governments, it is abused and used for the procurement and accumulation of wealth. In many countries, including, though not limited to, the Third world, political power is translated to wealth.[30]

A relevant question with regard to appointments is: since the President cannot know all potential appointees, who nominates them and what principles and mechanisms exist for ensuring that the right people are appointed to the right jobs ?

With regard to political appointees, notably ministers, commissioners and other high-ranking government personnel, the President should have a pool of people known to him from which to draw. The pre-constitution experience of the first seven years after independence, shows the President appointing without any mechanism of consultation, at least one known to the public.[31] It is worth repeating here that the Constitution provides that the appointment to some high-ranking positions which includes justices of the Supreme must be approved by the National Assembly. [See Art. 42(7) and (8)]

2. Legislative Power

Legislative power is constitutionally vested in the National Assembly. Nevertheless, there are three situations under which the Executive can exercise legislative power, indirectly.

First, the President can, in his capacity as Head of State, (in his annual Address to the National Assembly) provide the outlines of the legislative programs of his government, in virtue of Article 42(1) which authorizes him to speak "on the state of the country and the policies of his government."[32]

Second, he presents legislative proposals of his government to the National Assembly, on a continuing basis, in virtue of Article 42(15) of the Constitution. This is the commonest and significant way in which the Executive branch is involved in legislative matters. Eritrea is no exception. The Executive's command of expertise and other resources enables it to have legislative initiative in terms of preparing masses of legislation which the Legislature would not be able to do especially in countries with shortage of trained manpower and other resources. But the Legislature has the last word; th Executive proposes, the Legislature disposes.

Third, The President and his ministers can make laws pursuant to Acts of Parliament delegating legislative power to them. Such delegated legislation is a common practice arising out of realization that Parliaments cannot cope with the minute details that must, by their very nature, be left to the Executive which carries the responsibility of carrying out laws.

3. Quasi-judicial Power

What has been called quasi-judicial power here involves Presi-

THE MAKING OF THE ERITREAN CONSTITUTION

dential acts that are related to the work of the judiciary. Under Article 42(12), the President has the power to grant pardon and amnesty, or to reprieve convicted offenders. Acts of pardon usually involve commuting a sentence of death by a court of law to life imprisonment. Amnesty may be general or particular. When it is general, it may involve numerous persons that had committed offenses, such as rebellion, to whom the President extends amnesty in consequence of which they may live without fear of prosecution.

We should note an exception to this power of granting pardon or amnesty. Under Article 27(5) of the Constitution, the President cannot grant pardon or amnesty "to any person or persons who, acting under the authority of the State, have committed illegal acts" in an emergency situation.[33]

4. Diplomatic Power

In addition to his power of accrediting and receiving ambassadors and other diplomatic personnel, the President enjoys diplomatic power in his treaty-negotiating and treaty-signing function. Indeed, he is the principal player in the making and conduct of the nations foreign policy.[34]

5. Emergency Power

As we saw in the discussion on state of emergency in chapter eight, the President is given power to deal with emergency situations. Emergency situations as defined in Article 27 of the Constitution that may trigger the use of emergency powers may occur **when public safety or the security or stability of the State is threatened by external invasion, by civil disorder or by natural disaster in Eritrea or any part thereof.**

Note that under Article 27:

(a) the President is required to publish the declaration of a state of emergency in the Official Gazette.

(b) to become effective, the declaration has to be approved by a resolution passed by a two-thirds majority votes of all members of the National Assembly.

(c) in case of a declaration made when the National Assembly is in session, the declaration has to be presented within two days after its publication, or otherwise the National Assembly shall be summoned to meet and approve the declaration within thirty days of its publication.

(d) a declaration approved by the National Assembly continues to be in force six months after such approval. It may be extended for periods of three months at a time by a resolution of two-thirds majority vote of all members.

(e) the National Assembly may by resolution at any time revoke the declaration.

Note also the three prohibitions stated in Sub-Article 5 of Article 27.

Immunity from Civil and Criminal Proceedings

Article 43
Any person holding the office of the President may not be sued in any civil proceedings or charged for a crime, save where such civil proceedings concern an act done in his official capacity as President or proceedings involving Sub-Article 41(6)(a) and(b) hereof.

Commentary.
For clarity of exposition, let us start from the reverse, i.e., when a President can be sued in civil matters and charged in criminal matters.

Civil Suits. A President can be sued in civil matters where a civil wrong is involved arising from an act committed in his official capacity as President. An example may help; it is offered as a problem for students of Eritrean constitutional law to ponder.

An Example:

The President orders the minister of Energy and Mines to evict the inhabitants of village X from their traditional land in order to start a mining project on their farm land. The right of the villagers is recognized by the Land Proclamation. In the process of eviction, officials of the ministry demolish buildings used as cattle shed and watering equipment. A few months later, an explosion occurs caused by cigarette smoking by a ministry employee who threw an unstamped cigarette butt to a concealed pile of explosives. Unknown to the errant employee, the explosives had been stored by the ministry, for mining purposes, at the mining project site. In consequence, some villagers are injured and there is damage to property. The villagers sue the President for damages in terms of Article 43 of the Constitution and relevant Articles of the Civil Code and the Land Proclamation.

Examine Articles 2028, 2033, 2035, 2053, 2054, 2067, and 2069 of the Transitional Civil Code and the Land Proclamation of 1994.[35]

The attorneys of the villagers contend that the suit for civil damage is grounded on the constitutional article that makes the President liable because the order was given by the President in the course of exercising his constitutional duties. What say you, students of constitutional law?

What about civil suits not related to the President's official duties? According to the Constitution, the President is immune from such suits. The idea is to shelter him from vexatious litigation that might hamper the performance of his presidential duties. Does that mean that such civil suits can be brought against the President or his estate after he leaves office? Also, for comparative purposes, note Articles 2137 and 2138 of the Civil Code on legal immunity of the Sovereign and ministers and members of parliament of a different era.[36]

Criminal Charge.
On the hypothetical example cited above, is the President liable to criminal charge? The answer is no. According to Article 43, criminal charges can only be brought against a serving President in terms of the impeachment proceedings discussed above.

Can the President be subject to criminal prosecution after he leaves office for offences committed during his term of office?[37]

Privileges to be Given to Former Presidents

Article 44
Provisions shall be made by law for the privileges that shall be granted to former Presidents.

Commentary
There is an old adage in Eritrea: "Honor the departed so that the living may serve you well."

Opportunistic on the face of it, it is a wise saying. The honor or privilege bestowed upon past Presidents, or any public servant for that matter, is sound in principle, in and of itself, because honor and privilege should be given where it is due. This is one of the self-evident truths known in all societies. But there are special privileges reserved for people who performed special services. It is a way for society—the beneficiary of those services—to say thank you. The Constitution's provision on privileges to former Presidents is based on such natural considerations.

The Eritreans that have become known as the generation of freedom fighters have developed a culture of self-denial which was dictated by military necessity, by the requirements of a protracted and lonely struggle "against all odds." Many members of this generation, veterans of the struggle, expressed surprise and puzzlement during the constitutional debates, when this Article of the Constitution was raised. Why the special privilege? Why reward anyone with special privileges when he was only doing his patriotic duty? These were not perfunctory questions raised for theatrical effect; they were based on the movement's long-standing ethos—the freedom fighter's ethic.

Eventually, there was grudging acceptance of the necessity of according special privileges for special service. But it was accompanied with a universally expressed admonition that due care should be made to avoid abuse and the development of unjustified sense of entitlement on the part of the "political class" which would be contrary to the revolutionary, democratic culture of the freedom fighters. The admonition was equally, universally applauded and duly noted. Hence the foregoing remarks.

As to what kind of privileges will be accorded to former Presidents, Article 44 refers to a future law to be enacted by the National Assembly.[38]

In conclusion, let it be said that life after the presidency can and should be rewarding, as the examples of former Presidents Jimmy Carte, Julius Nyerere and Leopold Senghor demonstrate.

The Cabinet and Ministerial Accountability

Articles 46 and 47

First, the provisions of the two Articles will be listed separately. Then the commentary that follows will deal with constitutional points raised in both provisions.

Article 46

1. There shall be a ministerial Cabinet presided over

by the President.

2. The President may select ministers from among members of the National Assembly or from among persons who are not members of the National Assembly.

3. The Cabinet shall assist the President in:
   a. directing, supervising and coordinating the affairs of government;
   b. conducting study on, and preparing, the national budget;
   c. conducting study and preparing draft laws to be presented to the National Assembly;
   d. conducting study on, and preparing, policies and plans of government.

4. The President shall issue rules and regulations for the organization, functions, operations and code of conduct relative to the cabinet and the secretariat of his office.

Article 47

1. All cabinet ministers shall be accountable:
   a. individually to the President for the administration of their own ministries; and
   b. collectively to the National Assembly, through the President, for the administration of the work of the Cabinet.

2. The National Assembly or its committees may, through the office of the President, summon any minister to appear before them to question him concerning the operation of his ministry.

259

Commentary
1. The Cabinet in Executive Presidential Systems

Cabinet government in a presidential system is different from one in a parliamentary system of the Westminster variety. In executive presidency of the American variety, the President who is elected by the public, chooses his ministers and they serve at his pleasure. Their responsibility is to him and to him only. There is no collective, ministerial responsibility owed to him or to the Legislature. And the Executive branch is separate from the Legislature.

In contrast to this system, the cabinet in a parliamentary system, is formed by the leader of the party with majority seats in parliament. The leader of the party that won the preceding election, known as the Prime Minister, and his cabinet colleagues are members of parliament where they sit to explain and answer questions on their policies and programs as well as to present legislation affecting their ministries. One critical feature of cabinet government in a parliamentary system of the Westminster variety concerns what is called collective responsibility. The constitutional significance of collective responsibility is expressed in a motion and vote on censure. The opposition party may at any time on any issue challenge the government and put the issue on the agenda of parliamentary debate. If a motion of censure is tabled by the opposition and the government loses the vote on that motion, then according to accepted convention the government must resign and call for new elections. Thus the Cabinet as the nerve center of the government, stands or falls on the fate of an issue put to a motion of censure. Obviously, this does not occur frequently. Party discipline and survival considerations will dictate party unity and discipline. In the vast majority of cases the members of parliament of the government party vote for their party. On issues of morality and related social questions some may "vote their conscience." But then rarely, if ever, do such issues call for

260

motions of censure.

In the Eritrean constitutional dispensation, collective responsibility in the sense discussed above does not apply. Nor was the concept of binding no-confidence vote adopted; fearing the prospect of instability in government at this critical stage in Eritrea's young history, Eritrean constitution makers decided against it. Ministerial accountability is provided for at two levels: individual and collective. Each minister is individually accountable to the President for the work of his ministry, and the ministers are collectively responsible to the National Assembly, through the office of the President. Moreover, each minister may be summoned by the National Assembly or any of its committees to answer questions on his ministry.

What is the significance of individual and collective responsibility, and of parliamentary summons of a minister, in the Eritrean constitutional context?

After heated debate concerning the relative merits of a presidential versus a parliamentary system, Eritrea adopted a system with features chosen from both presidentialism and parliamentarism; the controlling idea was to select whatever seemed most relevant to the country's own particular needs and circumstances. The executive power is vested, as already noted, in a President who is required to exercise it "in consultation with" a Council of Ministers. The ministers are, needless to say, assistants of the President who appoints them and can dismiss them. The exercise of presidential power in consultation with ministers is conducted at the Cabinet level; the major consideration for the consultation requirement is to institute a culture of collective decision making and the coordination of policy that it implies. Given the powerful position of the President, the temptation is great for him to "go it alone" on questions of critical importance to the nation, including matters concerning war and peace. The consultation requirement is designed principally to check against precipitous action.

261

Unlike the Prime Minister in a parliamentary system, the President in Eritrea, is not accountable to parliament, on a daily basis; nor can he be concerned with fears of negative vote of censure, as already noted. But Article 47(1)(B) requires ministers to be collectively responsible to the National Assembly, **through the President** which is a second line of defense in checking presidential power. Two related questions arise in this regard. First, how would such collective responsibility be achieved in practice? Second, what does "through the President" mean and why was it considered necessary ?

In answering these questions, we should stress that the collective responsibility provided for in the Eritrean Constitution is a watered down version. The constitution makers decided against a binding vote of censure, as explained above, while at the same time introducing the idea of collective responsibility. The purpose of this half-way house approach is twofold: to institute shared executive responsibility and at the same time instill a sense of executive cohesiveness.

Collective, ministerial responsibility would be achieved in practice through a senior minister designated by the President to appear before the National Assembly to explain or answer questions on policy and practice concerning the government as a whole. Since matters affecting individual ministers are handled through the appearance of the concerned minister, the appearance of the President's designated minister to answer for the government would involve matters of government policy and decisions undertaken by the Cabinet.

The requirement for this collective responsibility to be exercised through the office of the President is obviously designed to ensure cabinet integrity and cohesion.

Finally, a word on parliamentary summons of ministers. This is a provision borrowed from presidentialism to ensure accountability in a concrete manner. Experience of presidential systems shows that congressional committees can perform a critical role in holding ministers to account for acts or omissions concerning their ministries. This provision is one of the most important in the Constitution.

Notes

1. Article 42(1).
2. Article 42(4).
3. Article 42(10)
4. Article 42(12).
5. Article 42(16).
6. Article 42(2).
7. Article 42(3).
8. Article 42(5).
9. Article 42(6).
10. Article 42(7).
11. Article 42(8).
12. Article 42(9).
13. Article 42(11).
14. Article 42(13).
15. Article 42(14).
16. 42(15).
17. Article 42(17).
18. Cf. the Constitution of Ethiopia in which there are two separate chapters—one concerning the Prime Minister, the other concerning the President
19. Cf. Constitution of Uganda. See also Bereket Habte Selassie, *The Executive in African Governments*, London, 1974.
20. In the Summer of 1994, the author discussed this topic, among others, with Professor Didier Maus, of the Sorbonne, who was one of the fifteen members of the Foreign Advisory Board of the Constitutional Commission of

Eritrea. To the question whether a dual executive and "co-habitation" as in the French system was a good idea, Maus instantly responded, *"Jamais! Evitez-le comme la peste."* {Never! Avoid it like the plague.] To my question, "Then how does it work in France" his answer was that the President and the Prime Minister, belonging to two different parties, had to cooperate because the French public would not tolerate any wrangling between them if as such wrangling would adversely affect the country's interest. They cooperate because the public wants them to cooperate.

21. Cf., for example, the Constitutions of Nigeria in which the minimum age of forty is specified as a requirement (Article131(b). Similarly, the Constitution of Egypt lays down an age qualification of forty (Article 75).

22. Article 3.

23. Among the nine ethnic groups of Eritrea, all but the Kunama have had patriarchal systems.

24. See Preamble and Articles 5 and 7(2).

25. The question frequently arises as it did during my interview series with Saleh A. Younis of Awate. Com in the spring of 2001 as to a cut-off date of citizenship: How far does one have to go to claim citizenship? The Eritrean law on citizenship was issued with the 1993 referendum in mind. As in much of Africa, Eritrean citizenship is linked to the country's origin as a nation state, which is Italian colonial rule. Eritrea was born in 1890, as already noted. Between 1890 and 1941, Eritreans were Italian colonial subjects. But the new law on citizenship requires residence of a person or his parents from an arbitrary cut-off date (1938).

26. The tendency of unlimited term has been to tempt incumbents to prolong their occupation of the office with the implication of abuse and corruption. Life time Presidents have been known to abuse power, the most notorious

examples being Dr. Hastings Banda of Malawi and Mobu-
tu of Congo (former Zaire). In Zimbabwe, Robert
Mugabe' sycophants have made attempts to turn him into
a life time President, so far without success..

27. Senghor was a poet of world renown. Nyerere was a pragmatic philosopher and a man of letters. He translated
Julius Caesar into Kiswahili.

28. During the parliamentary debate on the draft Constitution, Mr. Isaias Afewerki, who was chairing the meeting
answered critics of the term limit by asserting that it is a
good way of ensuring succession to the leadership in addition to its values as a mechanism of control. As Chairman
of the Commission, summoned to explain the draft, I was
so relieved to hear the President that I went home later that
day to write a poem of commendation in Geez, in the manner of classical scribes! Such was the trust we had, which
proved fatal.

29. For example, Ronald Reagan had apparently developed
Altzheimer while in office. The question arises as to how to
detect, evaluate and report mental incapacity. The press in
a free a society may be an answer; if so, why didn't the press
discover and report on Reagan's condition? The other side
of the issue is action taken to remove an ailing (or aging
and impaired) President from office, on the grounds of
infirmity in a coup style operation as happened to President Habib Bourguiba of Tunisia. In this matter, everyone
should be his brother's keeper because of the magnitude of
presidential power.

30. It seems that Eritrea, which started with a promising clean
slate, is no exception to the rule, much as we Eritreans
claimed exceptionalism because of the country's peculiar
history of lonely struggle and final triumph against impossible odds.

31. There is a widely held belief that the inner circle of the party

is involved in nominations to such high-ranking positions.

32. This lies in the tradition of parliamentary government in which the queen makes the annual speech from the throne.

33. The denial of pardon or amnesty to persons who commit illegal acts under the authority of the state is in order to discourage wrongs being committed under the cloak of legality and thus to instill a culture of restraint on the part of government personnel, especially the armed and security forces, in times of emergency.

34. The Algiers Accord, which was the result of protracted negotiations that broke down many times, was first initialed by the Foreign Ministers of the two countries before they were approved by the executive heads of the respective countries. There are unconfirmed reports that the then Eritrean Foreign Minister, Mr. Haile Woldetensae (Duru'e), initialed the Accord without calling the Eritrean President to do so because that he felt his powers as a Foreign Minister entitled him to do so without having to refer to the President. In any case, the latter has the prerogative of vitiating the initialed Accord. The story goes that the Eritrean President was angry at the Foreign Minister and that was one main reason for their falling out resulting in Haile's eventual arrest and detention with the other G15 reformers. As this book goes to press, the eleven detainees and others are held without charge and incommunicado.

35. The Transitional Civil Code, which is based on the Ethiopian Civil Code, has been under review since at least 1996.

36. Articles 2137 and 2138 of Transitional Civil Code.

37. The US experience in criminal prosecution of a former President after he leaves office was highlighted in former President Bill Clinton's case. After his impeachment was defeated in Congress, threats of criminal prosecution after he leaves office were heard but, to date, none have been forthcoming. [One civil suit was settled out of court before he left office].

38. The experience of other African countries varies in terms of the type of privileges from modest villas, a car and driver and related facilities, to palatial residence in the capital and a holiday home (not unlike a Russian dacha), two cars— one for the former President and another for the spouse— and two drivers, plus free tickets on the national airlines for travels abroad. All this is, of course, in addition to retirement benefits like pension and medical benefits.

ELEVEN
Administration of Justice

Roper: *I would cut down every tree in England to get at the Devil*
Thomas More: *"Oh, and when the last law was down, and the Devil turned round on you—where would you hide, Roper, the laws all being flat? This country's planted thick with laws...Man's laws, not God's laws—and if you cut them down...then d'you really think you could stand upright in the winds that would blow then? Yes, I'd give the Devil benefit of law, for my own safety's sake.*
(From Robert Bolt's *A Man for All Seasons*)

The Judiciary

Article 48

1. The judicial power shall be vested in a Supreme Court and in such lower courts as shall be established by law and shall be exercised in the name of the people pursuant to this Constitution and laws issued thereunder.

2. In exercising their judicial power, courts shall be free from the direction and control of any person or authority. Judges shall be subjects only to the law, to a judicial code of conduct determined by law and to their conscience.

3. A judge shall not be liable to any suit for any act or omission in the course of exercising his judicial power.

4. All organs of the State shall accord to the courts such assistance as they may require to protect their independence and dignity so that they may exercise their judicial power appropriately and effectively pursuant to the provisions of this Constitution and laws issued thereunder.

Commentary

The first point of Article 48 is to declare the locus of judicial power—in the Supreme Court and other courts which will be discussed under Articles 49 and 50 below. The constitutional significance of this first point is to clarify the uniformity of the judicial system. We shall see below the nature and jurisdiction of the "other lower courts" which form part of the unified judicial power.

In this regard, we should note the traditional close connection between religion and law, particularly with respect to Sharia law. Sharia law should be distinguished from "native" customary law; each enjoyed its autonomy and was administered by its appropriate judicial institutions—the Sharia courts for one and local (customary) courts for the other. During the constitutional debates, the place of Sharia and customary laws was raised consistently. In view of the fact that both enjoy a pride of place in Eritrean society and that the governing party as well as the Constitutional Commission recognise and respect their place and role, there was no occasion for conflicting views on their recognition, unlike situations in some other countries.[1]

However, there was divergence of views where it concerns certain rights of women, as was discussed before.

The other main points contained in Article 48 concern: a) judicial independence, b) immunity of judges from suit for their role while exercising their judicial function, and c) the duty imposed on all organs of the State to ensure the independence and dignity of judges.

a) Judicial Independence and the Rule of Law

The principle of an independent judiciary is the key-stone of the constitutional edifice, particularly as regards the Bill of Rights. A judiciary that is insulated from the pressures of powerful interests in society and that can render justice without fear or favor acts as the best guarantee for people to live and go about their business with a sense of security and a trust in the rule of law. In that sense, therefore, the rule of law and its custodian in the form of an independent judiciary is the foundation of peace and development.

This is connected to the fundamental right of equality under the law which is a cardinal constitutional, democratic principle, as we saw in an earlier discussion. The law is conceived as a neutral force, above all taint of class or clan, party or personal predeliction. But since such a lofty and impersonal conception of the law cannot apply itself, it demands institutions and mechanisms for its application. That is the job cut out for an independent judiciary. It is a noble calling which requires special qualities. Judgeship calls for rare intellect and character, especially supreme court judgeship.

It also calls for extraordinary discipline together with sagacious acceptance of a life of loneliness.

The words of the philosopher, Sir Thomas More, in Robert Bolt's play, cited in the epigraph, posit law as value, or as a neutral force. But the law as a neutral force does not always work fairly, raising a question about the difference between law and justice. If the human agency that applies the law—the judiciary—is truly independent, it cannot, in its judging, overlook the unequal starting point between the rich and famous, on the one hand, and the poor "nonentities," on the other. If judging is neutral for the powerful, it can sometimes be injuriously neutral for the weak. But redressing the balance in this respect takes us outside the judicial province into that of the active politician, as law-maker. Nonetheless, there have been instances in US jurisprudence, for example, in which an "interventionist" Supreme Court, during the Roosevelt era in the mid-to late thirties, and thereafter, sought to redress the class balance by judicial means. Indeed, this is one of the enduring debates in US constitutional politics—whether the Supreme Court should be interventionist or not.[2]

In Eritrea, the question of judicial independence and the role of the judiciary was repeatedly raised during the constitutional debates. How is judicial independence secured in actual practice? The answer lies, first and foremost, in the culture of the society—in its felt need to be aware of and support the principle of judicial independence—from the ordinary citizen to the highest ranks of political leadership. There must be a national consensus that the independence of the judiciary benefits everybody and deserves the support of everybody, irrespective of political views, ethnic or class background. And the second answer is that such consensus must have institutional expression, which is why we have a Judicial Service Commission. [See below.]

b) Immunity of Judges from Suits.
This principle is an extension of the doctrine of judicial independence. The idea behind it concerns the need to instill in judges a spirit of tranquility and fearlessness so that they perform their duties satisfactorily.

Might it not lead to judicial abuse of power? Would not

the immunity for omission, in particular, induce in the judges a certain delinquency in their functions? These questions were raised and discussed by the Constitutional Commission. Both judicial abuse and delinquency are subject to proper sanctions by the Judicial Service Commission.

c) The Duty of State Organs in Regard to Judges
The duty of State organs to assist judges flows from the need of a culture of support generally. The constitutional provision requiring State organs to assist in maintaining the independence and dignity of judges sends a clear signal to members of government and ordinary citizens alike on the weight of the judicial branch of government in the scheme of things. In addition to facilitating the proper exercise of judicial function, it helps secure their prestige. Certainly, judicial orders shall be obeyed, on pain of drastic sanctions.

Article 49, The Supreme Court
1. The Supreme Court shall be the court of last resort; and shall be presided over by the Chief Justice.
2. The Supreme Court shall have
   a) sole jurisdiction of interpreting this Constitution and the constitutionality of any law enacted or any action undertaken by government.
   b) sole jurisdiction of hearing and adjudicating upon charges against a President who has been impeached by the National Assembly pursuant to the provisions of Sub-Article 41(6) and (b) hereof; Article 41 hereof; and
   c) the power of hearing and adjudicating cases appealed from lower courts pursuant to law.
3. The Supreme Court shall determine its internal organization and operation.

4. The tenure and number of justices of the Supreme Court shall be determined by law.

Commentary
The Jurisdiction of the Supreme Court
The Supreme Court has both first instance and appellate jurisdictions. In the first instance jurisdiction it hears questions on the constitutionality of laws or executive acts. In its appellate jurisdiction, it sits as a court of last resort and, as such, it bears immense responsibility. The finality of its decisions means that any losing party to a case would have no further recourse, no remedy. This reason, among others, adds gravity to the work and life of the Justices.[3]

In its jurisdiction of interpreting the Constitution and the constitutionality of laws or executive actions, it acts as the Constitutional Court of the country. In a new country with no previous experience of challenges to the constitutionality of laws or government acts, the prospects of the Supreme Court handing down judgements that may be looked upon with disfavor by the government of the day, are at once exciting and hazardous. There is already growing consciousness of the gravity of the Supreme Court's role among citizens which was sharpened during the constitutional debate.[4]

Organization and Operation of the Courts
The Supreme Court is constitutionally authorized to determine its internal organization and operation. [Art 49(3)]

This is a departure from existing practice under which the minister of justice played a critical role. Under the new constitutional regime, the independence of the judiciary is the controlling concept in the organization and operation of the courts. Under the pre-existing system, administrative power which included the power to appoint, reshuffle, promote and demote judges of all ranks, placed in the hands of the Executive branch operated to undermine judicial confidence, and hence, independence. Moreover, the control of the purse strings—approval and determination of the budget for salaries of all court personnel—reinforced the executive control of the judiciary. The effect of Sub-Article 3 of Article 49 is to take such control from the Executive to the judiciary, although it is conceivable that a ministry of justice, jealous of its powers, will fight to retain control on the budget.[5]

Aside from budget and personnel, the Supreme Court has control over its internal organization. The Chief Justice, in his capacity as the administrative head of the court, will be responsible for the administration of the court, including organizing the structure of the different divisions of the court and assigning judges to them, and generally monitoring and supervising the work of the administrative staff.

The law to be enacted respecting the tenure and number of Supreme justices, as envisaged under Sub-Article 4, is expected to make their tenure for life, "during good behaviour," because this is a crucial element of judicial independence.

Lower Courts
Article 50
The jurisdiction, organization and function of lower courts and the tenure of their judges shall be determined by law.

Commentary
Courts other than the Supreme Court come under the rubric of lower courts which should not be understood to imply insignificant jurisdiction. To the contrary, as Sub-Article 1 of Article 48 makes clear, judicial power is vested in the Supreme Court and in other courts "to be established by law. The specific jurisdiction of the other courts is (to be) fixed by law as to quantum and geographical area.[6]

Removal of Judges from Office
Article 52

1. A judge may be removed from office before the expiry of his tenure of office by the President only, acting on the recommendation of the Judicial Service Commission, pursuant to the provisions of Sub-Article 2 of this Article for physical or mental incapacity, violation of the law or breach of judicial code of conduct.

2. The Judicial Service Commission shall investigate whether or not a judge should be removed from office on the grounds of those enumerated in Sub-Article 1 of this Article. In the event that a Judicial Service Commission decides that a judge be removed from office, it shall present its recommendation to the President.

3. The President may, on the recommendation of the Judicial Service Commission, suspend from office, a judge who is under investigation.

The Judicial Service Commission
Article 53

1. There shall be established a Judicial Service Commission, which shall be responsible for submitting recommendations for the recruitment of judges and terms and conditions of their services.

2. The organization, powers and duties of the Judicial Service Commission shall be determined by law.

Commentary
We will discuss th provisions of Articles 52 and 53 togeth-

er, but in a reverse order, because the entry of a judge into the judicial service comes before his removal on any ground.

The Judicial Service Commission
The thinking behind the institution of judicial service commission is to ensure that the process concerning the entry into, progress within and exit from the judicial service is insulated from the pressures of political or other interest groups. This is a critical element in upholding and maintaining the independence of the judiciary. To that end, the question of its composition and its leadership is relevant, and at the risk of being contradicted by the law that will deal with the organization, powers and duties of the Commission, we may hazard a guess that among its members will be the Chief Justice, at least another Justice of the Supreme Court, a prominent member of the Bar, and a member of the Civil Service Administration, among others. As noted before, during the debate on the Draft Constitution held at the transitional National Assembly, questions were raised as to the relationship of the Judicial Service Commission and the minister of justice. The novel idea of an independently operating judicial service commission inevitably raises concerns about an uncontrolled judiciary. It is, therefore, conceivable that the minister of justice will be the Chairperson of the Commission.]

It is of interest to note that according to the Judicial Service Act of Uganda any member of Parliament, or a member of a local government, or a member of the executive of a political party or political organization must relinquish that office upon his or her appointment as member of the Judicial Service Commission.[7]

Appointment. It will be recalled that among the government officials that the President appoints with the approval of the National Assembly, are commissioners. It is therefore reasonable and logical to expect that the members of the Judicial

Service Commission, including the Chairperson, will be subject to presidential appointment with parliamentary approval. The provisions of other constitutions such as that of Uganda lends support to this expectation. Clearly, given the central place of the minister of justice in the present scheme of things, her/his role will be critical in initiating and managing the choice of candidates for membership of the Commission.

But it will be an unwise minister indeed who does not involve the Chief Justice in this task.

Function. The Judicial Service Commission shall have the function specified in Sub-Article 1 of Article 53 of the Constitution, pursuant to which it will be charged with the search for, and short-listing of, qualified people for judicial appointment. The role of the Commission extends to prescribing the terms and conditions under which the judges will serve, including their rank and salaries and conditions for their removal from office or other disciplinary action falling short of removal. It will also surely play a key role in determining the examination that judges may have to pass, or in deciding whether past legal practice and/or the requisite diplomas or other documents certifying professional worth will be sufficient for recruitment.

Removal of Judges from Office

The norm is, or should be, life time tenure which assumes "good behaviour."[8]

The principle of security of judicial tenure implies that judges can only be removed from office for serious reasons. The Constitution lists these as:

- physical or mental incapacity;
- violation of the law; and
- breach of judicial code of conduct.

It bears reiteration that a judge may be removed from office by the President only. This means that other members of the government, be they members of the Legislature or the Executive, may not remove a judge. Secondly, the President can remove a judge only on the recommendation of the Judicial Service Commission. And who initiates the complaint against a judge before it ends up at the desk of the Judicial Service Commission?

Physical and Mental Incapacity. Complaints concerning physical and mental incapacity may originate from within the judicial circles, from colleagues with a chance to observe the infirmity or incapacity of the judge. If a consensus is formed as to an incapacitating infirmity among the colleagues whose opinions count, it would be pointless on the judge's part to challenge the consensus. If he does, technically, he may be allowed to have his day in court which in this instance is the clinic of a physician or psychiatrist. It would be a rare occurrence, indeed. Whether the issue goes to a doctor for final certification or not, before it can be cited as ground for removal, there must be a complaint. But whatever the source of the complaint of incapacity, it is the Judicial Service Commission that determines whether there should be a recommendation to the President for the removal of the judge. It will be recalled that in the case of the President's incapacity, it is the National Assembly that determines to initiate complaint and institute proceedings for removal. In the case of the President the constitution specifies that the incapacity must be such as to render him "incapable of performing the functions of his office by reason of physical or mental incapacity." [Art. 41(6) (c).]

Violation of the Law. This is a clear enough ground for removal. Not even a judge can be spared if he violates the law; indeed, a judge is expected to set a good example in observing the law. In this case, complaints may originate from diverse sources, not being restricted to his colleagues.

Breach of Judicial Code of Conduct. A code of conduct may be one which has been prescribed by law, or sanctioned by custom. Judicial code of conduct means that judges should

279

show conduct befitting the dignity of their function. Pending the enactment of a law or regulations providing for judicial code of conduct, we may use the analogy of the prohibition of the President against conduct that "brings the authority or honor of the office of the President into ridicule, contempt and disrepute." Even though the office of the judge is not as exalted as that of the President, a person who decides between life and death holds no mean office. His conduct must thus be commensurate with such power.

The Advocate General

Article 54
There shall be an Advocate General whose powers and duties shall be determined by law.

Commentary
The office of the Advocate General, sometimes also called Attorney General, has been part and parcel of the Eritrean legal system since Italian colonial times. During Italian colonial rule, the office was known as the Procurator-General, or *procuratore generale*, in Italian, also at times referred to as *procuratore del Re* (King's Procurator). With the advent of the British, following Italian defeat, in 1941, the office of the Attorney-General was created along the lines of the English legal system. In the English legal system, the Attorney-General is the preeminent legal advisor of the government and his office deals with all criminal prosecutions on behalf of the State. That system was introduced into Eritrea and continued through the federation period, with the Attorney-General of Eritrea functioning independently of his Ethiopian counterpart, and even pleading on behalf of Eritrea in the Federal Supreme Court. All this ended in November 1962 when the

federation was abolished, and the office of Attorney-General of Eritrea was incorporated into the Ethiopian one, becoming a provincial branch.

During the latter part of the liberation struggle when the EPLF undertook the task of establishing fledgling State institutions, the office of the Attorney-general was one of such institutions, as part of the Department of Justice. This was continued after liberation. The Attorney-General's function has been principally concerned with criminal matters.

Under the new Constitution, the function of the Advocate General is envisaged as both an officer of the courts (hence the inclusion of the office in the Chapter on the Judiciary) and an important arm of the Executive branch of the government. Thus, administratively, the Minister of Justice has oversight responsibilities on the office the Advocate General in the sense that she/he is answerable for, and represents, the work of the Advocate General at the Cabinet. Presumably, this responsibility extends to answering questions in the National Assembly in terms of Article 47(2) of the Constitution, although the National Assembly may conceivably insist on summoning the Advocate General himself.

When the Constitutional Commission discussed the nature of the function of the office of the Advocate General and his place in the government scheme of things, his independence from any pressure in performing his duties was stressed. He holds in his hands matters of life and death the determination of which should be made on professional, legal considerations. He must therefore be insulated from politics; he must not be used as an instrument for political or personal interests of powerful forces in society. Hence his semi-judicial status. In this objective, both the Judiciary and the Parliament, as well as the general public will surely be deeply interested.

Notes

1. The Nigerian experience is instructive with respect to the role of Sharia courts and their relationship with the civil courts of a country with a large Muslim population.. According to F.R.A. Williams, Chairman of the Constitutional Commission that drafted the Nigerian Constitution of 1979, the subject had "posed very serious and delicate problems for those on the Constitution Drafting Committee and for those in the Constituent Assembly. Indeed, so sensitive were the issues that each of the two bodies almost reached a deadlock on the issue..." In the end, Williams wrote, the proposal to set up a Federal Sharia Court of Appeal to deal with appeals from each of the Sharia courts of appeal in the northern states was not accepted by the Assembly. Extremists on both the Muslim and Christian sides can turn simple issues into a political crisis, as Williams observed in his presentation of the Draft constitution to the Constituent Assembly. [See F.R.A. Williams, *The Making of the Nigerian Constitution.* in Constitutions and Constitution Makers, Robert Goldman and Art Kaufman, (editors), 1988, pages 411-413].

2. Broadly speaking, the interventionists—at times dubbed as liberals—contend that the Constitution should be interpreted not only in terms of its original intent (Strict construction principle) but also as capable of adapting to changing circumstances. On the other hand the strict constructionists—dubbed as conservatives and today represented by Justice Antonin Scalia—argue that the intent of the original drafters must be followed.

3. The Supreme Court also sits as a court of last resort when being seized of issues as a court of first instance, such as interpreting the constitutionality of issues.

4. See James C.N. Paul and Clarence J. Diaz, *Law and Legal*

Resources in the Mobilization of the Rural Poor for Self-Reliant Development, International Center for Law in Development, July 1980 p. 21.

5. The provision of Article 49(3) of the Eritrean Constitution is a significant break from the past and a blow in favor of judicial independence in transferring the power of determining the internal organization and operation of the courts from the executive branch to the judiciary. Next to autonomy in matters of internal organization and operation is control o budget. Even in the United States, it took over a century for the Supreme Court to have control over its budget. This is the Executive's last prerogative, and it may take a long time for the Eritrean judiciary to have such control.

6. In the matter of the jurisdiction and functions of the lower courts, the Supreme Court will no doubt have a major say in drafting the law. Even before the ratification of the Constitution, the Supreme Court President had a major input, acting as the principal advisor of the Minister of Justice in such matters.

7. See the Judicial Service At of 1997, Article 4(1). It is worth noting that the Attorney General of Uganda is an ex officio member of the Judicial Service Commission. The other members and the Chairperson are appointed by the President with the approval of Parliament.

8. The selection of judges on merit basis is widely practiced. Compare, for example, the selection plan known as the Missouri Plan used by many states in the USA for selecting judges, notably Alaska, Arizona, Florida and Missouri. See *Carp and Stidham, Judicial Process in America 5th edition* (2001).

The term good behavior is a simple rendering of its Latin ancestor "*quam diu se bene gesserint.*"

TWELVE
Miscellaneous Provisions

Chapter VII of the Constitution on miscellaneous provisions deals with five subjects that could not be incorporated in the preceding chapters of the constitution. The five subjects are:

1. The Auditor-General's office;
2. the National Bank;
3. the Civil Service administration;
4. the Electoral Commission;
5. Constitutional Amendment

The responsibilities of the first four, endowed with autonomous status, place them apart from other branches of the government. Also, all four need to maintain their integrity in the daily discharge of their responsibilities. These institutions are important in any system of democratic government, for the health of the system depends to a large extent on their independence and efficient operation.

The Auditor General

Article 55

1. There shall be an Auditor General who audits the revenues and expenditures and other financial operations of government and who reports annually his findings to the National Assembly.
2. The Auditor General shall be appointed for five years by the President with the approval of the National Assembly and shall be accountable to the National Assembly.
3. The detailed organization, powers and duties of the Auditor General shall be determined by law.

Commentary

The basic function of the Auditor General is to ensure that government money is spent appropriately, pursuant to the law and in accordance with sound accounting principles. Different national systems may have differences in some detail, but in most democratic countries, the constitutional provisions for the Auditor General have many similarities and are based on the same principles. For example, the Auditor General in general enjoys autonomy to conduct his or her job without the control of any person or authority. Article 55(1) of Eritrea's constitution makes the Auditor-General accountable to the National Assembly and to nobody else, even though he or she is appointed by the President.

Auditor Generals are invariably required to submit an annual report to the national legislative body and to detail all expenditures of the government institutions audited during the preceding year. In order to perform this function well, the Auditor General and his or her auditors have the right of access to all books, records, returns and other documents relating or relevant to these accounts. The office must also have at its disposal the most competent professional staff of proven skills and integrity.

The office of the Auditor-General of Eritrea was established soon after independence, but there is no law providing for its powers and responsibilities.[1]

Most constitutions allot a certain amount of time for the legislative body to examine the Auditor General's report and debate any issues concerning the audit. In many jurisdictions, the constitution provides for the appointment of a separate committee to analyze the report and submit its findings to the larger body. In Eritrea, as elsewhere, the appointment of such a committee is left to legislation. Whatever the basis of the appointment, however, such committees perform the same task of analyzing and reporting to the larger legislative body which has the final word.[2]

The Auditor General is generally appointed by the President with the approval of the legislative body, as exemplified by Article 55(2) of the Eritrean constitution and Section 163(1) of Uganda's constitution. Exceptionally, Parliament appoints the Auditor General, as in Ghana [See Section 187 of the constitution of Ghana.] The term of appointment differs from country to country. Under the Constitution of Eritrea the term is five years.[3] In Nigeria it is six months.[4] In South Africa, the Constitution leaves the term of office to be determined by the National Legislative body but stipulates that the term must be a "fixed, non-renewable term of between five and ten years."[5]

With respect to the functions, terms and conditions of service of the Auditor General, some constitutions make detailed provisions, while others leave the details to legislation. Examples of the former are the constitutions of Ghana, Nigeria and Uganda. For instance, the constitutions of Uganda and Ghana contain provisions stating that the salary and allowances payable to the Auditor-General shall be charged to the Consolidated Fund.[6] The Constitution of Ghana goes into more detail giving the Auditor General power to disallow expenditure items that he deems to be contrary to law.[7]

Because Nigeria is a federal republic, the Nigerian constitution addresses the needs of the governments of the federating states in addition to the needs of the federal government. Provision is thus made for the appointment of an Auditor General by the governors of the several states with the approval of the state assemblies.[8]

The functions of the State Auditor General are practically congruent with those of the Auditor General of the federation, as provided for under the federal constitution.[9]

To turn to an example of mature democracies, in the United States, for example, the function of the Auditor General is exercised by the Comptroller General, who is head of the General Accounting Office. The latter was established by legislation.[10] The Comptroller General audits the government agencies and submits annual reports to the Congress of the United States. He or she has the same function as Auditor Generals of the African countries and, like most of them, he or she is appointed by the President. However, this appointment is made with the advice of the U.S. Senate, and the term is fifteen years.[11]

The current practice of the work of the Auditor-General in Eritrea is not available to comment upon. Apart from the lack of a requisite law, the practice is shrouded in mystery.

The National Bank

Article 56 provides

1. There shall be a National Bank, which performs the function of a central bank, controls the financial institutions and manages the national currency.

2. The National Bank shall have a Governor appointed by the President with the approval of the National Assembly. There shall be a Board of Directors whose members shall be appointed by the President.
3. The detailed organization, powers and duties of the National Bank shall be determined by law.

Commentary

The Constitution defines the functions of the National Bank and its principal officers in bare outline, leaving details on its organization, powers and duties to legislation. Sub-Article 1 states that the National Bank performs the function of a central bank, controlling financial institutions and managing the national currency.

Central banks are at the center of a nation's financial and economic life. To begin with, the central bank of a country (also known as the Reserve Bank in some counties, for example, in South Africa and the United States) is the only authority allowed to issue currency. Central banks have the responsibility for formulating and governing monetary, credit, and exchange-rate policies in a manner that ensures stability and facilitates sustainable economic development.

The following functions belong to all central banks:

a. Promoting and maintaining the stability of the national currency which includes the regulation of currency system in the interest of economic progress;
b. Acting as the sole custodian of state funds both inside and outside of the country. The Central Bank may, of course, authorize any other person or authority to act on its behalf as custodian of any such funds, as specified in an appropriate legal instrument;

    c. Encouraging and promoting economic development and the efficient utilization of the nation's resources through effective and efficient operation of a banking and credit system in the country;

    d. Monitoring transactions and transfers of funds involving any foreign exchange to ensure that it is not contrary to law.

In exercising these functions, particularly to find the right mix of interest rates to balance the effects of inflation and unemployment, central banks may be caught in a dilemma, torn between the demands of the politics of the moment and the politicians of the day, on the one hand, and the requirements of sound fiscal and monetary policies, on the other.

This raises the question of the operational independence of central banks. In an ideal situation, central banks would be insulated from politics, but the government of the day, represented by the President or Prime Minister, should have a say in the appointment of the principal officers of a central bank. In the Eritrean case, the President appoints the Governor of the National Bank, with the approval of the National Assembly, and he or she appoints the Board of Directors without such approval. Can the President remove the Governor of the National bank without the consent of the National Assembly? In most countries, there is security of tenure protecting the Governor of the central bank and the members against arbitrary removal. In Eritrea, if recent history and current practice is any guide, presidential intervention in the running of the bank's function seems to be likely for the foreseeable future.

The best guarantee against such interference is a law providing for security of tenure for a fixed term, in the manner of the Chief Justice and Justices of the Supreme Court. Indeed, Ghana's Constitution contains a provision to that effect.[12] Similarly, the Constitution of South Africa provides that the Reserve Bank "must perform its functions independently and without fear, favor, or prejudice."[13]

And in Uganda, the Constitution provides, *inter alia*, that "the Bank of Uganda...shall not be subject to the direction or control of any person or authority."[14]

Civil Service Administration

Article 57 provides

1. There shall be established a Civil Service Administration which is responsible for recruitment, selection and separation of civil servants as well as for determining the terms and conditions of their employment, including the rights and duties and the code of conduct of such civil servants.

2. The detailed organization, powers and duties of the Civil Service Administration shall be determined by law.

Commentary

Any discussion of modern civil service must begin with an explanation of the distinction between this kind of public service and the activities of the "government of the day." The former is professional, the latter political. Entry to the former is based on professional criteria like competence and experience, whereas appointment to the latter is based on political considerations, loyalty or ideological affinity with the governing party or its leader.

Why the need for such distinction?

The advent of modern civil service administration is linked to the development of party politics, and the requirements of criteria and rules governing the manner of entry and progress in the service and exit from it is designed to ensure the integrity and quality of service and hence, the stability of public administration as a whole. Governments come and go, but the civil servant continues in his or her post to serve the public.[15]

While "neutral" in their politics, civil servants are required to abide by any change of policy that may occur as a result of a change of government following an election. They must be loyal to and follow the instructions and guidelines of the new government, including new policies that change previous ones, even if there is disagreement with the new policies.

If leaders of a governing party insist that civil servants, especially those in the higher echelon, join their party the better to control them there is a serious problem. In the absence of legal prohibition, party bosses or their government ministers might make decisions that adversely affect the condition of service, salaries and careers of the civil servants. Indeed, the origin of the idea of a civil service insulated from the arbitrary power of capricious party bosses or government ministers can be traced to society's need to separate the service from party politics in order to ensure its quality for the common good, irrespective of party affiliation.

The idea of an independent civil service, whose autonomy is guaranteed under the constitution and laws issued thereunder, implies non-membership of any party and neutrality that refrains from participating in party politics or expressing any political opinion. Thus, civil servants enjoy the constitutional rights of voting in elections, but are in most systems, precluded from active participation in party politics. Governments or party bosses are not supposed to dictate the civil servant's duties.

There have been attempts to make civil servants members of a governing one-party, as in Tanzania in the late 1960's and 1970's. Julius K. Nyerere, the country's first President and arguably the most brilliant leader of Africa of the time, established a one-party State and was unapologetic for it. His contention was simple—some would say simplistic. He argued that a multi-party system was developed in Europe in circumstances in which society was divided by classes. In those circumstances, parties would form naturally to represent the interests of the different classes. Africa, he argued, was a classless society. There is no need for multi-parties, and it was a luxury that Africa could not afford. This argument was also used by other African leaders to foist one-party regimes upon their peoples.[16]

Nevertheless, Nyerere was too honest a man and incorruptible a leader to fail to see the damage of one-party regimes and, therefore, reversed the policy and installed multi-party democracy in Tanzania. The civil service that had been emasculated under the one party system regained its autonomy with its members no longer required to be members of political parties.[17]

One of the most instructive studies on the African Civil Service, from the stand point of the metropolitan influence, is by the Ghanaian scholar/civil servant, A.L. Adu.[18]

A common definition of the civil service from the metropolitan models is that it is a service comprising all servants of the state, other than holders of political or judicial offices, who are employed in a civil capacity and whose remuneration is paid out of moneys voted by Parliament. On the basis of this definition, A.L. Adu has written:

> A servant of the State, the civil servant's first loyalty is to the State. Since the government is charged by popular choice with the control and administration of the affairs of the State the civil servant's loyalty is to the government of the day and he should appropriately feel a positive and consistent responsibility to prosecute the interests of the government as his employer.[19]

In Eritrea selection and separation of civil servants is stipulated in Article 57(1) of the Constitution as the exclusive jurisdiction of the Civil Service Administration (CSA). Proper recruitment and selection is based on merit, meaning that the CSA must issue rules on the criteria for such recruitment and selection, including rules on job description, position classification and salary scale. CSA also determines the terms and conditions of the employment of civil servants and their rights and duties as well their code of conduct. The details on the CSA's powers and duties are left to legislation. Here, as in the case of the Judicial Service Commission, the legislative body that is to pass the law defining the powers and duties of CSA is expected to keep in mind the need for the autonomy of the Civil Service provided that the government of the day has regulatory powers including the power to issue guidelines and instructions to put into effect the promises of their election platform. However, the autonomy of the civil service and their function of ensuring that merit and not fear, favor or prejudice is the governing principle in the civil service administration.

Public personnel administration has been a specialized field of knowledge, just as business administration and management has become a specialized field in the private sector. The problems of public administration and of bureaucracy have long engaged the interest of many scholars. While insulating the civil service from political pressures by ensuring appropriate autonomy and integrity has been a historic preoccupation of scholars and statesmen alike, the problem of bureaucratic arrogance and "irresponsibility" raises not only administrative but also constitutional issues of concern. How transparent and accountable should the civil service be? How can its discretionary powers be controlled in a just and democratic society? What type of people are these "guardians" and "who will guard us against our guardians"? What principles and mechanisms should be put in place to secure the best possible public administration?

Syoum Gebregziabher, a long-time student of the subject contends that,

"By virtue of their primacy, government employees (the bureaucracy) have assumed the guardianship of the long-term public interest and they have become the keepers of the public trust. The members have tended to become the fourth branch of government although they are not democratically elected...What type of men and women are these guardians and who will guard these guardians is a continuous challenge of the body politic. This de facto (unavoidable) power of the bureaucracy creates a basic conflict that has to be resolved with the principle of government "by the people and for the people."[20]

Syoum also describes the challenges governments face as employers: the kinds of challenges that would be addressed in the appropriate legislation (to be) passed by the Eritrean National Assembly, pursuant to Articles 57 and 11 of the Constitution. As Seyoum asks,

1. What criteria and under what organizational arrangements would they select, train, discipline, promote and pay these public employees? What system can they develop to place the right person at the right place, at the right time, with the right adequate compensation to enhance service and productivity?
2. How would they motivate their civil servants to provide the highest level of performance with the highest ethics, morality and loyalty to the people they service?
3. How would they obtain and assure their loyalty to the nation and their willingness to cooperate with political leaders?
4. Should the government (the state) engage in col-

lective bargaining with its civil servants? Should they be given the right to strike and to organize their own unions or join other unions?

5. To what extent should the civil service in quality and in character be representative of the various groups and geographical area of the country?

6. How can they prevent or control the bureaucracy from becoming the Fourth branch of government outside the given constitutional provision?[21]

The challenges are to put in place the right mechanisms to ensure a properly working civil service and to make the civil service accountable. Coming under the chapter on National Objectives and Directive Principles, Article 11(1) of the Eritrean Constitution requires the civil service to have "efficient, effective, and accountable administrative institutions dedicated to the service of the people." Article 24 of the constitution gives citizens the right to seek redress in the event that their rights are interfered with or threatened by a public servant.

Electoral—Commission

Article 58 provides

1. There shall be established an Electoral Commission, operating independently, without interference, which shall, on the basis of the electoral law, ensure that free and fair elections are held and administer their implementation; decide on issues raised in the course of the electoral process; and formulate and implement civic education programs relating to elections and other democratic procedures.

2. An Electoral Commissioner shall be appointed by

the President with the approval of the National Assembly.

3. The detailed organization, powers and duties of the Electoral Commission shall be determined by law.

Commentary

Article 20 of the constitution gives every Eritrean citizen the right to vote and to seek elective office, provided that he or she "fulfills the requirements of the electoral law." The representation of the people in the national legislature is one of the fundamental requirements of a democratic system. The Constitution gives all citizens of eighteen years of age or more the right to vote. The Constitution leaves to future legislation the details regarding election, including the organization, powers and duties of the entity that would be responsible for organizing and managing elections.

Another issue to be settled by legislation concerns the electoral system that would govern elections in the country. As explained in chapter nine, basically, there are two types of electoral systems which may be chosen in accordance with the needs of a country—the majority system and proportional representation.[22]

In Eritrea, the committee established by the transitional legislative body to draft an electoral law seems to have opted for the majority system.[23] Members of opposition groups were adamantly against the holding of an election, as announced by PFDJ , at the end of 2001, for two reasons. First, the PFDJ did not permit the creation of multi-parties and as a result the election will be a sham. Second, the violation of the letter and spirit of the ratified Constitution and the absence of the rule of law make it imperative for opposition groups to boycott the election and insist instead on the rule of law and authentic democracy, which allows the existence of more than one party.[24]

Whatever the type of electoral system, the Constitution is clear as to the need for the operational independence of the Electoral Commission. This is crucial if the integrity of the electoral process is to be maintained and thus the proper functioning of democracy ensured. Following the publication of the draft Electoral Law of Eritrea, questions have been raised as to whether the draft law is consistent with the Constitution. The answer depends on whether the draft law, in any way, limits or otherwise derogates from the right of a citizen seeking elective office, or the right of the voting citizen. The Constitution charges the Electoral Commission with the responsibility of ensuring that free and fair elections are held.

The question whether the law is consistent with the Constitution turns on whether the law's provisions are such that fair and free elections can indeed be held. Assuming that more than one party competes in the election whenever it is held, the following specific questions need to be answered:

1. Will the Electoral Commission be independent: will it operate without the interference of the governing party, as the constitution requires?
2. Will there be a level playing field in which all the competing parties are treated equally, particularly in terms of financial resources?
3. Will the Media be accessible to all of the candidates without favor?
4. Will they have sufficient time to organize their supporters and conduct their campaign, especially the new parties, if there are any?

With regard to the independence of the Electoral Commission, the draft law seems to follow the requirements of the Constitution. However, at present there is one dominant party that is committed, on paper, to the establishment of a multi party system but seems to be, by all indications, reluctant to fulfill the commitment. An election to the National Assembly has momentous political implications, not least because it is the National Assembly that elects the President. A dominant party and its leader, used to assuming office without opposition, is naturally averse to competition, and a national election is a highly competitive affair.

According to the Constitution, the President appoints the Electoral Commission, albeit with the approval of the legislative body. In a post-constitutional situation and in circumstances in which the National Assembly is composed of various political parties, the general practice would be for different parties to have their own nominees represented in the Electoral Commission. At the time of writing, Eritrea's National Assembly does not have such representation; it is a body dominated by one party. Whether multi-parties emerge and whether they will have representation in the Electoral Commission remains to be seen. In the meantime, the Commission appointed by the President will no doubt be from among people considered to be loyal or sympathetic to the PFDJ party—possibly even comprising all members of the party. The election itself is seen by many as if it is already won by the PFDJ, even before it has occurred! This does not augur well for democracy in the short run; democrats who demand multi-party democracy will have to wait until a multi-party system is allowed with or without the concurrence of the governing party.

In the Eritrean case, the fact that the media are owned by the government is a big minus, even with the emergence of a few private newspapers that have valiantly fought for openness and democracy. The government media, especially the radio which is listened to by the greater mass of the populations, can be used in favor of government candidates.

Government candidates would have powerful backing by a well-heeled party and its enormous resources and better name recognition. New candidates need more to mount their campaigns, to get the message of their programs out and endeavor to persuade the public to elect them.

Most constitutional systems provide for an independent entity to be responsible for managing elections with powers to determine all issues related to the running and management of an election, including registration of voters. Such Electoral Commissions must ensure that free and fair elections are held in which all registered voters can vote for specific parties or persons. Constitutions differ on the degree of detail in assigning powers and responsibilities to the Commission. For instance in the South African Constitution, as in the Eritrean Constitution, the relevant provision is couched in generalities, leaving details to be determined by the national legislature.

In contrast, other Constitutions, such as those of Ghana and Uganda, go into more detail. These two constitutions require their respective Electoral Commissions

- To ensure that voting is held by secret ballots;
- To make sure that the number of registered voters increases if need be, due to increase of population in the voting district;
- To educate citizens on the electoral process;
- To register political parties;
- To manage election stations to provide a fair and impartial election.

The Constitution of Uganda contains provisions that require the Electoral Commission to divide the nation into constituencies where the number of inhabitants in each constituency is as close to the population as possible.[25] The Ugandan Constitution also makes provision allowing for appeal by any "person aggrieved by a decision of the Electoral Commission" to the Election Tribunal or eventually to the High Court.

Both the Constitutions of Ghana and Uganda provide for the independence of the Commissions. In Ghana, the electoral Commission, which consists of a Chairman and a Deputy Chairman and four other members, is appointed by the President. The Constitution of Ghana provides that the Commission "shall not be subject to the discretion or control of any person or authority."[26]

In Nigeria, the Independent National Electoral Commission [INEC] is responsible for "monitoring the organization and operation of political parties" and providing rules and regulations for these political parties.[27] In carrying out these duties, INEC has the right to "arrange for the annual examination and auditing of the funds and accounts of political parties, and publish a report on such examination and audit for public information.[28] In addition to INEC, which is a federal body, the Nigerian Constitution establishes a State Independent Electoral Commission for each State in the federation. The State Commission is given the power to "organize, undertake, and supervise all elections to local government councils within the State" and give advice to INEC on the registration of voters within the State.[29]

On the composition of the Electoral Commission, the Constitutions of Ghana and Uganda have similar provisions. In both, the members of the Commission are seven, with a chairman, a deputy chairman and four members. In contrast, the Constitution of Nigeria establishes the office of Chief Electoral Commissioner who must not be less than fifty years old, and twelve National Election Commissioners who must be at least forty years old.[30] In terms of the mandate, the constitution of Uganda specifies a seven years mandate with a renewal period of one more term.[31]

In the United States, unlike most systems, there is no formal Electoral Commission at the federal level. Instead, the US Constitution calls for all elections to be governed according to state laws. Within each State, an Electoral Commission establishes eligibility requirements for state officials, the date on which state and local elections are to be held, and qualifications for voters.[32]

The U.S. presidential election of 2000 demonstrated that the United States is not immune from the play of politics, notwithstanding rhetorical pronouncements to the contrary. That politics does impinge on the electoral process was demonstrated by the Florida election debacle in Election 2000.[33]

The 5-4 decision of the US Supreme Court to settle the election result will probably be remembered by some Democrats as a politically motivated decision. The jury is still out as to whether a state-wide recount of votes in Florida might confirm, or not, the election of Bush.

Amendment of the Constitution

Article 59 provides

1. A Proposal for the amendment of any provision of this constitution may be initiated and tabled by the President or 50 percent of all the members of the national Assembly.

2. Any provision of this constitution may be amended as follows:

   a. where the National Assembly by a three-quarters majority vote of all its members proposes the amendment with reference to a specific Article of the constitution tabled to be amended; and

   b. where, one year after it has proposed such an amendment, the National assembly, after deliberation, approves again the same amendment by four-fifths majority vote of all it members.

Commentary

Two basic points must be made regarding this provision. The first is the mechanism of amendment. Second, any part of the constitution may be subject to amendment—in theory at least.

The first point refers to the difference between the mechanism required for constitutional amendment and for ordinary legislation. Constitutional amendment is different from amendment of ordinary legislation for the simple reason that a constitution is a basic law on which the legal edifice and political system rest. The amendment of a piece of ordinary legislation—even one that contains some important legal matters such as articles in the penal code—is a matter to be disposed of during the normal legislative session and following the normal legislative process, requiring a simple majority vote of the members of the legislative body. Amendment of any article of the Constitution is more difficult before it can become a reality, as can be seen from the provision of Article 59.

The different mechanism contemplated under Article 59 has two aspects—the higher majority of votes required, and the length of time that must elapse before the initially tabled amendment can be reviewed and be submitted for further deliberation. The first time that an amendment proposal is tabled—be it by the President, or by half of the members of the National Assembly—it has to muster three-fourths of all the members. If the total members of the Assembly is 160, the vote required would be 120. Subsequently, the National Assembly has to wait twelve months before it can deliberate on the amendment proposal. Twelve months having elapsed, the initiators would then submit the proposal for debate for a second time. If after sufficient debate has been held on the proposed amendment, there is passage with not less than four-fifths majority vote of the 160 members (i.e., with not less than 128 votes), the amendment becomes part of the Constitution as First Amendment, Second Amendment, etc...

The second basic point of Article 59 of the Constitution is that any part of the constitution is subject to amendment. This naturally raises some pertinent questions. To begin with, if any part of the Constitution is theoretically subject to amendment, can't a ruling party change some of the fundamental principles on which a democratic constitutional government is based? With such a possibility in mind, why didn't the constitution-makers declare some of these principles "off-limits" to amendment in order to prevent the possibility of ant-democratic forces from tampering with democratic principles? Did the constitution-makers of Eritrea think through this carefully?

There must be a general understanding among the populace, especially including opinion leaders, that any such attempt must be condemned and resisted by all means possible. Any attempt to change the democratic basis of the government is like destroying the foundation of an edifice, and no inhabitant of an edifice wishes the building to crumble on them. In the last analysis, there must be a national consensus of what the basic values are and a general commitment to live or die by them. Any attempt by a governing elite to change them would, therefore, be resisted and fought to the bitter end. Many nations have been tested on this particular issue. Those who fail the test are condemned by succeeding generations, while those that pass earn the blessings of their progeny.

Are some principles "off limits" to amendment? The problem of such "exceptionalism" raises the question of which principles to include and which to exclude. If one or two principles are declared "off limits" other principles appear to be subordinate in the constitutional scale of values. But all constitutional principles have equal values; at the very least they reinforce one another. Nevertheless, a rare example of such exceptionalism was Article 16 of the UN-imposed Constitution of Eritrea of 1952. The framers of that Constitution, who agonized over the fact that a democratic unit (Eritrea) was being grafted on to a non-democratic and larger unit (Ethiopia), devised Article 16, which provided that the democratic basis of the government of Eritrea was not to be abolished by any authority. History showed, however, that a determined king sought to and did finally did away with that provision by abolishing the federal structure itself. History also witnessed an equally determined people whose democratic and human right to self-determination was violated and who waged war for thirty years to regain it from the aggressor nation. It is an open question whether, in the African context, these lessons of imperial tampering with a democratic principle and the consequent tragedy will be lost on would-be autocrats.

One method to which autocrats resort to change constitutions is the use of plebiscite or referendum. Yet a referendum was not adopted by the Eritrean constitution-makers for ratification of the Constitution. A complex subject like the Constitution cannot be decided by a simple "yes or no" formula, which would inevitably involve the simplification and distortion of very complex matters. The same argument holds for constitutional amendments, which is why article 59 does not resort to referendum.

Historically, referendum as a political concept—as a tool of constitutional engineering—has been used on rare occasions. As a legislative concept, it has been used by the Executive to side-track opposition only recently and has been riddled with controversies. The advent of such a ploy in Africa is courtesy of the French (Gaulist) constitution of 1958. But even under the Gaulist Constitution of the Fifth republic, the initiative to use referendum did not belong to the president but was imposed by the president at the request of the government of the day. Moreover, subjects that may be settled by resort to referendum are limited.[34]

Under the Eritrean constitutional dispensation, referendum is not an option as a method of amendment. The

Executive may be tempted to resort to extra-constitutional means in order to side-step legislative strictures ordained by the Constitution, but any President that tries to override the Constitution in this respect does so at his own peril.[35]

Notes

1. There is no law, to date, establishing the office of the Auditor General. Nor are there guidelines on budgetary and fiscal policy.
2. See, for example, the Constitution of Ghana, Section 187(6) and that of Nigeria, Section 85(5).
3. Article 55(2).
4. Section 80(3).
5. Section 189.
6. Section 163(8), and 187(11).
7. Section 187(7).
8. Section 126(1).
9. Section 125-127.
10. See the Budget and Accounting Act of 1921. In the United States, there is also the office of the Inspector General of the National Archives whose function is to ensure ready access to essential evidence by providing high quality audits and investigations.
11. See generally, Raymond A. Mosley, The General Accounting Office, the United States Government Manual, 2000/2001.
12. See Article 183 of the Constitution of Ghana: "The Chairman of the governing body of the bank of Ghana...shall not be removed from office except on the same grounds and in the same manner as the Chief Justice of the Supreme Court of the Judicature."
13. See Const of South Africa Section 225.

14. See Art 162.
15. See Julius K. Nyerere, *Democracy and the Party System.*
16. Kwame Nkrumah of Ghana was among the first to introduce the one-party regime.
17. Nyerere had the integrity to admit his mistake and restored the autonomy of the civil service and cleared the way for a multi-party system after his retirement.
18. See A.L. Adu, the Civil Service in the New States. 1965.
19. Ibid.
20. See Seyoum Gebreigziabher, *A Primer of Public Personnel Administration*, 2000, p.xiii.
21. Ibid pp. xiii-xiv.
22. See Chapter nine above.
23. See Draft Election Law 2001.
24. See Ismail Omer-Ali, *More Reasons Why the 2001 Election Should be Boycotted.* www. Awate.com.
25. Art. 63.
26. Art. 46
27. 1999 Const. Section III, Pt. 1, Sec 15.
28. Schedule III, Pt.1, Sec 15.
29. Ibid.
30. Schedule III, Pt. 2, Sec 3.
31. Section 60(3).
32. See *Elections in the United States World Book Encyclopedia* 1997 Edition.
33. Some Democrats bristle at the way that the election was handled by some Florida state officials whom they saw as helping George W. Bush.
34. They are limited to the following:
    (a) Bills involving the organization of public powers;
    (b) Bills involving the approval of an agreement;
    (c) Bills authorizing the ratification of a treaty, "*qui sans etre contraire a la constitution aurait des incidences sur le fonctionement des institutions.* [Article 11 of the Constitution].

35. For a more detailed analysis of the issue of referendum, see Bereket Habte Selassie, *The Executive in African Government*, London 1974.

Epilogue

The Constitution of Eritrea became a subject of a lot of controversy following the end of the 1998-2000 war with Ethiopia. Much of the political debate centered on the implementation of the Constitution. The general expectation was that the Constitution would be immediately implemented after its ratification, in May 1997. The fact that the government failed to implement it in 1997 or 1998 became a bone of contention between Eritreans, who expected its immediate implementation (the vast majority), and the central office of the ruling group (PFDJ), as will be explained below.

In the April 1998 issue of Journal of Democracy (Volume 9, Number 2), I wrote a brief report on the Eritrean experience of constitution making. In that report, I stated the following:

> The Constitution of Eritrea is expected to come into force in the summer of 1998. The exact date has been left open so that the government can 'clear the deck' by reviewing, and if need be, repealing, laws that conflict with the Constitution. The government has also appointed a committee to draft an electoral law. Once the Constitution is promulgated, a general election will be held and the people of Eritrea will begin living under the political institutions that they have been so actively involved in creating.

I had expected the Constitution to come into force much earlier than the summer of 1998, but was later led to believe that preparations were underway to enable the government to arrange for elections to be held immediately after the coming into effect of the Constitution in the summer of 1998. My report was thus a statement of faith: faith in the government, and faith in the integrity of a process of constitution making that had been the subject of a great deal of international attention and of generally favorable review. Not for one moment did I suspect that the government would delay the implementation of the Constitution.

Ratified in May 1997, the Constitution remained unimplemented a year later when war broke out between Eritrea and Ethiopia, in May 1998. When the government was later challenged by concerned citizens on its failure to implement the Constitution, the reason the government gave was the outbreak of the war. That explanation did not satisfy the majority of thoughtful observers. As we will see below, the behavior of the central organ of the ruling party, and especially of its Chairman, President Isaias Afewerki, in the ensuing months when challenged by high-ranking members of his party gives an indication as to the real reasons for such failure. Eritreans in general have persistently inquired about the fate of their Constitution. Among the most frequently raised questions with constitutional implications of relevance to the present study are the following two:

1. How does one explain the behavior of the Eritrean government: why did it fail to implement the Constitution following ratification?
2. Why did the Constitutional Commission decide not to insert an effective date in the Constitution?

Raising the question why the government did not implement the Constitution after the war ended in July 2000, implies raising a related question: can a duly ratified Constitution be considered to be in full force and effect, despite the failure of the government to implement it, as in this case?

The Government's Behavior After Ratification

It is paradoxical that a government that was fully supportive of the constitution making process and whose National Assembly approved the draft constitution would drag its feet in implementing a ratified Constitution. Why did this happen?

In a long piece titled, "The Disappearance of the Eritrean Constitution and its Impact on Current Politics in Eritrea," posted in the INTERNET, early in 2001, I argued that the most likely explanation of the government's failure to implement the Constitution following ratification was fear of loss of power—fear "in case the multi-party system envisaged by the Constitution enables opposing parties to win in future elections..." [See Asmarino.com, February 2001] I reminded readers that, six months after the ratification of the Constitution, the government had appointed a committee to prepare the ground for elections pursuant to the Constitution. According to one of its members, the committee met twice, the second and last meeting being in early January 1998. Nothing of substance was discussed at the two meetings and the public was never informed as to the terms of reference of the committee. Nor was the identity of its members published. An intriguing silence descended upon the nation on the fate of their ratified Constitution for a whole year. And a committee that was supposed to clear the ground for the establishment of the primary institutions to move the nation to constitutional government kept silent and did nothing. In view of all this, it is not unreasonable to wonder whether the committee got a hint to keep quiet and do nothing.

The government was dragging its feet for reasons best known to itself, but not explained to the public. The government preferred to remain silent rather than respect the public's right to know and provide an explanation such as it needed more time to clear the deck of dockets in its special court. The

THE MAKING OF THE ERITREAN CONSTITUTION

Eritrean public would have understood, provided there was a "sunset provision" in the measure extending the life of the special court. It is reasonable to expect interested people to ask hard questions as to why this happened and many Eritreans did ask and are still asking such hard questions. The government's response giving the war as an excuse is not persuasive. It does not explain the silence and lack of action of the months following the ratification of the Constitution. Nor does it explain the strange behavior of the electoral committee that it established which met only twice and dispersed without doing anything. The public was kept in the dark throughout.

The Absence of an Effective Date in the Constitution

With respect to the decision of the Constitutional Commission of Eritrea not to insert an effective date in the Constitution, I reported in the above-mentioned article posted in the INTERNET that the Commission decided not to mention a date on which the Constitution was to come into effect in order to give the government a chance "to clear the deck:" to remove laws from the statute book that were contrary to the Constitution. One such law was the law establishing the so-called special court, originally created to deal with corruption. This law is in clear violation of the Bill of Rights chapter of the Constitution. The implicit understanding was that the law would be removed by expediting the cases in the special court's dockets, that the Constitution would be implemented within a few months and election held by early-to-mid 1998. The Commission's decision was based on trust: trust that the government would honor the people's will as expressed in the ratified Constitution. Indeed, there was no reason to believe otherwise. [See also my article in the INTERNET on this, titled "Eritrea's Special Court and Universal Principles of Justice"]. In hindsight, it is now clear that the Commission made a mistake in not inserting an effective date. It was a mistake based on trust and, in retrospect—in view of the political fallout that ensued—there is no question but that it was a serious mistake. The explanation given by the government about time constraint is clearly unacceptable.

Two lessons can be learned from the Eritrean experience in this respect. First, no constitutional dispensation should be based on trust only. If we must trust it is prudent to follow the wise Russian saying, "trust but verify." The clear lesson for those involved in drafting constitutions is that they should insert an effective date in the Constitution. The second lesson concerns legislation that curbs civil liberties, as the Decree creating Eritrea's special court does. Even though they may be conceived originally as temporary measures to deal with specific situations such as corruption or terrorism, such legislative measures are difficult to get rid of. Of course, in a constitutional democracy with judicial review, legislative oversight and the scrutiny of a free press, there would be a way out of such problems. But Eritrea is not a constitutional democracy—yet.

The End of the 1998-2000 War and Constitutional Politics

The war came to an end in July 2000 with the ceasefire agreement signed in Algiers. The ceasefire was brokered by the active role of the United States government, the United Nations and the European Union, with the OAU acting through the good offices of Algerian President, Abdulkadir Bouteflika. Although some of the technical details are still to be worked out, including the application, on the ground, of the verdict of the Arbitral Commission on border demarcation, the first important step has been taken towards normalization of relations between these neighboring countries.

Turning to the status of the ratified Eritrean Constitution, le me deal with the question of whether the Constitution can be considered as in effect after its ratification. With respect to the Bill of Rights of the Constitution—the whole of Chapter Three—I am of the opinion that it can indeed be considered as being in force. The government would no doubt dispute this and the matter is a constitutional issue. Under the Constitution, such an issue would be decided by the Supreme Court. For the rest, the principal institutions of state, such as the National Assembly, must be formed. For that to happen, the implementation of the Constitution would need the passage of laws such as an electoral law, the election of the National Assembly and the formation of a government on the basis of the Constitution.

The end of the war with the signing of the ceasefire agreement was expected by many Eritreans to clear the way for implementing the Constitution. Many Eritreans felt that it was time to fulfill the promise of transition to constitutional democracy. Indeed, demands for implementation of the Constitution began to be heard. Of particular historical and constitutional significance in this respect was the call made by high-ranking members of the governing party for convening meetings of the party's Central Council, of the party's Congress, and of the National Assembly with a view to making a thorough review of the events of the previous few years. At the first meeting of the Central Council following the end of the 1998-2000 war, members complained that meetings had not been held regularly as mandated by the party's constitution and demanded that future meetings be held on time.

In September 2000, the National Assembly passed a resolution that general elections be held in accordance with the Constitution, before the end of 2001. To those ends, the National Assembly created two committees, one to prepare a draft law on elections, the other, to prepare a draft law on political parties. Both committees prepared the draft laws. What happened next may be regarded as a turning point in the recent political history of Eritrea.

The Committee on political parties, having completed the draft law on political parties, was about to start public consultations on the draft law, through its chairman, Mr. Mahmud Sherifo, when President Isaias ordered the latter to cease such consultation and instead to report the matter to him. Presumably the President did this in his capacity as Chairman of the National Assembly or as head of the governing party, or both. Mr. Sherifo did not accept the President's order, contending that his mandate was given to him not by the President but by the National Assembly, which had required the draft to be enriched by input from the public before its submission to the National Assembly. The President dismissed Mr. Sherifo from his Chairmanship of the Committee and also from his Cabinet position as Minister of Regional Government. [Being minister of Regional Government also made Sherifo, *ex officio*, Vice President of the country]. Deprived of its Chairman, the Committee was left suspended in the air, its function was taken over by presidential appointees and the work mandated by the National Assembly ceased.

Sherifo's refusal to accept the President's order was a first in that no one before him ever defied the order of Mr. Isaias Afewerki. The challenge posed by Sherifo's defiance was based on legal grounds but the challenge and the consequent dismissal of a man who was a *de facto* Vice President of the government must be analyzed against a backdrop of general dissatisfaction of President Isaias' leadership style and his party's governance, particularly on the part of some prominent members of his colleagues and former comrades-in-arms. Such dissatisfaction had been concealed behind the President's popularity and his leadership during the armed struggle. Things came to a head after the disastrous war with Ethiopia in 1998-2000, and especially after the "third offensive" in the spring of 2000. The causes of the war, including the question of who is to blame must be left for historians to settle. Its relevance to the present discussion is that it had an impact on current Eritrean politics and society. Simmering tensions surfaced as hitherto inhibited government and party cadres began to voice their dissatisfaction and offer criticisms, at first timidly. The timidity disappeared following the publication of the so-called Berlin Manifesto.

Civil Society, Cyber Space and the Constitution

The "Berlin Manifesto" was not a manifesto; it was a private letter written in September 2000, to President Isaias by thirteen Eritrean academics and professionals concerned with the predicament facing their homeland in the aftermath of the war. Respectful but highly critical of the President's policies and politics, the letter was meant to be a private communication designed to induce change in the president's rule from autocracy to a collective style of decision making in accordance with the Constitution. Among the letter's recommendations, immediate implementation of the Constitution figured prominently. For reasons that are not yet clear, the letter was leaked and published by Dehai, a website generally believed to be sympathetic to the government. The publication of the Berlin Letter—so called because the group met in Berlin in September 2000—created two types of reactions. On the one hand, there was immense relief accompanied by numerous commentaries supportive of the Berlin Letter and calling for change in governance as well as implementation of the Constitution. Opposition Groups and a large number of supporters of the ruling party fell into this group. On the other hand, supporters of the government were critical of the Berlin letter on the grounds of its tone and timing. The cyber space thus became the most critical medium of political debate as never before. New websites emerged, including one created by the PFDJ. The battle of the media was on, with the government putting more resources in defense of its policies.

Meanwhile, within the ruling party, fifteen high-ranking members of the Central Council wrote a letter to President Isaias to convene meetings of the Council, of the party Congress and of the National Assembly. The President's response was a one-line dismissal of the request and this was repeated, whereupon the G15, as they became known, wrote an open letter to members of the Central Council of the party. Failing a positive response from that quarter, they wrote an open letter to the general membership of the party and eventually to the Eritrean public.

In explaining why they wrote the open letter to the party members, the fifteen leaders stated:

> All legal means to solve this crisis in the legislative bodies have been blocked, frustrated. The President has refused to convene meetings of the legislative bodies, but continues to express his views and taking illegal action…We shall continue to struggle to establish the rule of law. We shall continue to struggle to implement the sacred ideals and principles of the Front (party) and our national Constitution. We shall continue to struggle using every legal and democratic means available. We have no ambition other than making these sacred ideals a reality. We take this opportunity to call on all PFDJ members and the Eritrean people in general to express their opinion through legal and democratic means and to give their support to the goals and principles they consider just.

The above communication was written in March 2001. The letter that the group sent to the President was dated February 20, 2001, and his response, addressed to Mr. Sherifo, was written On March 12, 2001. In his last response, the President wrote: "This morning you sent me a letter with signatures. If it is for my information, I have seen it. In general, I only want to say that you all are making a mistake."

Eritrean communities throughout the Diaspora were divided into two camps—those who support the Reformers and those who stick by the government. The debate was raging over cyber space when on September 18, 2001 the President ordered the arrest of eleven of the fifteen members who were in Eritrea. Three of them were abroad and, following the arrest of their comrades, vowed to continue the struggle for democracy, the rule of law and constitutional government. One of them, Mr. Mesfin Hagos, gave several interviews on the Internet and international media and addressed Eritrean communities in England, Sweden, other countries in Europe and the United States of America and Australia. Others began similar activities in the United States and Canada. The government's response was to condemn such activities as those of traitors.

The arrest of the eleven officials was followed by the detention, again without charge, of the elders and reporters of the only private newspapers in the country, as well as the closure of the newspapers.

Thus, amid great expectations of democratic transition into constitutional government, frustrated by unforeseen political developments, the Constitution remained unimplemented. The election promised before the end of 2001 did not take place, and no explanation was given by the government. And the Chief Justice of the country was dismissed for voicing criticism about undue executive interference in judicial matters. The condition and whereabouts of the arrested officials and journalists remains unknown. The verdict of the Hague

Tribunal had raised yet another hope that it might lead to some relaxation of the tense situation in the country. Many expected the demobilization of most of the young people in the trenches as well as the notification to parents of those who were killed during the two-year war—numbering 19,000, according to government statement, but estimated to be more. The government announced that it would demobilize 5,000. No detail is given as to why 5,000 only are being demobilized, or who they are. The fate of those who remain un-demobilized in addition to the question of notification of the war-dead will likely continue to be one of the issues of contention.

The detention without charge of eleven reformers, of many others previously detained, of journalists and of elders, whose only sin was to try to mediate a settlement, provoked highly critical response both domestically and internationally. The most emphatic denunciation came from the European Union as well as from individual member governments of the Union. The Italian ambassador to Eritrea, Mr. Bandini, made representations to the government, expressing the European Union's demarche, in his capacity as doyen of the European ambassadors. He was ordered to leave Eritrea.

The reaction of the U.S. government, although critical, has been characterized by ambiguities. While the Department of State is consistently critical, the Department of Defense seems to be less so. This is presumably due to the Defense Department's interest in the Red Sea region and the unseemly blandishments of the Eritrean government hoping to enter into a "defense pact" with the United States. If this should come to pass, it would constitute a betrayal of what Americans consider their core values, i.e. justice, democracy and the rule of law. It will mean rewarding autocratic rule at the expense of democracy and human rights. It is sincerely hoped that whatever happens, the concerned U.S. authorities will do as the European Union has done, to bring appropriate pressure to bear on the Eritrean President to honor the will of the people, implement the ratified Constitution and open up to democratic governance and the rule of law.

Index

Z